Benjamin Artom,

Sermons preached in several Synagogues

Benjamin Artom,

Sermons preached in several Synagogues

ISBN/EAN: 9783743349209

Manufactured in Europe, USA, Canada, Australia, Japa

Cover: Foto ©Lupo / pixelio.de

Manufactured and distributed by brebook publishing software (www.brebook.com)

Benjamin Artom,

Sermons preached in several Synagogues

SERMONS

PREACHED IN SEVERAL SYNAGOGUES

BY

THE REV. BENJAMIN ARTOM,

Chief Rabbi of the Spanish and Portuguese Congregations of England.

בשפתי ספרתי כל משפטי פיך

"With my lips have I declared all the judgments of Thy mouth."

PSALM cxix. 13.

PUBLISHED BY REQUEST.

LONDON:
TRÜBNER AND CO., 57 & 59, LUDGATE HILL.

1873.

CONTENTS.

LETTER BY THE WARDENS TO THE AUTHOR. . . . vii

ANSWER BY THE AUTHOR viii

SERMON I.

PAGE

THE JEWISH PASTOR IN THE PRESENT AGE.—Preached at Bevis Marks Synagogue on Tebet 8, 5627—December 16, 1866, on the occasion of the author's installation as Chief Rabbi (Haham) of the Spanish and Portuguese congregations. 1

SERMON II.

THE SHOFAR. *A New Year's Day Sermon.*—Preached at Upper Bryanstone Street Synagogue on Sabbath, Tishri 8, 5632—September 23, 1871, שׁ׳ שובה האזינו. . . 2

SERMON III.

CONFESSION. *Day of Atonement Sermon.* Preached at Bevis Marks Synagogue on Sabbath, Tishri 10, 5633—October 12, 1872, יום כפור׳. 38

SERMON IV.

THE SUCCAH. Preached at Upper Bryanstone Street on Sabbath, Tishri 16, 5629—October 2, 1868, יום ב׳ של סכות. 54

CONTENTS.

SERMON V.

THE LULAB. Preached at Upper Bryanstone Street Synagogue on Thursday, Tishri 15, 5633—17 October, 1872, יום א׳ של סכות. 68

SERMON VI.

WOMAN AND PASSOVER. Preached at Bevis Marks Synagogue on Sunday, Nisan 16, 5630—April 17, 1870, יום ב׳של פסח. 82

SERMON VII.

THE MESSIAH. *A Passover Sermon.* Preached at Upper Bryanstone Street Synagogue on Monday, Nisan 21, 5632—April 29, 1872, יום ז׳ של פסח. 97

SERMON VIII.

THE ANSWER OF ISRAEL. *A Feast of Weeks Sermon.* Preached at Upper Bryanstone Street Synagogue, on Sunday, Sivan 6, 5630—June 5, 1870, יום א׳ של שבועות 113

SERMON IX.

JACOB'S DEATH. Preached at Upper Bryanstone Street Synagogue on Sabbath, Tebet 14, 5631—January 7, 1871, ש׳ ויחי. 129

SERMON X.

THE WAR. Preached at Bevis Marks Synagogue on Sabbath, Elul 21, 5630—September 17, 1870, ש׳ כי תבא. . 144

SERMON XI.

THE BURNING BUSH. Preached at Upper Bryanstone Street Synagogue on Sabbath, Tebet 19, 5633—January 18 1873, ש׳ שמות. 159

CONTENTS.

SERMON XII.

KNOWLEDGE OF GOD. Preached at Bevis Marks Synagogue on Sabbath, Tebet 26, 5633—January 25, 1873, ש׳ וארא. . 176

SERMON XIII.

EDUCATION. Preached at Bevis Marks Synagogue on Sabbath, Hesvan 29, 5629—November 14, 1868, ש׳ תולדת. 189

SERMON XIV.

ISRAEL'S CHARACTERISTICS. Preached at Bayswater Synagogue on Sabbath, Nisan 8, 5633—April 5, 1873, ש׳ צו הגדול 207

SERMON XV.

ILLNESS OF THE PRINCE OF WALES. Preached at Bevis Marks Synagogue on Sabbath, Tebet 11, 5632—December 23, 1871, ש׳ ויגש. 224

SERMON XVI.

MANNA. Preached at Bevis Marks Synagogue on Shebat 11, 5633—February 8, 1873, ש׳ בשלח. 236

SERMON XVII.

THE HOME SANCTUARY. Preached at Upper Bryanstone Street Synagogue on Sabbath, Adar 2, 5633—March 1, 1873, ש׳ תרומה. 251

SERMON XVIII.

THE HEIFER AND THE CALF. Preached at Upper Bryanstone Street Synagogue on Sabbath, Adar 18, 5631—March 11, 1871, ש׳ כי תשא פרה. 268

SERMON XIX.

THE OMER. Preached at Bevis Marks Synagogue on Sabbath, Sivan 2, 5632—June 8, 1872, ש׳ במדבר . . . 283

SERMON XX.

RELIGIOUS MAJORITY. An Address to Three Youths, on their being received as responsible members of the Jewish community. Delivered at Bevis Marks Synagogue on Sabbath, Shebat 18, 5629—January 30, 1859, ש׳ יתרו . . . 298

VESTRY ROOM,

SPANISH AND PORTUGUESE SYNAGOGUE.

BEVIS MARKS, E.C.

Shebat 21, 5633—*February 28th,* 1873.

REV. AND DEAR SIR,

Moved by the same feelings of satisfaction as are uniformly expressed, not only by the Members of our Congregation but by all who have had the advantage of listening to those eloquent and powerful Discourses which impress so forcibly the sublime teachings of our religion, the Wardens are anxious that you should consent to publish a selection of your Sermons, feeling assured that it would be productive of very happy results.

Hoping that their request will meet with a favourable response,

I have the honour to be,
Rev. and Dear Sir,
Yours faithfully,
S. ALMOSNINO,
Secretary.

To the REV. DR. ARTOM,
Chief Rabbi of the Spanish and Portuguese Congregations.

OFFICE OF THE CHIEF RABBI OF THE SPANISH
AND PORTUGUESE CONGREGATIONS.

Adar 1, 5633—*February* 28, 1873.

GENTLEMEN,

THE request which you have, in flattering terms, conveyed to me to publish a selection of the sermons which I have delivered in our Synagogues, has deeply gratified me, since it constitutes an eloquent proof that, with the assistance of God, I have not spoken or taught in vain.

Yet it is with the utmost reluctance that I accede to your wish, for I am fully aware of the difficulty of speaking and writing in a language which is not my own, in a language so peculiarly expressive and vigorous as the English, in a language which, some years ago, was unknown to me.

May my earnest, though unadorned, discourses meet with the indulgence of the reader, and spread among our brethren a greater knowledge of, and a stronger love for, the religion of Sinai.

I am, Gentlemen,

Yours very truly,

BENJAMIN ARTOM.

To the Wardens of the
Spanish and Portuguese Congregation,
London.

THE JEWISH PASTOR IN MODERN TIMES.

INSTALLATION SERMON.

כי שפתי כהן ישמרו דעת ותורה יבקשו מפיהו כי מלאך ה׳ צבאות הוא :

"For the priest's lips should keep the covenant, and they should seek the law at his mouth: for he is the messenger of the Lord of Hosts." MALACHI ii. 7.

אם הרב דומה למלאך ה׳ צבאות יבקשו תורה מפיהו ואם לאו אל יבקשו תורה מפיהו :

"If the religious head is really the messenger of the Lord, they should seek the law at his mouth; if he is not, they should not seek the law at his mouth." *Talmud*, HAGIGAH 15.

My DEAR BRETHREN,—Do you see that noble hoary-headed figure rising before our mind's eye from the mists of antiquity; those illumined features which inspire us with mingled feelings of reverence, admiration and sympathy? It is the historical figure of an aged man, who, oppressed by cares and sorrow, and overwhelmed with fatigue, is yet hurrying his steps onwards and onwards to an unseen goal. All around him is solitude, all as gloomy as a desert. He has not as yet come to the burning sand of Arabia driven up into destructive clouds by the terrific Simoom, but to a desolate plain which leads to it. No green sward to rejoice the eye, no flower to perfume the air; all that can be seen is a stunted shrub here and there, lifeless and sad. The venerable old man, hardly able to walk any farther, looks about for shelter from the fiery rays of the sun; he perceives a juniper tree from a distance and hastens to it; and there, overcome by lassitude, he falls asleep. But soon an Angel appears, who touches him and says, "Arise and eat." The sounds of the heavenly voice awaken the traveller, and behold! bread and water are before him. He eats and quenches his thirst, but he still feels so overpowered by fatigue that he again lies down and falls asleep. Then the Angel touches him again, and, with an irresistible voice, bids him "Arise and eat, for the journey thou hast to perform is too great for thee."* קום אכל כי רב ממך הדרך

Who is, then, that wondrous man whom Angels feed and heavenly Messengers cheer on? No doubt you have recognised him already, my Brethren; he is Elijah, the Prophet Elijah, who had just achieved one of those wonderful deeds, the influence of which is felt throughout all ages. He had caused a fickle, unsteady, and rebellious people to acknowledge and proclaim in the most solemn manner the Lord God of Israel as the Only, True, and Eternal God; he had confounded the idolaters and their priests; he had delivered his country from the abominations of the worship of Baal, and compelled a faithless king to bow to truth, and to acknowledge that with Providence alone rested the power of fertilising the earth, or withholding the rain. Yet Elijah feels weary and dispirited; he sees that in his mission, not yet fulfilled, he will have numberless obstacles to encounter. He is surrounded by powerful enemies,

* 1 Kings xix. 7.

while his friends are cold and unnerved. His confidence and courage begin to fail; and whilst a prey to doubts and hesitation, and to sad reflections caused by a true love for his people, he flees to the desert where he falls asleep from exhaustion. But the Angel arouses him, infuses into him a new spirit, a new life. "Arise and eat" are but a few short words, but they are pregnant with meaning and thoughts such as the following—"Consider the loftiness, the sacredness of the cause committed unto thee: draw from it fresh courage and zeal; this is the spiritual food that shall sustain thee: thou canst not abandon the career on which thou hast entered, whatever be its length, its difficulties, its struggles; for thou art a messenger of God unto His people. The more thou perseverest on thy path of duty, the greater shall be thy merit."

Elijah obeys; and we see him again on the march. His submission is at once rewarded. The nourishment—the spiritual nourishment—just received imparts to him strength and power to travel forty days and nights, until he arrives at the holy mountain of Horeb. There, after a sublime vision, such as his great master Moses was familiar with, he hears a "still, small voice," a sweet and tender call, by which he is greatly awed, and he wraps his face in his mantle. The voice asks, "What doest thou here, Elijah?" To which the Prophet replies: "I have been very jealous for the Lord God of hosts," etc. והנה אליו קול ויאמר מה לך פה אליהו ויאמר קנא קנאתי ליי' אלהי צבאות וכו'"*

Be not surprised, my Brethren, if, on an occasion so solemn and affecting as the present, I have recalled to your memory an ancient epoch, since which many cen-

* 1 Kings xix. 14.

turies have rolled away. In this episode of the Sacred Scripture there are points which naturally apply to the Jewish Pastor, whose career should be a shadow of the life of a Prophet. The duties of that mission, before which the greatest Prophets, including even Moses himself, hesitated and trembled, and from which they wished to be relieved, as from a task exceeding their powers, seem to be vividly characterised by the fears, the flight, and the discouragement of the Prophet Elijah. How much greater then, must be the trepidation, the terror of a very humble and unworthy teacher like myself, who accepts the burden of the divine service, though in a limited sphere, who undertakes the noble but most difficult task of leading on the path of truth a large community, equally renowned for its antiquity and for the respect with which it surrounds the law and tradition. I hear within the deepest recesses of my soul the echo of a mysterious voice crying—*קום אכל כי רב ממך הדרך "Arise and eat, for the journey thou hast to perform is too great for thee. Prepare thyself, by solid moral and intellectual nourishment, to carry out worthily the high functions to which thou hast been called." Agitated and oppressed by fear and confusion in contemplating the heavy duties before me, what subject am I to develop in my discourse ? On what can I touch more appropriately than on my own task, on the duties, the grave and solemn duties, imposed on the Jewish Pastor in modern times—duties in which alas! so many disappointments may be involved, but which may yield a harvest of so much glory ? You, who among this congregation may understand the language in which I am speaking,§ I

---

* 1 Kings xix. 7.
§ This Sermon was delivered in the French language.

entreat you to listen to me attentively. My words are of importance to us all; for you may judge from what I say all that you may expect of me—all that I ought to do in order that I may enjoy the happiness which attends the practice of virtue—ומצא חן ושכל טוב בעיני אלהים ואדם*—"to find grace in the eyes of God and man." And may He who hath said, "Who has made man's mouth?" §מי שם פה לאדם be with me while I speak, and graciously inspire my humble words, lending them that force which human power alone can seldom attain.

I.

I believe, my dear Brethren, that there are few vocations or missions more solemn and more difficult than that of a Rabbi in the present century. Permit me to examine the nature of this mission and its various duties, and to enquire into the history of the rabbinical vocation from early times. For this purpose I propose to cast a glance on the annals of the past—on history, the mother of wisdom and the light of truth.

When the hour had at last arrived at which the prophecies of the seers were unhappily about to be fulfilled by the chastisement of the people of Israel—the race that had sinned again and again, and had been as often forgiven; when Jerusalem was taken, the altar overthrown, the Temple consumed, and the priests and sacrifices disappeared with all the rites of that glorious form of worship on which all nations of the earth had looked in wonder; when exile had become the fate of the people from whom wearied heaven had at length withdrawn its smile, though only for a short time, as the

---

* Prov. iii. 4. § Exod. iv. 11.

Prophet Isaiah had said, ברגע קטן עזבתיך* "For a small moment have I forsaken thee;" when by one sad blow their ancient joys were shattered, and around them loomed hatred and contempt, oppression and persecution, they still found one refuge, one consolation amid all their cares and troubles—one source of peaceful happiness when the arduous labour of the day was past and the hour of rest had come. This refuge, this comfort lay in the study of the Law and the traditions of the fathers! In those days every man received a religious education. The head of every household became a teacher of the faith, and every home became a school, and at the head of all was the spiritual chief—the teacher of the teachers. His mission was truly a holy one; and when to the zeal of faith he added wisdom and learning, his task was easy. When he spoke all listened. He was understood and obeyed. Then religion reigned supreme; on her hallowed breast the weary exile rested, and was comforted! There he found the peace of mind which was doubly grateful to him since all other peace had fled. And when at one time the sanguinary Roman emperors—who feared our faith because it taught its votaries to be patriots and heroes—sought to crush it by cruel threats, and pronounced the penalty of death on the Rabbi who taught the Law, the Rabbi's mission became more perilous than before, but its nature was unchanged. He remained still the teacher of the people. He had no foes except those who were without the pale of his communion; foes whom he could confront and resist. He had no need to fear apostasy, no suspicion of artful snares, of enticing attempts on his flock, through the condition

* Isaiah liv. 7.

described by the king-prophet's words, ויתערבו בגוים וילמדו מעשיהם "They were mingled among the heathens and learned their works;"* for a wide abyss yawned between the oppressed and the oppressor, between the captive and his ruler! And when at length Christianity, discovering that spiritual sway alone was not sufficient to secure dominion, grasped the sceptre of temporal power; when the creed of Islam arose, sword in hand, and usurped the morality of Judaism, though its doctrine of fatalism separated it irrevocably from the law of Sinai, the condition of our people became still more distressing; for though contact with the gentler manners of the south had softened the fierceness of the northern hordes, and the nameless cruelties of barbaric times had ceased, yet a new and still more terrible enemy arose—I mean Fanaticism! Fanaticism, which distorts the true feelings of humanity, and visits liberty of thought with the scaffold and the rack. Thenceforward the Rabbi's task became more arduous; he saw his flock imperilled by a new danger, a danger with which it was difficult to grapple, for the last-threatened malediction of Moses was fulfilled—והיו חייך תלאים לך מנגד—" And thy life shall hang in doubt before thee." §

It was then that the sword of Mahomet in Asia and Africa, and the Inquisition in Europe made fatal havoc amid the ranks of our exiled people. Yet, persecutions such as these, far from repressing their attachment to their ancient faith, added fuel to the flame of their pious enthusiasm. Our fathers suffered, but they would not yield. They perished readily in the agonies of martyrdom, but they perished without a murmur, without a cry! נגש והוא נענה ולא יפתח פיו ||

* Psalm cvi. 35.   § Deut. xxviii. 66. || Isaiah liii. 7.

And still, in those heroic days, the Pastor remained the father of the faithful, and to him his brethren turned their tearful eyes for justice, for comfort, and for the hopes and promises of religion. His task in those days was full of peril; but yet it was an easy duty, for his words were welcomed with reverence and submission.

But with the fifteenth century a great change, brought about by remarkable public events, affected the social condition of the civilised world. The discovery of America and the Reformation imparted a new direction to the minds of men. Liberty of conscience awoke to life in the Netherlands, and beneath its incipient influence our fathers at once looked forward to safer and brighter days. Their hopes were not frustrated, and from this epoch, the position of our people gradually improved, until this happy age, in which, as regards our social position, civil emancipation and equality form the rule, and oppression and suffering the exception.

Yet, singular as it may appear, the duty of the Jewish Pastor became more difficult as the civil, social, and political condition of our people improved. Alas! that firm union of heart and mind, which is a safeguard to the oppressed, vanished with the chains which had bound them in their days of sorrow! The religious ardour which inflamed our fathers' breasts, and afforded them so much consolation in their adversity, passed away with the persecutions of an intolerant age. That blind obedience to the master's voice which has preserved the sacred heirloom of the Law and tradition intact through centuries, gave place to a new-born spirit of enquiry and cavil—a spirit which is so perilous only because it is too often tainted with malevolence and disingenuousness. The old anxious and general desire to acquire a knowledge of our national language, and through it, of the majestic productions of the genius and learning of our great authors and teachers, yielded to a craving for the thousand superficial trifles which constitute the glittering surface-education of modern days. It became the evident duty of the Jewish Pastor to resist, to check the threatened danger—the tendency which menaces with ruin our national literature, national sentiment, and national bond. And this is still his task! Perhaps, the mission is beyond his restricted powers. But no! this cannot be; for religion warms the heart with fervour, and endows the mind with a force which shapes into practicability aims that seem unattainable at first! This fervour, this force, inspired and animated the Prophets of old, who dared to correct and to denounce the proud monarchs of the earth. For the blessed spirit of God was with them! רוח אדני אלהים עלי—"The spirit of God is on me,"* cried Isaiah: and thus armed, thus protected, he defied all human dangers and vanquished every human foe!

II.

And now, my dear Brethren, let us examine what duties in these days belong to the Jewish Pastor. The condition of the human mind which, as time advanced, became more and more impressed with the tendencies of truth, has attained a stand-point which offers a striking aspect to a reflective spirit. Perhaps at no previous time has there been so much religious indifference, yet never has there been so much written on religious questions. Philosophers first kindled the spark of liberty of

* Isaiah lxi. 1.

judgment, and governments have been obliged to follow in their wake in affairs of public policy; and at length the minds of the masses awoke to a terrible doubt—doubt in matters of religious belief. Much of that which men believed to be absolute truth lost the halo which rendered it divine. Dogmas to which men bowed in blind obedience, seem no longer invulnerable to the questioning eyes of criticism. The religion which pretentiously asserted itself to be the successor of Judaism, assailed by the spirit of enquiry, trembles under the attacks of reason—and well it may; for beneath that searching light, it has all to lose. And even its sister faith, which protested against Catholicism, quivers on the brink of a chasm opened by its own hands. It is a force which has been able to destroy but which cannot rebuild. And as in all things in which the original fount has spread into less pure channels, men go back to the source from which they sprang, so in the question of religion, men look back enquiringly into the original faith—the simplest and purest of all—the creed of Sinai. And thus Judaism again becomes a subject of anxious study. At no former period of their career was it ever more needful than at present for the Jewish people to be well instructed in, and thoroughly acquainted with, the principles and practice of their faith, in order to be able to teach them and to defend them. This duty is especially the mission of the Rabbi, who should strain every nerve to expel religious ignorance from the Congregation which he guides—and this task has been truly described in the Talmud—תלמידי חכמים אין להם מנוחה "Religious teachers can aspire to no repose." *

* Talmud Berachot, 64.

Unfortunately, among our people, religious instruction does not receive the attention which it merits. Instead of its being considered as a main element of education, it has become, even in our schools, but especially in our families, a mere subsidiary isolated branch, and is held at the best as equal—though more usually inferior—to other subjects of study. Yet religious instruction, rightly understood, should be the focus—the centre of activity and power, whither all other studies converge, and whence they should derive their strength and vitality. In this matter, school and home should work hand in hand; school and home influences should aid and strengthen each other. Our children should hear in their schools the elucidation of principles first instilled into their young minds at home; and they should see at home the rigid practice and observance of the laws and rules of conduct inculcated at school. Combined action, and unison of feeling and responsibility would thus impart increased authority both to parent and to teacher. Religion would take firm hold of the heart of youth, and form an impregnable bulwark against temptation and corruption. Alas! this golden age of Judaism is but a dream. It has no real existence anywhere—I suspect, not even in your own community, in which the meritorious endeavours of so many are directed to the preservation of religion. The want of religious instruction, and of united action of home and school, is, in my opinion, the true cause of the scepticism, indifference, superstition and materialism which prevail. But it is vain to deplore the evil. Let us rather try to remedy it. And this is one of the duties of the Jewish Pastor. צפה נתתיך לבית ישראל "I make thee guardian of the house of Israel,"* said the Lord to Ezekiel. Yes! the Pastor

---

* Ezekiel iii. 17.

should be, in truth, a warder of the holy trust confided to his guardianship. In the homes, in which he should strive to be an ever welcome guest by reason of his sacred calling and his spotless life—in these homes he should watch these holy interests, and be ever ready to counsel and guide parents of families in the religious training of their children: he should help them, by his influence, to place their little ones on the right path! It is his duty to urge the firm, inseparable connection of moral, secular and religious education. If these be divided, the true aim of neither will be attained in the Israelite. Your education should be such as to train a child to become, at the same time, a good man, a good citizen, and a good Jew. But if secular instruction be the sole object of attention, the boy thus taught will become a heartless man—a man cold to all the higher sentiments of our nature—a man who will easily repudiate his faith, his nationality, the past glories and the future promise of his race. From the home the Pastor's way lies to the school; there his duty is to supervise education, and encourage master and pupil—to guide the teacher, who must be not only a *good* Jew, but an *educated* Jew; for the creed of our fathers is not taught by the dry maxims of the Catechism alone! From all the treasures of knowledge, but more especially from the mine of history, he should bring to light the immortal truths of our faith, and its glorious morality, which is the source of the moral teachings of all later creeds. He will urge the most careful attention to the education of young girls, for it especially depends on woman to render home a hallowed temple.

While enjoying the happy position of civil equality which we have attained by the advance of civilisation and the progress of political freedom, let us never be unmindful of the glories of our past. We are citizens, and let us by all means act as good citizens; but we must not forget that we are Jews also; nay, Jews before all—above all other titles and qualifications. Then let us strive earnestly to fulfil the twofold duty which is laid upon us. Believe me when I tell you, that the world will only respect us so long as we accept our sacred mission — so long as we are the faithful custodians of our nationality!

But if we would in truth retain our nationality, we must assuredly retain our oral law—the law which teaches us in detail all the domestic and social virtues, and the mode of application of the general principles inculcated in the dispensation of Sinai. That law we must respect. It is a chain whose links are closely welded together, and if we attempt to break but one link, we imperil the whole. And if we would retain our nationality, we must also retain our sacred, our national language—the language which has been for centuries our bond of union—which, though for ages we have been scattered over the broad face of the earth, has kept us together, and gathered our dispersed masses into one family, one people, one heart; separated by clime and distance, but united by one hope, one promise, one sacred aspiration!

III.

I have hitherto referred to the education of our young children, but the duties of the Jewish Pastor do not end at this point. There are among us men and women who have attained years of maturity, but whose youth may unhappily have been deprived of the blessings of a spiritual education. They know their religion—but in its material aspect only. They are acquainted with its forms and ceremonies, conversant with its practical observances, but here their religious knowledge ends. They know not the *spirit* of the practice—the signification of the rites which they perform—the true intent of the laws which they obey. Hence their hearts are cold to the true consolations which spring from intelligent faith; their minds are devoid of the sublime thoughts which rise from religion spiritualised. When their children crave for the knowledge they would willingly impart, alas! they must be mute in their young presence, for they themselves have all to learn. There are many too, who in the cares and struggles and changes of varied and troublous life, have forgotten the lessons of their youth, and would willingly hear again the truths which still are dear to them—the lessons which are borne again to their manhood laden with many a tender memory of childhood. Again, there are some who go to Synagogue with sorrowing or heavy hearts, seeking comfort and instruction from the living lips of a preacher, which they are unable to find in a mere Prayer-book, the lofty expressions of which they perhaps do not understand. For all these the Rabbi has many and serious duties to fulfil. All these demand his care and anxious energy.

My dear Brethren, when I speak of preaching, I mean that religious instruction which is, in fact, of all ages — the instruction which dates from the days of the Prophets, and the imparting of which was almost their only mission—at least it was the mission in which they shone so gloriously. "Go," said the Lord to Isaiah—"Go preach! cry out! fear nothing; raise thy voice with a

THE JEWISH PASTOR.

sound loud as the trumpet, and reveal to my people its transgressions, and to the house of Israel its iniquities." But God laid a still heavier duty on Ezekiel, and therefore on all future ministers of religion. If he who would be a warder of the faith, sees the anger of God about to burst on His people, and the sword about to descend, and if he fail to sound the alarm, then he shall be accountable for the blood of him on whom the sword may fall! והצפה כי יראה את החרב באה ולא תקע בשופר והעם לא נזהר ותבא חרב ותקח מהם נפש הוא בעונו נלקח ודמו מיד הצפה אדרש : *

From this awful warning we may judge of the solemn importance of the preacher's duty; for it is the PREACHER who henceforth must sound the trumpet of warning in the hour of a sinful people's peril; it is the preacher who must call the sinner back to the paths of virtue, who must explain the majesty of religion and denounce the misery of sin! But for the power given to the Pastor thus to uplift his voice among the people, his mission would be a vain, a fruitless work. כי שפתי כהן ישמרו דעת §

From the Pastor's lips the truth must go forth to his flock, and it is from the pulpit that he has to declare it to the faithful. For if we appreciate the preacher's mission with intelligence and sympathy, surely we must feel that it is a solemn hour—that in which he stands amid his silent auditors and utters the message of everlasting truth; teaching men the ordinances of faith, and the precepts of civil life; teaching men their duty to their neighbour, and to the fatherland which is so dear to them; their duty to its sovereign, and the respect due to its laws; teaching them the rules and precepts which

* Ezekiel xxxiii. 6.   § Malachi ii. 7.

render life happy on earth below, and promise undying happiness in the world to come! From his lips, as the congregation throngs silently around him, must flow words of advice, admonition, reproof, and warning, and words of hope, comfort and promise!

The preacher must fulfil his duty fearlessly, and tell his solemn truths unflinchingly to the rich as well as to the poor, to the powerful as well as to the humble. For God, as Isaiah has told us, will inspire him: every day must he devote to learning and teaching that Law which strengthens his words—and upholds the fallen, the feeble and the dejected. In obeying the inner voice that calls him to his work, he may unhappily, in the course of his sterner duties, meet with resentment, anger, scorn, and obloquy; but he must not yield nor tremble. God will be with him. He will help him; and he may cry, with the Prophet, "I shall not be confounded; I have set my face like a flint, and I know that I shall not be ashamed."

ואדני אלהים יעזר לי על כן לא נכלמתי על כן שמתי פני כחלמיש ואדע כי לא אבוש: *

He will never be put to shame, for he is only the interpreter of the immutable and incontrovertible truths of our Divine Religion!

Yes, my dear Brethren, I firmly believe that preaching is one of the most important duties of the Jewish Pastor; and that duty I will take earnestly to heart. I bear deeply in mind that I am the spiritual guide of a congregation whose glory has long been to have preserved inviolate the inheritance bequeathed to them by their honoured ancestors. I am the firm custodian of our hallowed traditions. I bear in mind that I am the pastor of a congregation which builds a holy joy on the

* Isaiah l. 7.

rigorous observance of our ancient rites and festivals; which devotes much care to the duties of charity, and which extends a maternal affection to all its children—even to those who are at a distance from it, to whom it sends a kindly greeting: שובו אלי ואשובה אליכם—"Return unto me, and I will return unto you."* Assuredly I shall be understood when henceforth on this sacred spot, I deliver the words of religion; when, seeking instruction from the rich literary treasures of our oral law, I shall endeavour to show how this law harmonises with the various conditions and epochs of social existence, and the varied requirements of humanity, even so as we have been assured, אשר יעשה אתם האדם וחי בהם:, which if a man do "he shall live in them."§ I shall be understood when I narrate the exemplary lives of the sages of our people, some of whom were friends of kings and emperors, yet remained strict adherents to our faith; when I explain their precious maxims, to love our neighbours as ourselves; to forgive our enemies; to be patient and gentle towards the sinner, and to strive to recall him to the pale of faith by tender and affectionate persuasion. And if by the grace of God, my humble words be received by you with kindness and sympathy, I shall ever heartily and earnestly seek to promote a spirit of love, concord and brotherhood; and say from the depths of my heart: "O brethren of the house of Israel, let there never be disunion, never divisions amongst us! Let us love and cling to each other! Let us rivet still more closely the links which bind us together! Let us remain firmly and lovingly united, until the day when we shall be still more firmly, still more lovingly united

* Malachi iii. 7. § Levit. xviii. 5.

in our own land, whither we shall be gathered as one people under the sceptre of one only King! ועשיתי אותם לגוי אחד בארץ בהרי ישראל ומלך אחד יהיה לכלם למלך ולא יהיה עוד לישני גוים ולא יחצו עוד לשתי ממלכות עוד *

Such then, I believe to be the mission of the Jewish Pastor in our days. If he fulfils his duty, the pulpit will be to him a source of glory and consolation, for it will enable him to carry religion triumphantly and victoriously through the ranks of her enemies; to labour zealously for the welfare of his flock, for the instruction of his brethren; to give joy to the righteous, and to win back the sinner. According to the words of the Prophet, which our sages have interpreted so admirably, it should be said of him: "The law of truth was in his mouth, there was no iniquity found on his lips; he walked with me in peace and righteousness, and brought many sinners back from their transgression." תורת אמת היתה בפיהו שלא טמא את הטהור ולא טהר את הטמא, ועולה לא נמצא בישפתיו שלא אסר את המותר ולא התיר את האסור, בשלום ובמישור הלך אתי שלא הרהר אחר דרכי המקום, ורבים השיב מעון שהשיב פושעים לתורה: §

But if there is no radical reform necessary in our religion, there is yet much to be done. There is much ignorance to be dispelled, and a religious sentiment to be rekindled by a true Jewish education. Our mode of worship may be rendered more dignified and suited to its purpose, by conducting it with the order and reverence which command respect. It is the Rabbi's duty to initiate all improvements, to remove all abuses if he would indeed honour the Holy Name before the world מקדש שמו ברבים:

* Ezekiel xxxvii. 22.
§ Medrash Yalkut, chap. DLXXXVIII., commenting upon Malachi ii. 6.

And with God's help, I will strive to do these things; and I will devote all my powers to my work; for indeed I ardently hope that this congregation may be true to its holy title and bear it bravely before the world, so that it may be truly said—אין זה כי אם בית אלהים וזה שער השמים—"This is none other but the house of God, and this is the *gate of heaven*."*

Let us so act that our brethren who dwell in foreign countries, that our fellow citizens of other creeds may commend us for the manner in which we conduct our worship and celebrate our rites; let us retain the holy charm of religious song—the vocal harmonies with which the Temple of Jerusalem was filled, and which ever impart a heavenly beauty to the words of prayer.

It is moreover, the Rabbi's duty to superintend all works of public charity, the accomplishment of which will render him, "the father of the orphan, the protector of the widow." The Pastor should be ever open to the appeal of the poor and wretched,—the distressed father of a family who may have fallen low, whether by his own fault, or by the force of circumstances—the unhappy woman who may have been deserted, despite her innocence, or by reason of her guilt. He must not shrink from contact with misery and squalor, from the abode of poverty and the house of suffering; he must not shun any spectacle of pain or grief—the pallet of the dying, or the infection of disease. These sights and sounds may lacerate his heart, but they will not deter him from his duty. As he feels no repulsion from the hovel of the indigent, so he should feel no attraction for the mansion of the wealthy. And if at times his steps lead him to the gilded halls of wealth

---

* Gen. xxviii. 17.

and luxury, he should go thither, not for the sake of joining in their revels and their banquets, but in order to bespeak help for the poor, or to give hope and comfort in the hour of pain and sorrow, from which neither wealth nor grandeur can protect. He should endeavour to soften every grief, to wipe away every tear. He must be the friend of every family, of every home; he must seek out the sufferer, if the sufferer does not come to seek him; he must try to discover the hidden source of discord, the concealed injustice and secret wrong, and strive to remedy the evil. He must be ready to give advice and counsel; he must promote good works, and be the living link between the rich and the poor, and thus maintain the loving spirit which has rendered the Jewish character the type of true charity. But when he helps the poor, he should discourage idleness, and urge self-reliance and industrious exertions.

All works and institutions of beneficence and philanthropy should receive help and protection from him. He must be the most ardent and zealous promoter and supporter of all that can tend to the moral and religious benefit and progress of his congregation. In the words of prophecy, "He must open the eyes of the blind, release the captive from his bonds, and deliver those who are plunged in darkness!"—לפקח עינים עורות להוציא ממסגר אסיר מבית כלא יושבי חושך:*

I have attempted to give you a sketch of what I conceive the duties of a Rabbi to be in the present age, for

* Isaiah xlii. 7.

he is now the apostle not only of religious truth, but also of every other truth which can be useful to mankind; he is a moving spring in the great moral machine which works always in the same direction and towards the same end—human improvement and happiness. I wish I could have made myself fully understood by you, my dear Brethren, for I want your assistance in the work before me. I am here in the presence of my new congregation, of my new flock, which I must endeavour to lead to good pastures. I am here in the sacred house of the God of Israel, of the Almighty Himself, who hears the words of men, and sees the innermost recesses of their hearts. And in this place, and in this moment which is, perhaps, the most solemn in my life, I hesitate not to promise to devote all my thoughts, all my attention to the great work, for the performance of which I was elected, though young and unworthy. I will spare no effort and shrink from no labour for the moral benefit of this congregation. I will work to promote our holy religion, that Judaism so often misunderstood through ignorance or malignity. I will venture to repeat on my part what Judah said to Jacob when the patriarch refused to let his dear Benjamin depart for Egypt, אנכי אערבנו מידי תבקשנו אם לא אביאתיו אליך והצגתיו לפניך וחטאתי לך כל הימים "I will be surety for him; of my hand shalt thou require him; if I bring him not unto thee, and set him before thee, then let me bear the blame for ever."*

But, I repeat, I shall require your assistance. In all human concerns union gives strength and insures the success of great undertakings. It is necessary that labourers in this holy field should aid and animate each

* Gen. xliii. 9.

other; אִישׁ אֶת רֵעֵהוּ יַעְזֹרוּ וּלְאָחִיו יֹאמַר חֲזָק "They helped every one his neighbour, and every one said to his brother, Be of good courage."* From you principally, who are the educators and teachers of our children, I must crave help and support that we may work together. The rising generation ought to be imbued with a strong Jewish feeling, and no exertion should be spared to attain so noble an end. The human mind is now eager to acquire extended knowledge. Let us direct these favourable tendencies on the good path, and towards the loftiest aims, and we shall triumph. And you who lead this congregation with your influence and wisdom, you also, I trust, will assist and encourage your Pastor, to whom all is new in this foreign land. You will find me ever willing, and your example will strengthen my hands. Be my friends and brethren, all you around me, and I will be to you both a friend and a brother. To-day I ask from you only a word, the word with which the elders of our nation greeted Ezra, when he undertook the re-establishment of our nationality, קוּם כִּי עָלֶיךָ הַדָּבָר וַאֲנַחְנוּ עִמָּךְ חֲזַק וַעֲשֵׂה "Arise, for this matter belongs unto thee; we also will be with thee: be of good courage, and do it."§ O my Brethren, repeat to me this word, and all fear and hesitation will vanish, and the hope of success will gladden my heart!

But unto Thee, O Lord, I raise my eyes with all my soul, for "the steps of man are only strengthened by Thee" מה׳ מִצְעֲדֵי גֶבֶר כּוֹנָנוּ‖ I pray Thy Divine Providence to assist me in my holy mission, to grant me an eloquent and persuasive tongue, to bestow upon me the power of convincing of their error those who transgress,

* Isaiah xli. 6.   § Ezra x. 4.   ‖ Psalm xxxvii. 23.

and to crown with success my efforts for my brethren's welfare and for the glorification of Thy holy name.

O Lord, my God and the God of my fathers, bless this country and its Sovereign; bless this free people, which gives such glorious examples of toleration and religious liberty, and venerates the Jewish faith as the mother of the creed of the most civilised nations.

May He, who blessed our ancestors, Abraham, Isaac, and Jacob, bless this holy congregation and all the Jewish community; them, their wives, their children, and all belonging to them; bless those who establish oratories for prayer, and those who go thither to pray; the pious men who contribute with their offerings to the lustre of Thy worship; those who administer food to poor pilgrims, and liberal alms to the indigent; bless the venerable philanthropist who has so often endangered his own life to accomplish the holiest works of brotherly love and charity. May God protect those who devote themselves faithfully and piously to the welfare of their congregation; may He reward them, forgive their sins, and heal their wounds. May He grant success to the work of our hands. May He bestow happiness upon all the children of Israel our brethren, and extend His mercy to all mankind. "The Lord will give strength unto his people, the Lord will bless his people with peace."

ה׳ עוז לעמו יתן ה׳ יברך את עמו בשלום ׳ אמן :

THE SHOFAR.

A NEW YEAR'S-DAY SERMON.

והרעתם בהצצרות ונזכרתם לפני ה' א‌‌להיכם :

"Ye shall blow an alarm with the trumpets, and ye shall be remembered before the Lord your God."

NUMBERS x. 9.

אף על פי שתקיעת שופר גזירת הכתוב רמז יש בו כלומר עורו ישנים מישנתכם ונרדמים הקיצו מתרדמתכם וחפשו מעשיכם וחזרו בתשובה :

"Besides its Scriptural object, the New Year's trumpet has a profound meaning. It says: 'Awake ye that sleep; up, up ye that slumber; investigate your actions and be repentant.'"

MAIM. *Treatise on Repentance.*

MY DEAR BRETHREN,—Have you ever found yourselves alone in a wild tract of land, when instead of a gentle breeze, a violent wind blows, which howls and roars like the beast of the forest, and in its fury "rends the mountains and breaks in pieces the rocks, before the Lord?"* מפרק הרים ומשבר סלעים לפני ה' : Does then your courage remain firm? No, it does not; you are frightened, and in your terror you exclaim: That, that is the voice of the Almighty. Yet, "the Almighty is not in the wind." לא ברוח ה' And when an earthquake visits us, its terrible vibration shaking the foundations of houses and towers, of cities

* 1 Kings xix. 11.

and villages, while its rumbling noise fills our heart with alarm, do we not repeat again: That is the voice of the Lord? Yet "the Lord is not in the earthquake." לא ברעש ה׳ So, when the bosom of the earth bursts violently open and ejects fire, lava, and melted metals with fearful and deafening clash, do we not then whisper with dismay: That, that is the voice of the Lord? And yet "the Lord is not in the fire." לא באש ה׳ Winds, earthquakes and volcanic eruptions are the Lord's messengers, but they are merely the agents of the physical world and natural phenomena. The voice of God is "a still small voice." * קול דממה דקה A still small voice which delights and agitates, awes and consoles man's heart.

We may recognise a symbol of the voice of God in the strange sounds which have echoed within these sacred precincts on the New Year's day, and which shall again echo before the greatest day of the Hebrew year has entirely elapsed. Yet the Shofar has not frightened or agitated us. We have heard it without the least emotion, nay, with all the indifference with which we perform a constantly repeated act, a thing "taught by the precept of men." § מצות אנשים מלמדה If the sound of the Shofar is not the voice of the Lord, it is its representative, the effect of His express command. Like the drums which beat at the head of a battalion of soldiers and lead it onward, their hurried or heavy roll making the soldiers' march quick or slow, so our trumpet's sounds determined in the days of old the departure and the advance of the camp of the Hebrews. "When ye blow an alarm, then the camps shall go forward." ותקעתם תרועה ונסעו המחנות ‖ Even in the present they lead

* 1 Kings xix. 11.   § Isaiah xxix. 13.   ‖ Numbers x. 5.

the legions of Israel onward on the path of religion and duty. That march was begun amidst the marshes of the Nile, continued on the sands of the wilderness, and on all the roads of the earth. And it is not yet over. Its object was, and still is, only one: the fulfilment of the compact of Sinai, and the perfecting of the human race. Thus understood, the Shofar is really the trumpet of the Lord, the sounds of which awaken the sleeping, rouse the sluggard, give movement to those who stand still, and urge forward the slow.

I have already treated this subject in its general aspect. This morning I intend to explain the meaning of the three touching prayers which in the additional service of New Year's Day, are preceded and followed by the sounds of the Shofar, and which are respectively called מלכיות *Malchiot*, זכרונות *Zichronot*, שופרות *Shofarot*. No ideas can be more elevating, more beautiful and impressive than those which they convey to us. But we cannot find them out, we are unable to appreciate them, unless we thoroughly devote both our mind and our heart to their consideration, unless we withdraw for a while from our worldly cares and every day's exertions.

אמר הק"בה. לישראל אמרו לפני בר"ה מלכיות זכרונות ושופרות · מלכיות כדי שתמליכוני עליכם · זכרונות כדי שיעלה זכרונכם לפני לטובה ובמה בשופר: "The Lord said unto Israel: Let me hear the *Malchiot*, by which you accept my sovereignty; let me hear the *Zichronot*, which may recall you favourably to my remembrance. You can attain this double object by means of the *Shofar*."* These are the explicit words of tradition, and naturally mark the three parts of my meditation.

* Talmud Roshashana 16.

I.

The first hour of the New Year strikes, that hour which men have expected with eager desire, and is immediately the sign of pleasures, rejoicings, and revelry. It announces among nations that the time has come when they may indulge in amusements of all kinds, even those which border on intemperance and the frantic excitement of the senses. But how different is its character in Judaism! The first hour in the year is for us an appeal to new thoughts, to new habits; to unwonted reflections. It reminds us of Creation—of the time when the Universe was not yet formed, and its materials exhibited a state of chaos; when the elements, mixed with each other, the earth with the water, and the atmosphere with fire, were suddenly called by the commanding voice of the Master into order, harmony and beauty; when boundaries were set both to the ocean and the atmosphere, and the world was enveloped in the charming blue vault adorned with sparkling stars and crowned with the sun, "the highest minister of nature." According to Judaism, the New Year's Day is the anniversary of Creation, and we ought to commemorate it with all possible solemnity. We often celebrate the anniversary of pigmean events, the centenary of authors, artists or warriors; we dare to solemnise the annual returning of bloody revolutions and cruel victories; and ought we not to solemnise with greater eagerness and more splendid ceremonies the sublime fact of Creation, which was prompted by love, carried out by the means of love, and had only one object: love? *Malchiot* is the name of the first of the three-mentioned prayers, and it means the proclamation of the sovereignty of the Lord, the Lord's coronation; as David said: "The Lord reigneth, He is clothed with majesty; the Lord is clothed with strength wherewith He hath girded Himself: the world is also established that it cannot be moved."* ה׳ מלך גאות לבש לבש ה׳ עז התאזר אף תכון תבל בל תמוט And by celebrating Creation, of which God was the sole and omnipotent Agent, we proclaim Him the king of the Universe, we break the idol of human conceit, we remind man that, compared to the Eternal Maker, he is nothing but a powerless creature.

And is it not necessary to remind him of his weakness? He remembers too well the power which his intellect gives him upon the earth, in accordance with God's words: "Replenish the earth and subdue it," § ומלאו את הארץ ולבשה He has conquered it and subjected it to his iron rule. He levels mountains, raises valleys, crushes rocks, pierces lofty Alpine chains, and opens roads through their virgin bosom: he scorns distances, and by a spark of invisible fire he communicates his thoughts and orders from one end of the earth to the other, even through the depths of the sea. He penetrates the mysteries of nature, and at his imperious call, the very lightning falls obediently at his feet. He knows and avails himself of his power; but he forgets the insignificance of his origin, he thinks himself omnipotent. His pride grows daily, and like the tide, rises over its boundaries. Intoxicated with power, he says: "By the strength of my hand I have done it, and by my wisdom, for I am prudent, etc., and my hand has found as a nest the riches of the people; and as one

* Psalm xciii. 1.   § Gen. i. 28.

gathereth eggs that are left, have I gathered all the earth," etc.* כי אמר בכח ידי עשיתי ובחכמתי כי נבנותי וכול׳

He is like the astrologer of old who, while pretending to foretell the future from the position of the stars, did not see the pit open before him, and endangered his life by falling into it. He attributes his success to no other being but himself, and thinks his power unbounded, while a trifling circumstance can cut the thread of his existence and reduce his sounding boast to the silence of the grave.

Then the voice of the strange trumpet echoes suddenly through the air, and rouses us from our repose; it is not the trumpet blown by the victor to announce his joy and triumph, not the trumpet which sounds mournfully to tell defeat and shame.§ אין קול ענות גבורה ואין קול ענות חלושה It is the Shofar which warns us against dangerous sleep, and says: "Up ye that sleep, awake ye that slumber, recall to your mind the Creator, whose remembrance you have set aside; think of the truth which you have forgotten in the midst of worldly vanities, false pleasures and hallucinations." ‖ The Lord whom we always call a Father, is now designated by His attribute of justice. He is metaphorically described as holding in one hand the balance, in the other the sword. "Before Him," says the Talmud,¶ "pass all human creatures like sheep before the shepherd," בר״ה כל באי עולם עוברים לפניו כבני מרון; and "the Lord of hosts shall be exalted in judgment."** והאל הקדוש נקדש בצדקה. These ideas of throne and judge, of balance and sword, of trial and judgment produce a profound impression upon our

---

* Isaiah x. 13.   § Exodus xxxii. 18.
‖ Maim. "Treatise on Repentance."   ¶ Roshashana 18.
** Isaiah v. 16.

heart and imagination; our eyes seem to open to fresh light, and we recognise that our mental powers, although great, are limited and fallible; we see the miseries to which we are subject, we think of the terrible diseases which only leave in us consciousness enough to make us aware of our decay. What rain is to a dry and thirsty land, this doctrine is to our own mind and heart. It infuses into us new vigour, it forces us to acknowledge the tribute of praise which we owe to the "Master of all, the Maker of the Universe," *עלינו לשבח לאדון לכל לתת גדולה ליוצר בראשית, who by means of revelation placed our lot above the lot of the nations of the earth, and ennobled us by commanding us to adore the King of kings, the Holy One of Israel. Let us then repeat the *Malchiot*, let us blow the trumpet and announce the coronation of the Lord, and His sovereignty upon the earth: let us proclaim that he has ascended His throne and grasped the sceptre of justice. "How great are His signs and how mighty are His wonders! His kingdom is an everlasting kingdom, and His dominion is from generation to generation." § אתוהי כמה כברבין ותמהותי כמה תקיפין מלכותה מלכות עלם ושלטנה עם דר ודר:

II.

The second prayer, the *Zichronot*, begins by these impressive words: "Thou rememberest the work of the world and visitest all creatures; unto Thee all mysteries are revealed, and things secret from the day of Creation are known, for there is no forgetfulness before the throne of Thy majesty, and nothing remains concealed from Thy eyes." אתה זוכר מעשה עולם ופוקד כל יצורי קדם.

* Morning Service on New Year's Day.   § Daniel iii. 33.

How grand are these ideas, how useful is the lesson they convey! They can be summed up in one word: Remember.—Remember that there is an eye above which sees everything, actions, thoughts, intentions; an ear which hears every sound, every word, every whisper; and a hand which registers all our achievements and exploits in ineffaceable characters.* May this recollection be unto thee a wholesome warning, and a powerful restraint from the commission of transgression, ungodliness, and iniquity.—Remember: retrace in thy mind the road of the past, throw a glance on bygone days, embrace with a rapid look all the circle of thy actions and of accomplished events. Another year has elapsed and sunk into the abyss of the past. The winter with its sad retinue, the spring with its gay dress of flowers, the summer with its blessed harvest are gone, and another autumn has come with its manifold gifts. But the fall of the withered leaves, the long evenings, the cool nights, and the aspect of nature tell us that another winter is not far away. Remember how you have employed the year. All things around us, both animate and inanimate, have fulfilled their task. They have done that to which they were bound by the Divine Law, or to which they were led by their instinct. The sun has given light and heat to the earth which in her turn has completed her annual revolution around him. The moon in her monthly course has twelve times hidden her face and re appeared, and while lessening the gloom of the night, has governed and regulated the tides. The fields have given their corn, the trees their fruit, the gardens their ambrosial flowers. The animals have done their work: the birds by destroying pernicious insects, wild

* Talmud, Abot.

beasts by devouring each other, even the small ichneumon by hunting out the eggs of the crocodile. But thou, O man! what hast thou done? Where is the useful labour which thou hast achieved? Three hundred and sixty-five times hast thou had the opportunity of doing either good or evil; which way hast thou chosen? Condemned to the eternal law of labour, hast thou tilled the earth and forced it to yield the treasures hidden in its bosom? Hast thou eaten bread in the sweat of thy brow, by work and industry, or hast thou listened to the voice of sloth and stretched out thy hand in order to implore thy neighbour's help, thus renouncing thy dignity and covering thy face with the indelible blush of shame?* כיון שנצטרך לבריות נעשה פניו ככרום Another field was placed before thee; hast thou tilled it and made it productive? Hast thou educated that intellect which can conceive so many ideas, and acquire so much knowledge? Hast thou taught it truth? Hast thou raised it by the study of the law which draws man nearer to the Divinity? Hast thou improved thy heart and caused it to beat with noble feelings, with enthusiasm for what is good? Remember, remember, hast thou sown in thy way tears or smiles, joy or despair, love or hatred, benevolence or cruelty? How many of thy fellow-creatures hast thou assisted, how many consoled, how many raised by kind advice from the mire of degradation, from the abomination of vice, from the depth of dejection? Because thy actions are to be weighed in the balance of justice, and the sentence is to be pronounced, as we read in the second prayer: "For these the sword, for those peace; for the one famine, for the other abundance; and all creatures are

* Talmud Berachot, 6.

visited, and their name is mentioned for life or for death." * איזו לחרב ואיזו לשלום אוזו לרעב ואיזו לשובע ובריות בו יפקדו להזכירם לחיים ולמות:

The announcement and imagery of the divine justice may be formidable and terrifying; but together with it, we ought to remember the divine mercy which is as inexhaustible as God's justice is inflexible. With our faults He remembers our good will, the stubborn resistance which many a time we opposed to evil temptation, the few victories which we have gained over this internal enemy; and with kindness and love He calls us to repentance, for "His hands are always stretched out to receive those who return." § ידו של הק״בה פשוטה לקבל שבים: He is still our Father, and Israel is His son. He said, "I do remember him still: therefore my bowels are troubled for him; I will surely have mercy upon him, saith the Lord." ‖ זכר אזכרנו עוד על כן המו מעי לו רחם ארחמנו נאם ה': This, my brethren, is the real meaning of the *Zichronot*. Let us declare it before the Lord by sounding the mystical trumpet, "and we shall be remembered favourably by Him."

III.

It is thus our duty to proclaim on the New Year's Day that the Lord is King of the universe, and to remember our past conduct. "And by what means?" says the Talmud. "By the Shofar." ובמה בשופר The new sounds which the Shofar produces signify that new words and expressions which, unfortunately are not familiar to us, ought to be uttered by our lips; words by which we sincerely and humbly confess our misdeeds, expressions of ardent prayer, supplications revealing our

* Ritual.   § Talmud Pesachim.   ‖ Jerem. xxxi. 20.

longing for forgiveness. "Seek ye the Lord while He may be found; call ye upon Him while He is near."*
דרשו ה׳ בהמצאו קראהו בהיותו קרוב: Always accessible to the entreaties of human creatures, the Lord seems to have pointed out to us these ten penitential days as the best adapted to our moral regeneration. It was in these days that Abraham, with a courage unparalleled in history, was ready at the Lord's command to sacrifice his only son; it was in these days that the Lord, who had pronounced a sentence of destruction upon the incorrigible Hebrews, listened to Moses and uttered the great word "Pardon." And it is in these days that if we sacrifice on the altar of duty that which is often unto us dearer than a son—I mean our selfishness and our passions—He who disposes of life and death will accept our prayers and satisfy our wants. Let us then, have recourse to prayer which, if we are true to ourselves, will be our adviser, our consoler, our rescuer.

But this prayer, which has been preceded by the acknowledgment of the Lord's sovereignty, and by the remembrance of all our actions, must also be strengthened by the firm intention of repairing what we have damaged, and of rebuilding what we have wilfully destroyed. It may be a principle in other creeds that *faith without good actions* is sufficient, and that prayer alone has the power of soothing the Divinity. In Judaism, on the contrary, there is no forgiveness for those who pray and fast and thus usurp public consideration, unless the day be marked by reparation for injuries, and reconciliation between man and man; none for those who oppress their neighbour by their intolerable pride; none for those who, according to David, "speak with two hearts;" "those whose

* Isaiah lv. 6.

THE SHOFAR.

hands, according to Isaiah,* are defiled with blood and their fingers with iniquity, whose lips have spoken lies and their tongues have uttered perverseness" שפתותיכם דברו שקר לשונכם עולה תהגה; for them there is no forgiveness, unless they promptly shield themselves under the three combined virtues of penitence, prayer, and charity.

My Brethren, if in the *Malchiot* we acknowledge and adore, if in the *Zichronot* we remember and repent, if in the *Shofarot* we pray and promise to give reparation, then, when the peal of the Shofar is again heard in this holy place, in the last hour of the Day of Atonement, that sound will not be a threatening voice, but will proclaim glorious and delightful tidings. It will be the prophetic Shofar of Mount Sinai, which announced the freedom of Israel to the world, and declared him the bearer of the Lord's standard, of the religion of mankind. It will be the great trumpet of religion and liberty which in *that day* "shall be blown, and they shall come who were ready to perish in the land of Assyria, and the outcasts of the land of Egypt, and shall worship the Lord in the holy mountain of Jerusalem."§ It will announce to us that the offerings of our heart are agreeable to God, that our sins are forgiven, that our *camp may start*, but only for the land of victory—that we shall see a time of prosperity and peace. It will finally reveal, according to the prophet, the arrival of "Him that bringeth good tidings, and publisheth peace. O Judah! keep thy solemn feasts, perform thy vows, for the wicked shall no more pass through thee; he is utterly cut off."‖ הנה על ההרים רגלי מבשר משמיע שלום חגי יהודה חגיך שלמי נדריך כי לא יוסיף עוד לעבר בך בליעל כלו נכרת:

---

* Isaiah lix. 3.   § Ib. xxvii. 1, 3.   ‖ Nahum ii. 1.

SERMON II.

PRAYER.

ALMIGHTY God, after this appeal to my brethren, by which I have proclaimed Thee the omnipotent king and the upright judge of the universe, I feel myself even more deeply impressed with the idea of my insignificance, and of the unworthiness of my conduct. My heart is agitated by terror, rather than animated by hope. And it is unto Thee, O Lord, as a father, that I address my humble and ardent supplication, like the priest of old, both in behalf of myself, and of the community entrusted to my spiritual guidance. In the midst of the reefs and shoals of existence, Thou alone keepest up our vacillating steps, and raisest us when we have fallen. Thy help is indispensable unto us. Oh! bestow it upon us, so that we may successfully pursue our mortal career unto its close. The year just elapsed has been saddened by many a gloomy event, and some among my brethren have been tried by heartrending misfortunes. The vacant seats which I see before me show that more than one of us have been summoned to the life of eternity. Give, O Lord, rest and beatitude to the dead: but, we pray, keep the living under Thy divine protection, for the living, and not the dead, can praise and worship Thee. Grant us a more auspicious year, during which those that are in mourning may be consoled, and those that are sick may return to health. The year is gone, let also "its miseries and curses be gone for ever." תכלה שנה וקללותיה. A new year has just begun, Oh, let it be the "bearer of blessings." תחל שנה וברכותיה Remembering Thy mercy more than our deserts, our good intentions more than our actions, Oh, bless the work of our hands, and let it be the source of prosperity; bless our houses, and let them be the dwellings of health and abundance, of light and consolation. Bless us in everything that surrounds us, in our family, in our relations, in our friends. Open unto us the gates of prayer, the gates of virtue, the gates of devotion, the gates of atonement, the gates of pardon, the gates of success, and inscribe us in the book of peaceful life. For "who is a God like unto Thee, that pardoneth iniquity, and passeth by the transgression of the remnant of His heritage; He retaineth not His anger for ever, because He delighteth in mercy. He will turn again, He will have compassion upon us: He will subdue our iniquity: and thou wilt cast all their sins into the sea."*

ישוב ירחמנו יכבוש עונתינו ותשליך במצולות ים כל חטאתם:

AMEN.

* Micah vii. 18, 19.

CONFESSION.

DAY OF ATONEMENT SERMON.

חטאתי אודיעך ועוני לא כסיתי אמרתי אודה עלי פשעי לה׳ ואתה נשאת עון חטאתי סלה :

"I acknowledge my sin unto Thee, and mine iniquity have I not hid. I said, I will confess my transgressions unto the Lord, and Thou forgivest the iniquity of my sin. Selah!"

(PSALM xxxii. 5.)

כל הזובח יצרו ומתודה מעלה עליו הכתוב כאילו כבדו להק״בה בשני עולמים העולם הזה והעולם הבא :

"He who makes the sacrifice of his tendencies and confesses his sins, is considered as if he had honored the Lord in this life and in the next." (*Talmud*, SANHEDRIN 43.)

ONE of the most remarkable features of our religion, of the laws which Moses derived from the Divine source, as well as of the commentary upon them which constitutes tradition, is this, that they are adapted to all countries, to all climates, to all stations of human progress, and to all ages, so that they provided for the period in which they were proclaimed, and at the same time for the most distant future. But there is another characteristic which, though it does not belong exclusively to our doctrines, invests them with a high degree of beauty, I mean the envelope of beautiful parables, striking metaphors, and charming legends, with which they are clothed and expressed, and which delight the mind and touch the heart. Our sages intended, for instance, to teach us that the penitential days are austere and terrible ימים נוראים, that then the Almighty pronounces the reward or the punishment which will be our lot during the ensuing year as the natural consequence of our good or bad actions; and employing an impressive parable, they described the Almighty like a Judge seated on His adamantine throne, having the accuser at His right hand and three books before Him. He opens them, and having with one glance seen the conduct of all men, and with one movement of His eternal justice determined on that which each of them has deserved, He writes in one book the name of those who, absolutely wicked, shall die; in the other book the name of those who, absolutely righteous, shall live; and in the third book the name of those who, still on the brink of the abyss of impiety, may by a sincere repentance escape the terrible doom of misery and death,* צדיקים גמורים נכתבים ונחתמים לאלתר לחיים · רשעים גמורים נכתבים ונחתמים לאלתר למיתה בינוניים תלוין ועומדין מר״ה עד יום הכפ׳ זכו נכתבין לחיים לא זכו נכתבין לאלתר למיתה The sentence, say our sages, continuing their graphic parable, is written on the New Year's Day, it is sealed on the Day of Atonement, yet the heavenly messengers do not start for its execution till the seventh day of Tabernacles, the great Hoshaana Rabbah.

All Israelites are aware, as well as our ancestors, that this is the period of judgment, or if they do not know it through study, they feel it by their Jewish instinct, and like their ancestors, they prepare themselves for this terrible solemnity. But is what they do sufficient to cause the Divine balance to drop in their favour? And of what does their preparation consist? They regularly attend for a few days the house of prayer; even those attend regularly who during the year forget that a house of prayer exists. They seem to recite their supplications

* Talmud Roshashana, 16.

with devotion, and some in a more respectful attitude than usual. They distribute some of what is superfluous to them among the poor, and finally they come here to devote a whole day unto the Lord. They subject themselves to the hard trial of fasting, they weaken their frame by voluntary and heavy privations, which they trust may be accepted by God as a true personal sacrifice. All these acts of piety are certainly useful, nay, they are necessary; but is that all? If you have done that only, I am sorry to declare that you have not undergone the proper, the prescribed, the efficient preparation. You are like a man whose house has caught fire and who, instead of working for his own rescue and the preservation of his house, loses precious time in trying to save some insignificant pieces of furniture. You have forgotten the vital part of your duty.

My brethren, nearly all of you are merchants, and you must know the rules of book-keeping. In your social intercourse, you must often open your day-book, or your ledger in order to verify either your debtor or creditor account; therein you register what you sell and what you buy, what you lend and what you borrow, and to those books you address every evening your last thought, for they contain the true account of what you have gained or lost, and what you possess. But there is another ledger which you ought to consult every evening, and which it is your strict obligation to read before the day of judgment has elapsed. That is not the book of your commercial bargains, but of your actions, of your conduct, and of your thoughts. To peruse that book and to practise the lessons that you learn from it, is to carry out the real preparation for the Lord's judgment.

CONFESSION.

Put aside your prayer-book for a few minutes, and take in your hand the book of moral accounts. I do not address these words to a particular part of my audience, but to all those who are here; to men and to women, to the young and to the old, to workmen and to bankers, to merchants and to literary men, to masters and to servants, to the idle among the poor and to the idle among the wealthy, to all those "that stand here with us this day before the Lord our God, etc.,"* את אשר ישנו פה עמנו עומד היום לפני ה׳ אלהינו ואת אשר איננו פה Take that book into your hand; it has a dark cover, and a word is written upon it in red characters—Confession. Open it, and you will see that it consists of three large leaves. At the top of the first a striking word is registered—God. At the top of the next a second—Our Neighbours. At the top of the next a third—Ourselves. And now let us read together what is registered in those three different leaves, for it is for this that we are here to-day. והתודו את חטאתם אשר עשו § "Then they shall confess their sins that they have done." We are here to obey the recommendation of our sages that to give a pledge of sincere repentance, a man should publicly "confess his sins and minutely avow his transgressions." ‖ ושבח גדול לשב שיתודה ברבים ויודיע חטאו ומגלה הטאו My Brethren, my Sisters, let us rid ourselves of our false shame, let us go through the first leaf of our confession book. But remember that just as a mirror is only good when it reflects our figure in a perfect manner, so our confession is real and true only when it is the mirror of our mind and of our heart; when it frankly repeats all that we have thought, all that we have spoken, all that we have

* Deut. xxix. 14.   § Numbers v. 7.   ‖ Sepher Hassidim.

done, however blamable we may have been. My words will therefore personify no one, and yet they will be everyone's confession.

I.

What have we done, how have we acted towards God during the year that has just expired? Have we shown unto Him more devotion and love than in former years? Have we opened our eyes, so often covered by a thick bandage, have we looked at the magnificent works of the Almighty? Have we considered those grand phenomena which pass every day rapidly before us, and to which through their constant repetition we pay no attention whatever? The Universe is an immense sphere, the throne and at the same time the footstool of the Almighty.* It is an immense chain, the last link of which is held by the Lord's hand, and although many of its treasures and charms are concealed from the human eye, yet it is a real theatre of beauty. But alas! we have remained indifferent to that which reveals the infinite power of the Lord, we have not burst out in David's enthusiastic exclamation, "O Lord, how manifold are Thy works! in wisdom hast Thou made them all, the earth is full of Thy riches." מה רבו מעשיך ה' כלם בחכמה עשית מלאה וכול' § No, the sight of the wonders of the animals, the plants, and the minerals have not awakened in our mind the idea that everything belongs to God, and His praise has not been uttered by our lips. We have not said, "Let the great name of the Lord be blessed for ever and ever, Who by His wisdom gave existence to the whole world." ‖ But have we at least thought of His mercy, of His providence, of the goodness with which He rules the innumerable army of

---
* Isaiah lxvi. 1.   § Psalm civ. 24.   ‖ Abot. R. Nathan, chap. xxxi.

created beings, and carries out His own laws of order and harmony? No, we have not. "He feeds His flock like a shepherd; He gathers the lambs with His arm, carries them in His bosom, and gently leads those that are with young." כרעה עדרו ירעה בזרעו יקבץ טלאים ובחיקו ישא עלות ינהל :* He has guided us in security on a path of life often beset with dangers. He has given us bread for the preservation of our existence, He has granted us sleep for the restoration of our strength, He has sent the rain which fertilises our land and produces our corn and our fruit, He has opened his hand, and satisfied the desires of every living being: and we . . . . . We have readily picked up the fruit, we have gathered in the harvest, we have drunk the waters of His springs, we have reaped the effects of His beneficial dew, we have delighted in our sleep, we have availed ourselves unsparingly of the boons profusely displayed before us; yet not a word of thanks has sounded in our mouth. The source of our enjoyments was forgotten, the distributor of our comforts was set aside, we have had no remembrance of Providence, we have been such as Moses depicted our forefathers: § "Jeshurun waxed fat and kicked; thou art waxen fat, thou art grown thick, thou art covered with fatness: then he forsook God that made him, and lightly esteemed the rock of his salvation." ויטש אלוה עשהו וינבל צור ישעתו Consequently we have transgressed the Law, the expression of His will. This year will be marked with a black sign, for we had never been so irreligious. The name of God came upon our lips, but without due veneration; we have spoken of His commandments but without due submission; we have talked about His

* Isaiah xl. 11. § Deut. xxxii. 15.

ministers, but without due respect. How many times when the hour came to obey the will of the Almighty, to serve Him, to offer unto Him the words of our lips, to devote unto His praise and glorification one of the numerous days which we lavishly spent in useless amusements— how many times have we not exclaimed with Job* מה שדי כי נעבדנו ומה נועיל כי נפגע בו " What is the Almighty that we should serve Him? and what profit should we have if we prayed unto Him?" Yes, even in the Divine worship which ought to be the expression of abnegation, we have looked for our material interest, we have asked: " What profit should we have by it?" This year, therefore, saw us seldom in the place of worship; while our brethren were engaged in supplications, we were labouring for worldly objects, sometimes for unworthy undertakings; we have become strangers in that place which we ought most frequently to visit. Neglectful of the public worship, we have equally overlooked its domestic observance, and our house which ought to have witnessed the practice of the acts of our religion, and in which we ought to have spoken of the words of God, § ודברת בם בשבתך בביתך has only been the theatre of useless pastimes, of profane conversations, of discord and quarrels and sometimes of still more condemnable scenes. Oh, what a year, what a year! How can we ask for the Lord's protection? How can God look upon us with mercy? Therefore " we have not the courage to speak, we dare not raise our head." אין לנו פה להשיב ולא מצח להרים ראש ‖

II.

Let us now turn over, and read the second leaf of our confession book; perhaps there will be a less

* Job xxi. 15. § Deut. vi. 7. ‖ From the Ritual.

discouraging account. How have we acted all this year towards our neighbours? From the beginning till the end of the year, we have cried out with all the power of our lungs: שלי שלי "*My rights, my rights!*" * "None shall damage my rights! no one shall lay his hand on that which is my sacred property." But have we said at the same time: ושלך שלך "*Thy rights, thy rights!*" § "The rights of others shall be equally respected!" Have we refrained from grasping at that which belongs to others? Have we thought of our duties as we have thought of our claims? The most beautiful sentence ever written in any religious code stands engraved in our Law, and it is expressed by these immortal words: ואהבת לרעך כמוך "Thou shalt love thy neighbour as thyself." ǁ But alas! we have not always practised it. No, we have not loved our neighbours according to justice, we have not loved them according to charity. We have not loved them according to justice, because prompted by covetousness, by unjust animosity, by even baser passions, we have outstepped the limit of what is honest and true. We have coveted their property, and what have we not done in order to usurp it! We have had recourse to low and heinous subterfuges and stratagems in order to rise at the expense of people of good faith. Conspiracies, fraud, breach of promises given on our sacred honour, usury, gambling, ignoble impositions, deceit practised at the cost of our friends, of our relations, of a brother, even of a father, unjust lawsuits, false pretences, intimidation, all, all has seemed proper to us in order to hoard wealth, in order to gain in the world a position which we had no fair means of attaining. Oh! we dare

* Talmud, Abot. § Ibid. ǁ Lev. xix. 18.

not look at those whom we have ruined; we dare not look at those families which have fallen by our fault; at those tender beings who, born in the midst of comforts, have become indigent by our wickedness; at those fathers of families who have lost their reputation, not by any crime of theirs, but because they relied upon our honour, our honesty, and our word. No! we dare not look at those whom we have approached with a smile upon our lips, whose hands we have grasped with apparent friendship while we were placing a stone on their way in order to cause them to stumble, while we were preparing a snare in order to entangle them, while we were treacherously spreading calumnies which might damage their name, ruin their credit, and destroy their fame. No! we dare not look at those respectable houses, which we entered with the title of friends, and on which we have brought shame as well as the contempt of society. We cannot help blushing when we think of the use which we have made of the noble faculties with which we are endowed, and especially of that of speech. Our words, which ought to have been the bearers of friendship and consolation, have, like arrows, opened deep wounds; they have, like poisoned daggers, pierced in the dark and caused death and destruction. We have been of those who "bend their tongues like their bows for lies." * וידרכו את לשונם קשתם שקר We have been of those who "deceive every one his neighbour, and will not speak the truth, who have taught their tongues to speak lies, and weary themselves to commit iniquity." § How many have we not grieved by our unguarded or cruel expressions? How many have we not offended by our pitiless and unjust

* Jerem. ix. 2.   § Ibid. ix. 4.

reproaches? How much harm have we not done by divulging the secret faults of our neighbours, by trumpeting their failure, by reporting delicate communications and intimate conversations, by repeating words pronounced innocently, but to which we attributed a malignant signification. Oh! we see now that we have done a great deal of harm by our flattery, by praises entirely devoid of truth; that is the way by which we practised the greatest deceit, by which we have most often imposed upon man, so sensible to adulation. Ah! quite true is the saying of the sages:* "Justice began to be outraged on the day when flattery became prominent among men." מיום שגברה הגופה נתעותו הדינין Unable to comply with the exigencies of justice, we see that we have been equally incapable (are we to say unwilling?) to act in accordance with the demands of charity. Always to do to others what we should like to receive, is a precept constantly recommended by the law; but our selfishness stood in the way. We have more than once put a silver coin into the hand of a poor man; more than once we had a large offering for a philanthropic purpose publicly announced, when a smile of approbation on the part of a large audience rewarded us for our liberality; but how many times this year have we not disregarded real misfortune, rejected the appeal of unfeigned need, and been deaf to the timid prayer of modest and respectable indigence! And if we have occasionally loosened our purse, we did not open our heart. We gave alms, but we did not practise charity which raises those whom poverty has humbled and which, coming from the heart, goes straight to the heart of the recipient, and

* Talmud Sotah, 47.

establishes between the various conditions of men that which should ever unite them, a bond of love. And even when we did good we did it with arrogance and pride, so that we feel that our merit has been as small as the beneficial results of our liberality. Oh, mercy upon us "for our iniquities have gone over our head; as an heavy burden they are too heavy for us"* כי עונתי עברו ראשי כמשא כבד יכבדו ממני :

III.

We have arrived at the third leaf. Let us continue our confession, which now regards ourselves, and which will not be less interesting. Have we this year been more enlightened as far as our real interest is concerned? Have we learnt from God how to choose the way of life, §ובחרת בחיים the way of our true happiness? Have we, in a word, loved ourselves? We have always felt in us the elements of a man, and the elements of a child: those of wisdom and those of ignorance, those of good and those of evil, those of what is spiritual, and of that which comes from the dust of the earth. We have often felt in our heart that terrible struggle and contrast between these opposite influences, between the good temptation and the evil one: יצר הטוב ויצר הרע Which of them have we then let rule over us? The man or the child, the spirit or the body, wisdom or folly, good or evil? Have we been victorious in the moral fight? Have we, by being slow to anger, been better than the mighty, and by "ruling our spirit, been braver than he who takes a city?"‖ טוב ארך אפים מגבור ומשל ברוחו מלכד עיר There are many causes in the material order which bring about illness of body, and many

* Psalm xxxviii. 5.   § Deut. xxx. 19.   ‖ Prov. xvi. 32.

causes in the moral order, which produce sickness of spirit. Have we shunned either of them in order to preserve in the best possible state what the Lord has lent us, and in order to restore it unto Him, improved and perfected? Alas! alas! our eagerness for sensual pleasures has prevented us from keeping our machinery in order, and our delicate frame in health. Oh! we well remember our immoderate gaiety, we well remember how many times we have gratified our voluptuous desires; we remember our excesses at the table, our frequent libations to the idol of wine; we remember how many times we have, by our debauchery, undermined our existence. Therefore our body is weak, our health threatened, therefore infirmities afflict us, and we see at a distance the terrible ghost of a miserable old age. Unfortunately, we have also let our soul become diseased and infirm. We have not been able to control our temper, to check our irritability. We have let pride creep into our heart. We have let some slight success become the source of stupid vanity, which has blinded us, and concealed from us our real insignificance. We have been immoderate in our joy, despondent in our misfortunes, intolerant of the inevitable trials of life, and ready to murmur against Providence, and we see now that we have still to learn the noble virtues of patience, resignation, modesty and humility. If we are to speak truly, we can register no progress in our religious tendencies, no progress in our morals, no progress in the knowledge that is most precious upon the earth, the knowledge of ourselves. Oh, why have we not employed our time better? Why is it not in our power to boast of noble acts? Why are we forced to say, " I have nothing to relate but iniquities; I can only be grieved, for I have sinned" * כי עוני אגיד אדאג מחטאתי; and we are obliged to confess that we have acted towards God as a perverse son acts towards his father, as a rebellious servant towards his master, as an ungrateful pupil towards his teacher. We have declared unclean what God has pronounced pure, and pure what He has pronounced unclean: we have permitted what He has forbidden, and forbidden what He has permitted: we have hated what He has loved, and loved what He has hated: and all this we confess this day after a searching examination of ourselves, after having laid bare our moral wounds, in order to obey the saying of the Prophet: "Let us search, and try our ways, and turn again unto the Lord." § נחפשה דרכינו ונחקרה ונשובה עד ה':

Here we close the book, and our confession ends. And what can our feelings be now but those of shame? For, if none of us can be so wicked as to have indulged in all these sins, yet each of us has done his share, each of you, my brethren, and each of you, my sisters. More than one among us has already borne the inevitable penalty of his misconduct, and can the others flatter themselves that they will not bear their own punishment?—In a certain manner they may, provided they cause their confessions to be followed by sincere repentance and reparation, since reparation and repentance are the only means by which we can reach the true aim of the Day of Atonement, forgiveness. To undergo hard material privations for twenty-five hours, to devote the whole day to prayer and religious meditations, to remain from morning till evening entirely separated from our worldly cares, to withdraw even our

* Psalm xxxviii. 19. § Lament. iii. 40.

CONFESSION.

ideas from that which forms the occupation of the whole year, to raise our mind to spiritual thoughts, to the consideration of death and of a future life, is surely to obey the law; but if all these ceremonies and all that piety are not followed by repentance and reparation, they are useless, they are a mockery; they are like a watch without spring, like a ship without pilot, like a house without roof, like a bridge without solid foundations; they are an impossibility. Oh, my brethren, it is only when we have wiped the tears that we have caused to be shed, when we have returned that which we have usurped, when we have rebuilt what we have ruined, when we have consoled those whom we have grieved and healed those whom we have wounded, when we have restored cleanliness to that which we have made impure, it is only then that the glorious announcement of the Almighty by the mouth of Moses will be verified :* "For on that day He shall make an atonement for you, to cleanse you, that you may be clean from all your sins before the Lord." כי ביום הזה יכפר עליכם לטהר אתכם מכל חטאתיכם לפני ה' תטהרו:

The subject of my discourse having been confession, it is only by a solemn act of contrition that we can bring it to a close. Arise therefore, my brethren, and follow my solemn utterances with your hearts :—

ACT OF CONTRITION.

אלהינו ואלהי אבותינו

Our God and God of our forefathers, let our prayers reach Thee. Turn not Thy face from our supplications. Thou seest it, we are neither impudent nor obdurate; we shall not say, we are innocent and have not sinned;

* Lev. xvi. 30.

we confess it, both we and our forefathers have sinned. Listen, O Lord, to our confession which flows from our heart, beating from the emotion of sincere regret and uncontrollable remorse:

אשמנו We are greatly culpable.

בגדנו We have been rebels to Thine eternal will.

גזלנו We have abused our fellow-creatures' trust; we have deceived those who relied on us.

דברנו דופי We have not controlled our tongue, we have uttered blasphemies.

העוינו Not content with sinning, we have induced others to be irreligious.

הרשענו The cause of the righteous was placed in our hands, and we have condemned them.

זדנו We have let the demon of arrogance rule our actions.

חמסנו We have practised fraud in our social transactions.

טפלנו שקר We have spread falsehood, and misled credulous people.

יעצנו רע We have given bad advice, we have treacherously pushed a man to his ruin.

כזבנו We have told untruths to those who depended on our information.

לצנו We have ridiculed that which is sacred, we have been scoffers.

מרדנו We have openly disobeyed constituted authorities.

נאצנו We have abhorred Thy law, which we ought to have loved.

סררנו We have been consciously perverse.

עוינו We have committed iniquitous actions.

פשענו We have sinned for no other aim than that of sinning.

CONFESSION.

סררנו We have oppressed our neighbours.

קשינו ערף We have been stiffnecked, and turned a deaf ear to wise reproaches.

רשענו We have acted with wickedness.

שחתנו We have fallen into corruption and debased our immortal souls.

תעבנו תעינו ותעתענו We have altogether walked on a disreputable, dishonourable, and shameful path.

We have gone astray from Thy Commandments, but we have not profited by it : ולא שוה לנו

And how can wickedness result in the joy of its followers, how can he who sows destruction reap anything but ruin? Thou hast been just and merciful to us, and yet we have disregarded Thee and sinned. O Lord, what was I before being created? and now that I have been created what am I but dust? Yes, I am dust in my life; I shall be dust and vermin after my death. Therefore I come before Thee, O Lord, covered with shame and humbled by remorse. The heavens are Thy abode, and Thou knowest both what is open to human eyes and what lies concealed, both the hidden things of the Universe and the mysteries of the human heart. Thy power is infinite, but Thy goodness is equally unbounded. Oh, preserve me, O Lord, from falling again into sin, but save me also from the punishment which my past transgressions have called down upon me! Let thy mercy be my salvation. "Let the words of my mouth and the meditation of my heart be acceptable in Thy sight, O Lord, my strength and my Redeemer." *

יהיו לרצון אמרי פי והגיון לבי לפניך ה׳ צורי וגואלי :

AMEN.

* Psalm xix. 15.

THE SUCCAH.

בסכת תשבו שבעת ימים כל האזרח בישראל ישבו בסכת וכול׳:
"Ye shall dwell in booths seven days; all that are Israelites born shall dwell in booths. That your generations may know that I made the children of Israel to dwell in booths when I brought them out of the land of Egypt: I am the Lord your God."
LEVIT. xxiii. 42, 43.

למה ישראל עושים סוכה • לנסים שעשה להם הקב״ה בשעה שיצאו ממצרים שהיו ענני כבוד מקיפין אותם ומסככות עליהם:

"Why does Israel erect tabernacles? It is in remembrance of the miracles worked for them by the Lord on their quitting Egypt, when the divine clouds surrounded and protected them."
PESIKTA xxiv.

MY DEAR BRETHREN,—The imposing chorus of hundreds and hundreds of voices has uttered with ardour and emotion within these sacred walls the last word of the sublime hymn, the last note of the affecting song: "O Lord, terrible and great, let us obtain thy pardon now that we have reached the end of our fast." אל נורא עלילה המצא לנו מחילה בשעת הנעילה:* And we returned to our homes with the heart deeply moved, as if relieved from a heavy burden, and beating under the influence of the sweetest hopes. The time of anxiety is over, and we may give ourselves up to joy. But even

* Penitential Prayers.

THE SUCCAH.

this joy must be chastened and holy. Unlike other nations which after a long series of light fasts and forced acts of penitence, try to seek compensation in all the enjoyments that they can obtain, Israel who is austere, though moderate, in his self-imposed privations, must be so temperate in his joy that he may not endanger the merit which he has secured by his religious exertions. Nothing indelicate or impure ought to be found in our festivals, not even in those that are most joyous; nothing that goes beyond the limit of what is becoming; nothing that is not elevating and does not bear a moral signification. So five days after the great Day of Atonement, the dawn of another religious solemnity, the Feast of Tents, appears. We banish all the sad thoughts which may trouble the serenity of our soul, because this is called זמן שמחתנו, "the time of our exultation." Once more repose from our daily labour is bestowed upon us. It is a time when we may feel the blessings with which the divine mercy has surrounded us, in accordance with the words of the Law;* "And thou shalt rejoice in every good thing that the Lord thy God has given unto thee and unto thine house." ושמחת בכל הטוב אשר נתן לך ה׳ אלהיך ולביתך :

But are we to believe that if we have been cheerful, we have done all that is required of us, and celebrated the festival according to the precept of the Law? Do our houses present the delightful spectacle offered by the dwellings of Jerusalem? Innumerable tents were there erected. Every house was crowned with its tent of branches and flowers and brilliantly coloured draperies; charming during the day, but not less beautiful

* Deut. xxvi. 11.

during the night, when adorned with sparkling lights! There is to be seen little, alas! of all this now-a-days. It is said that in many countries the climate is opposed to the fulfilment of this law. But it is equally true that man allows himself to be guided by the society in the midst of which he lives. The ideas which prevail become his own and decidedly influence his conduct. When the tide of predominant opinions sets against the practice of religious acts, pretexts for their neglect are easily found, and all the fault is attributed to the *force of circumstances*. To explain the reasons of the difference between the past and the present, as well as of the religious indifference which is one of the characteristics of this age, would carry me too far. Yet I must ask you: If you do not observe all the ordinances which the Feast of Tabernacles imposes, do you at least comply with its moral import? Do you practise with your spirit that which is not done by your hands? Do you meditate upon the meaning of this festival? Do you comprehend it? Do you grasp with your mind the cause which gave rise to it, and the effect which it ought to produce? My text teaches that the object of the Lord's precept was to remind us that the Hebrews dwelt in booths when they were delivered from Egypt. But ought an annual solemnity to be necessary for us to recall to our mind that which we should not overlook? Oh, God knew that a time would come when the Israelite would forget his providential origin, misunderstand his glorious destiny, and have no faith in the brilliant future of his race. Therefore He rigorously insisted upon an annual solemn commemoration. Let, then, the moral signification of the *Succah* be this day the subject of our short meditation.

THE SUCCAH.

I.

Why should we, even for seven days, exchange our lofty and elegant apartments, our spacious halls, in which everything tells of comfort, for the small incommodious tent, which is declared unlawful if it goes beyond certain proportions, and in which everything is narrow, circumscribed, and limited? In a moral sense there is the same difference between the mansion and the Succah that exists between a palace in a town, and a cottage erected at the summit of a hill. We enjoy many more comforts in the former, but in the latter we breathe purer air, and delight in a beautiful extensive view, in the display of the various treasures of nature, and the transparent atmosphere allows our eye to survey the most distant parts of the landscape. In the Succah we live in a purer region, and our mind is pervaded by elevated and holy thoughts, by reflections which are to the soul what salubrious air is to our lungs. Like the cottage at the top of the hill, it allows us to see far around; it tears the veil which covers the past, and places it before us as though it were present. We remember, we see such events as may somewhat correct the failings of our heart, and make us proud of a greatness which we had almost forgotten. The first object of the tent is to force Israel to think what he was, in order that he may learn what he ought to be.

When Moses, standing at the foot of the mountain on which he was to die, spoke unto Israel as a dying father unto his children, he warned them above all things against forgetting their origin. "Remember the days of old," he said, "ask thy father." * זכור ימות עולם And it is not surprising, for Israel's charter of nobility is sanctified by the dust of remote ages. Israel's best title to glory is to be sought in his origin, which, unlike the origin of all other ancient races, is not hidden in impenetrable mist, but exhibits clear and well-defined outlines, illuminated by the light of undeniable wonders. "Look unto Abraham your father, and unto Sarah that bare you; for I called him alone, and blessed him and increased him." § הביטו אל אברהם אביכם ואל שרה תחוללכם כי אחד קראתיו ואברכהו וארבהו: That was the root of the Hebrew tree which produced so many luxuriant branches, and so much nourishing fruit. The Patriarch was a model of hospitality, charity and justice, of those virtues which ought to adorn both individuals and peoples, and which can alone secure their prosperity and greatness. But why did not the Lord select a powerful nation, the Romans for instance, who filled the earth with terror, and who would soon have made the Lord's precepts the law of the world? Why a simple shepherd, who had narrowly escaped death by Nimrod's fire? Why a people of slaves, who did not merit the name of a nation? It was, first of all, because the Lord wished to be the father of His own nation, to form it, to establish it in the portion which he had already pointed out when He fixed the boundaries of all races. He wished to lead Israel, to instruct him, to keep him as the apple of His eye, to show him the tenderness with which an eagle surrounds its nest. ‖ יסבבנהו יבוננהו יצרנהו כאישון עינו And just as a man is strongly attached to his protector, and his affection increases in proportion to his protector's devotion, so Israel, constituted by God himself, had not

* Deut. xxxii. 7.   § Isa. li. 2.   ‖ Deut. xxxii. 10.

only the most noble origin, but was to be united to his Creator by ties of filial love. It was, secondly, because the Lord's words were not like a human law, which is imposed all at once upon the members of the same empire. It was to be slowly enforced by the influence of example. The select race was to practise it, and after many centuries was to say to the other nations: "Come and see the harvest of blessings and civilisation which I have reaped by means of this law; come, accept and follow it, and your future will be like mine." No powerful nation, in the third place, could have been selected, because the people of God was never to be politically great. Made the depositary of institutions the destiny of which was to modify the world, Israel acquired by them the supremacy of intellect and wisdom. He had the mission of communicating to all men that treasure of great principles, but of keeping at the same time a passive attitude. He was to teach by example, and not by the sword. He was to endear his religion to mankind by peaceful words, and not by violence. He was to force men to "call them the holy people, the redeemed of the Lord,"* וקראו להם עם הקדש גאולי ה' by the strict morality of his actions, the temperance of his habits, and the domestic virtues which have always been his characteristics. He was to win the hearts of his enemies, and turn the fiercest among them into friends by forbearance and humanity even in the midst of oppression, and not by coercion, or by equally condemnable efforts for proselytism.

In the book of remembrance that the humble tent discloses to Israel, he will see that in spite of many failings, his ancestors walked on the path thus

* Isa. lxii. 12.

traced before them; that, small in number, they became great by the importance which their spiritual mission gave them, by the influence which they exercised, by the cruel persecutions and indescribable torments inflicted on them; and above all, by the wonderful vitality which animated them, and made them proof against time and events, against men and their implements of war, against the wiles of serpents and their venomous bite. In his humble tent, Israel will see the greatness of his prophets, the heroism of his martyrs, those who illustrated his name by deeds of war, those who gave him glory by achievements of peace, and those of his children who, impelled by the undying genius of the Hebrew race, ascend to the highest steps of the social ladder as scholars or orators, as judges or statesmen, as soldiers or financiers. And with feelings of deep gratitude he will recognise the divine clouds which have surrounded and protected him through thirty-six centuries, as a correct and literal fulfilment of the announcement of the prophet:* "And there shall be a tabernacle for a shadow in the daytime from the heat, and for a place of refuge, and for a covert from storm and from rain." וסכה תהיה לצל יומם מחרב ולמחסה ולמחסה ולמסתור מזרם וממטר:

II.

Were that the only signification of the Feast of Tents, it would be sufficient to endear it unto us; but that is not all. We cannot help being struck by the fact that we are commanded really to dwell seven days in a temporary house, in a frail tent, while, with regard

* Isaiah iv. 6.

to many other remarkable events of old, a simple mention of them is held as sufficient for their commemoration. God intended the law to remind us of the hardships which our ancestors had to endure in the wilderness; but He knew that men, by their nature, really feel the discomforts and sufferings borne by others only if they have themselves to experience them. Therefore He says unto us: "Go out of your wonted residence, and remain for a while in a temporary abode." *
צא מדירת קְבַע ושב בדירת עראי: Leave that place in which you are surrounded by comforts, in which you constantly enjoy the sight of ease and luxury, in which you can find a delightful shelter against the inclemency of the weather, in which neither severe frost nor melting heat can subject you to injury, and in which you are so thoroughly absorbed by your enjoyments, that the recollection of the miseries which past ages inflicted upon your fathers, produces upon your heart less effect than the mildest breeze upon the surface of the placid sea. The wind which shakes the frail walls of your tent, the rain which penetrates through its thin roof of branches and leaves will cause you better to understand what a sojourn in the wilderness meant, and the toil, the fatigue which forty years' wandering in a wild and desolate land imposed upon scarcely organised tribes: "All the travail that had come upon them by the way, and how the Lord had delivered them." §
את כל התלאה אשר מצאתם בדרך ויצלם ה': And naturally you will comprehend how wonderful was the protection afforded by Providence, how great was the love which the Almighty displayed towards the rescued slaves and the nation still in its cradle, when their

* Talmud Succah i. § Exod. xviii. 8.

"raiment waxed not old upon them, neither did their foot swell these forty years." * שמלתך לא בלתה מעליך ורגלך לא בצקה זה ארבעים שנה:

It was the Lord's will that the Hebrews should not forget Him, it is His will that man should think of His gracious favours, not for His sake, but for the sake of mankind. What is in fact our moral condition when we do not think of God? Self-reliance, conceit, pride, haughtiness, selfishness, hardness of heart, these are the defects which then become prominent in us. Then we are everything and our neighbours are nothing, all to ourselves and nothing to our neighbours; these are the two principles which then rule all our actions; they take possession of our mind and our heart, and soon identify themselves with our being. And could society fall into a more wretched and miserable state? If we are successful in life, if from a low position we are able to raise ourselves until we are called the powerful of the world, then we think ourselves demi-gods. We overlook how much hazard has favoured us; we forget that circumstances, which we could neither have foreseen nor mastered, persistently assisted us. We bow before our own image, we worship our great ability. But our religion warns us against pride and sends us every year to dwell seven days in the tent. "Go, go into that humble cottage," it says unto us, "remain therein for a while, as your forefathers dwelt in their booths, and learn modesty. Divest yourselves for a short time of your false pride. Remember the humble condition of our forefathers in the wilderness. There were among them no princes, no nobles, no titled individuals, no privileged classes. When they stood at the foot of Sinai, they were all equal

* Deut. viii. 4.

to each other, they had only one name—that of brothers, who appeared before the presence of their common Father. Ye who are now so great among men, and who, through the flattery of your fawning neighbours, have come to think yourselves superior and privileged beings, look into your genealogy, examine your pedigree, and you will probably find that your grandfather, or great-grandfather was a simple merchant, an artisan, or a workman. Enter in spirit for a few moments their workshops, look at their tools, and you will surely become humble and unassuming. Think of what our forefathers were, exclaims Judaism, and dwell in their tent.—When the Romans bestowed upon their victorious commanders the honour of a triumph, the hero of the day, bearing a sceptre in one hand and a branch of laurel in the other, rode in a chariot drawn by four horses, and followed by the Roman nobles, the magistrates and the captives. But behind the hero stood a slave, who continually repeated to him: "Man is but dust; be warned against pride."—Our religion speaks unto us in gentler words: "Your ancestors dwelt in booths: sojourn ye also in a humble tent, and ye will learn to be humble. Leave your luxurious mansions; go for seven days where the labourer dwells during the whole year, and your vain-glory will disappear, or it will at least diminish;" you will, according to our sages, "be truly great, for you will be humble." גדולים נמוכי רוח * You have promised humility on the Day of Atonement; practise it then, in the Feast of Tents, and your New Year will have been nobly begun. The Succah, to which this beautiful meaning is attached, says unto us: "Come,

* Talmud Sotah 5.

come, and in spite of thy worldly success, thou wilt not forget the Lord thy God; though thy silver and thy gold be multiplied, thine heart will not be lifted up, thou wilt not say: 'My power and the might of mine hand hath gotten me this wealth.' But "thou shalt remember the Lord thy God, for it is He that gives thee power to get wealth, that He may establish His covenant which He sware unto thy fathers, as it is this day"*

וזכרת את ה׳ אלהיך כי הוא הנתן לך כח לעשות חיל למען הקים את בריתו אשר נשבע לאבותיך כיום הזה:

III.

We have now arrived at the third signification of the Succah, which is as elevating as, and perhaps even more touching than, the two former. Autumn is the most delightful season of the year. Towards it the desires of most men, whether rich or poor, are turned, of those that spend their time in idleness, and of those who unceasingly undergo the hardest labour. In autumn the blessings of the Lord are poured upon man. In autumn the plain and the hill, the field and the forest echo with the merriest songs, with the most joyous sounds, and are the scene of the honest pleasures of the peasant. Then we gather in our corn, by which our food for the whole year is secured, we gather in our wine which will restore our decaying strength and give joy to our heart. At that season we see our wants satisfied, we can think of the future of our family, we can put aside our savings for remote contingencies; and then our religion commands us to celebrate the Feast of

* Deut. viii. 17, 18.

THE SUCCAH.

Tents. "Thou shalt observe the Feast of Tabernacles seven days, after that thou hast gathered in thy corn and thy wine"* חג הסכת תעשה לך שבעת ימים באספך מגרנך ומיקבך: In this blessed season we must dwell seven days in the tabernacle; then, according to the Law, we shall rejoice in our feast, we, and our son, and our daughter, and our man-servant, and our maid-servant, and the Levite, the stranger, the fatherless, and the widow, that are within our gates § ושמחת בחגך אתה ובנך ובתך וכול׳: We must try to enjoy happiness, and to spread happiness around us. But this happiness must come from a noble and pure source. We are not to seek it in the noisy pleasures of society, in those amusements which offer much more excitement than joy, and which are often of an objectionable nature. Our religion desires us to derive our joy from the beauties of nature, or at least from their symbol, from the peaceful gathering of our family, of those beings who are a part of ourselves. A father and a mother, and around them their children, all attached to each other by tender affection, and above them garlands of flowers, interwoven with green branches and hanging fruit—Oh, can there be a sweeter spectacle, a more delightful picture, a more pleasing group?

But when we have fully enjoyed domestic happiness, when our family has both contributed to, and shared in, our delight, when our servants have had their part in our rejoicings, we must not forget the three classes of our fellow beings whom the Law mercifully recommends, "the stranger, the fatherless, and the widow." והגר והיתום והאלמנה ‖ The simple Succah recalls to our mind that there are destitute creatures who not only lack a

---

* Deut. xvi. 13.   § Deut. xvi. 14.   ‖ Ib.

mansion as gorgeous as ours, but who cannot even afford to provide themselves with a poor cottage, and have no shelter; who, subjected to all sorts of privations, wander about and pray for assistance; who, besides the agony of hunger, are often made to suffer the more piercing agony of humiliation. The festivals, as established by the Mosaic law, are the expression of joy, national and religious joy; but they are so constituted as to establish an indispensable link between them and the idea of charity, so that they suggest that if the poor are not remembered, the festival cannot be rightly solemnised. Passover was marked by the harvest of barley; the Feast of Weeks, by the harvest of corn; and the Feast of Tents, by the gathering in of all kinds of agricultural products, the fruit of the trees and of the vine. In truth when man has plenteous store before him, he feels inclined to give largely and without grudge; then he experiences real pleasure in calling the needy to take shelter in his house, to sit at his table, and to cover their flesh with his garments. So the true Jew must be benevolent; spontaneously, liberally, and generously benevolent, for he ought to remember the words of his immortal lawgiver: "Thou shalt surely give him, and thine heart shall not be grieved when thou givest unto him; because that for this thing the Lord thy God shall bless thee in all thy works, and in all that thou puttest thine hand unto"*

נתון תתן לו ולא ירע לבבך בתתך לו כי בגלל הדבר הזה יברכך ה׳ אלהיך בכל מעשיך ובכל משלח ידך:

And now that we have briefly and graphically

* Deut. xv. 10.

described the three meanings of the Succah, which really vie with each other in elevation and grandeur, can we still be reluctant to enter the humble tent, can we still feel ashamed of one of our most charming institutions? No, that cannot be the case with thoughtful Jews; and to those who transgress through ignorance we will say with our sages: צא ולמד "Go out and learn," and the poetry of our ceremonies will render them precious in your sight. The stranger who sees "Israel and Judah abide in tents,"* וישראל ויהודה ישבים בסכות will admire a race which thus keeps alive the genius of its glorious past; he will bless the ancient people which preserves in its integrity the tradition of the great intercourse between God and man; and dismissing from his mind all secular prejudices, he will repeat with enthusiasm the words of the prophet of the Gentiles, Balaam, who at the sight of the innumerable tents of the Hebrews, stretched on the plain as far as his eyes could reach, rapturously said: "How goodly are thy tents, O Jacob, and thy tabernacles, O Israel! as the valleys are they spread forth, as gardens by the river's side, as the trees of lign aloes which the Lord hath planted, and as cedar trees beside the waters. Blessed is he that blesseth thee, and cursed is he that curseth thee" § מה טבו אהליך יעקב משכנתיך ישראל : כנחלים נטיו כגנות עלי נהר כאהלים נטע ה' כארזים עלי מים : מברכיך ברוך ואריך ארור :

AMEN.

* 2 Samuel xi. 11.   § Numb. xxiv. 5, 6, 9.

THE LULAB.

ולקחתם לכם ביום הראשון פרי עץ הדר כפת תמרים וענף עץ עבת
ועבת וערבי נחל ושמחתם לפני ה' אלהיכם שבעת ימים :

"And ye shall take unto you on the first day the boughs of goodly trees, branches of palm trees, and the boughs of thick trees, and willows of the brook; and ye shall rejoice before the Lord your God seven days."

Lev. xxiii. 40.

אלו ד' מינין שבכל אחד ואחד מישראל הולך ולוקח לו מהן להלל
להקב"ה הם נראים קטנים בעיני אדם וגדולים לפני הקב"ה :

"These four kinds of plants, with which every Israelite pays a tribute of devotion to the Almighty, appear before men as insignificant, but they are important in the sight of the Lord."

Vaikra Rabbah, 30.

My dear Brethren,—At the recurrence of our sacred festivals, we cannot help our thoughts reverting to the time when Jerusalem, the princess of cities, shone in her glory, when from all parts of the kingdom our forefathers, the male part of the population, hastened to the central point of national meeting, to the temple of the God of Israel, and naturally we think at the same time of the pilgrimages practised by other nations, we institute comparisons, we wish impartially to decide which had a nobler source and more beneficial results. We recall to our memory that which we know about the ancient times of Egypt, when the Feast of Neith, or the Feast of Lights, attracted to Said once a year an immense number of people, or when half the inhabitants of Egypt crowded the royal city of Memphis for the consecration of the image of their principal divinity, Api. We remember when millions of Hindoos made their devout pilgrimages to the subterranean Pagoda of the Island of Elephanta on the coast of Malabar, where immense buildings are allotted to the idol and its priests. We look on the eastern shores of the Mediterranean, at the few ruins which remind us of the celebrated city of Hierapolis, in which was worshipped the goddess Syria, and in which great was the concourse of pilgrims from India, Egypt, Ethiopia, and Armenia. Illustrious writers have sent down to us the history and description of the ancient Temple of Diana at Ephesus and of that of Apollo at Delphi, enriched by the presents which the admiring visitors from all nations devoutly offered. We think of the Caaba, the square tent, which, according to the Arabs, had been built by Ishmael, and in which the three hundred and sixty Genii said to preside over the three hundred and sixty days of the year, were worshipped under as many hideous forms. And when we reflect that the object of all such pilgrimages was the performance of idolatrous rites and ceremonies, we cannot help sighing, for we detect the depth of degradation to which the human reason can sink. But there are other pilgrimages of a more recent date to which the epithet of bloody will be attached for ever; I mean the crusades, when the religious rage of the ignorant populations of Europe was kindled by the preaching of a fanatic friar, when hundreds of thousands of human creatures, men and women, old and young, moved towards Jerusalem, marking their progress with horrible acts of cruelty, sacrificing on the altar of intolerance numberless human victims, the proscribed Jews, and hoping to gain the favour of God by the slaughter of His children. And there are even now, in this time of enlightenment and progress, pilgrimages which cannot stand the examination of reason, and can be prompted only by the most absolute blindness, by the most profound ignorance. Statues are now exposed before the followers of so-called spiritual religions, statues, the toes of which I have seen worn away by the friction of the lips and the hands of millions of devout pilgrims.

And can there be any doubt as to the result of the comparison, however impartial this may be ? The spirit of a religion can be known by the laws and the rites which it establishes, and in the same manner the character of a nation is revealed by the customs which constitute its daily life. The religions above mentioned are, so to say, judged by the pilgrimages which they instituted. But a different impression is produced upon us when we read the simple words of the book of Deuteronomy: " Three times in the year shall all thy males appear before the Lord thy God in the place which He shall choose, on the Feast of unleavened bread, on the Feast of Weeks, and on the Feast of Tabernacles, and they shall not appear before the Lord empty "* שלוש פעמים בשיה יראה כל זכורך את פני ה׳ אלהיך במקום אשר יבחר בחג המצות בחג השבעות ובחג הסכות ולא יראה את פני ה׳ ריקם:

The three pilgrimages of the Hebrews meant neither superstition nor immoral rites; they were edifying, elevating. The object of the first pilgrimage was to celebrate the anniversary of the triumph of religious

* Deut. xvi. 16.

and moral as well as national liberty; the object of the second was to commemorate Revelation, which sanctioned liberty; the object of the third was to commemorate the wanderings of our ancestors in the wilderness, and to celebrate the power which gives the earth both wealth and beauty. The three pilgrimages were eminently useful, for they served to make the Hebrew worship dignified, to promote brotherhood between the citizens, to increase the moral strength of the kingdom. Such was the general character of those great national gatherings; but the third pilgrimage, that of the Feast of Tabernacles, seemed to be enlivened by a display of greater rejoicings, by the expression of deeper happiness. It was the most mirthful of the three, not only because the season was so beautiful, but because there were additional joyous and impressive ceremonies. Oh! what a sight from the walls of Jerusalem! the numerous pilgrims who, unable to find room in the city, had been obliged to erect tents without the walls in the surrounding plains and hills, formed a great procession in order to go to the Temple, but they had the appearance of a real army, an army of peaceful soldiers, for they carried in their hands the four prescribed plants, the citron or orange, the palm tree, the myrtle and the willow; and while they went on their way, they sang the joyous hymns of the Hallel, they sang: "Glory be, glory be," to the Lord of Hosts, from whom all glories are, "praise ye the Eternal, whose goodness and mercy are everlasting!" : הודו לה׳ כי טוב כי לעולם חסדו

But what is the signification of those so called "four species" ארבעה מינים? What do they symbolise? What do they represent? That ceremony is still so dear unto us, we handle the Lulab with such pleasure, that we cannot think it a senseless symbol. According to my Talmudical text, these four species may be lightly esteemed by men who are unable to raise their mind to the sublime meditations of religion, but they are great in the sight of the Almighty."* הם נראים קטנים בעיני אדם וגדולים לפני הק"בה They must, therefore, have a deep significance. Yes, it is so, and there is a passage in the Medrash, a beautiful passage, which will strikingly answer our question, and which will surely charm your ears. It will give us, besides, an idea of the present religious state of our nation.

"The boughs of goodly trees," says the Medrash, "symbolise Israel. Just as the אתרוג, *citron*, possesses both a sweet smell and a fine flavour, so there are in Israel men who are in every way praiseworthy, who join together religious science and good actions." § פרי עץ הדר אלו ישראל : מה אתרוג יש בו טעם ויש בו ריח כך ישראל יש בהם בני אדם שיש בהם תורה ויש בהם מעשים טובים : And this is a consoling announcement. Yes, there are, in spite of the strong winds of incredulity and scepticism, there are those who by their religious and social virtues cause Judaism to be respected and cherished, because they show with what vigour it is still endowed after thirty-three centuries of existence. There are those who, Jews in the noblest conception of the word, are able to keep their eyes fixed on the earth and on heaven at the same time, and to carry out an auspicious union between religion and social exigencies. They know that the fear of God is the beginning of all wisdom ‖ ראשית חכמה יראת ה', that the highest point of perfection to which a man may aspire is that one sought by Moses, when he said to

---

* Vaikra Rabbah, 30.   § Ibidem.
‖ Psalm cxi. 10.

God: "I pray Thee show me now Thy way"*
הודעני נא את דרכך: and they study and meditate on the religious truths which open before them the immense and brilliant horizon of religious science and intimate conviction. They labour for the fulfilment of Isaiah's prophecy that "The earth shall be full of the knowledge of the Lord" § ומלאה הארץ דעה את ה': But they are at the same time men of action, they join to the greatness of the theory, the efficiency of the practice. They do their best to carry out rigorously the principles that they have learnt; the principles of truth and honour, of justice and morality, so that their deeds may always be the reflection of their belief, and their acts be always consistent with their words. In the midst of their cares and their daily labours they do not forget that their religion cannot be complete and perfect unless they become efficient members of society, unless they contribute to its welfare. Therefore, whatever their station and fortune may be, they constantly think of the improvements that can be introduced into the condition of men, they fearlessly work in order to perform the duty which they have prescribed to themselves, and very often their generous ideas, and their unbounded philanthropy are successful; they ameliorate industry, they improve legislation, they promote sanitary measures, they enlarge the field of science, they advance and accelerate the march of mankind towards its true vocation, that is to say, the perfecting of individuals, families, and nations. Oh! these righteous men are well represented by a citron, a fruit in which we delight, and in which everything is good and useful; so everything in them is good and useful to themselves and to

* Exod. xxxiii. 13.   § Isaiah xi. 9.

others; their body, their mind, their soul. "Blessed," says the Talmud, "blessed are the righteous who are able to render themselves and their fellow-creatures meritorious" : אשריהם לצדיקים שזוכין ומזכין They render themselves meritorious, because they fulfil the double mission which is assigned to man, to be a child to God and a brother to human creatures, the useful dwellers on earth while working in order to become the rightful guests of heaven. They render others meritorious, because nothing impresses more than true disinterestedness and virtue. They are the standard-bearers of both religion and civilisation, and their noble boldness is sure to make proselytes in the camp of the timid, to whom it gives strength, and in the camp of the wicked whom it will convert.

"The palm-tree," continues the Medrash, "is equally the symbol of Israel; in fact the fruit of this tree, the date, has a pleasing taste, but no smell at all; thus in Israel there are those who with social virtues, do not combine religious observances" : כפות תמרים אלו ישראל מה תמרה יש בה טעם ואין בה ריח כך ישראל יש בהם בני אדם שיש בהם מעשים טובים ואין בהם תורה: * This, my brethren, is the difficulty under which Judaism labours in modern times. The period of oppression is over, justice seems to have triumphed in the midst of all civilised nations; our brethren are no longer subjected to exclusion and isolation, they are called to the social banquet, admitted to the full enjoyment of the rights of citizens; but many Israelites think it necessary that they should give all their exertions to the performance of social duties, in order to prove themselves worthy of their new position. They would consider it as a stain on the Jewish name

* Vaikra Rabbah, 30.

were they to break the eighth commandment, were they to be brought before a court of justice; they think that a Jew should never give rise to accusations of deception and fraud; and they are right. But then they fall into a deplorable extreme. They come to think lightly of all religious doctrines and all religious practices; they conclude that religion is practicable only in its moral bearings, in its laws as to what is mine and what is thine. Alas! this is the fault which I find in the young generation; our young men who could by their energy and vigour, by their education and abilities, achieve so much good, allow themselves to be entirely absorbed by the claims of society, and put aside the immortal inheritance of their ancestors. They, as the Talmud truly says, do forsake eternal life, and occupy themselves with the life of the moment מניחין חיי עולם ועוסקין בחיי שעה:* They follow the habits of the people in whose midst they live, and would feel ashamed to be believed to be observant of, and faithful to, the practices which have been for three thousand years the heirloom of our race; nothing in their daily life speaks of Judaism, as they fear lest it would make them ridiculous in the eyes of society, and all their piety, all their observance is limited to a rare appearance in the house of worship. But they, as well as all those who think that a rigorous obedience to the principles of morality is sufficient, forget that, as the Talmud teaches,§ אם אין תורה אין דרך ארץ: "If there is no religion, there can be no social virtue;" that morality of any kind, either that of a son towards his father, or a servant towards his master, either of a merchant towards his customers, or of a solicitor towards his clients, if not inspired and sanctioned by religion, rests on so weak a basis that it has

---

* Talm. Shabbat, 10.   § Abot iii. 21.

no chance of durability. No, אם אין תורה אין דרך ארץ:
"If there is no religion, there is no real social virtue."
Morality without religion is limited, incomplete, and
imperfect, because it derives its origin from human institutions and laws which necessarily are limited, incomplete and imperfect; it is sometimes induced by
vanity, sometimes exists merely through fear of human
punishment, or through hope of human reward. It is,
therefore, extremely weak, and cannot secure the welfare
of either the individual, or of society. But that morality
alone is true and lasting which is the child of religion, and
goes hand in hand with religion; it has a mission of infinite
love, and it alone can make men better than they are,
and change the face of the world by removing corruption, fraud, and cruelty, and by giving rise to kindness,
honesty and brotherhood. When you hear of fraudu-
lent acts committed by Israelites whom you had always
thought respectable and moral, you may safely conclude
that their former morality fell because it was not united
with religious belief; you may then decide that it is not
right to be like the date, with flavour but without perfume, that good actions are insufficient when religion is
not their partner.

The Medrash, continuing its comparison, asserts "that
Israel is also represented by the third plant, the myrtle,
because as the myrtle has a sweet smell but no taste,
so, in the midst of Israel, there are those who devote
their life to the study of the Law, but have no good
actions to register in the book of their conscience."
וענף עץ עבות אלו ישראל : מה הדס יש בו ריח ואין בו טעם כך
ישראל יש מהם ב"א שיש בהם תורה ואין בהם מעשים טובים *
The greatness of the fault of this third class of Israelites

* Vaikra Rabbah, *ib.*

is even more strikingly apparent than that of the second. It awakens both our antipathy and disgust to see men who profess to be religious, who proclaim great principles of devotion to the Almighty, who act piously as far as religious ceremonies are concerned, who dare to assume the office of criticising their brethren, but who practise so little in their social intercourse, and exhibit so little inclination for the performance of our sacred duties towards our neighbours. Such men unfortunately do exist in society, and are to be found amongst the followers of every creed; they exist now as they existed in the ancient times of our nation, and against them Isaiah thundered his reproaches with unparalleled energy and fiery indignation. It is to those who were pious without doing good actions that he said with crushing eloquence * : לא אוכל און ועצרה I cannot bear to see iniquity coupled with religious celebrations, a life of pious practices and unscrupulous acts; prayer on the lips, while the hands are full of blood, is an abomination unto me, I will not bear it § גם כי תרבו תפלה אינני שמע ידיכם דמים מלאו: You fast, but your fast is not agreeable to me, because you find pleasure in it, because your object, apparently religious, is to make your voice heard on high and to exercise oppression, because you make your fast consist in bowing down your head as a bulrush, in spreading sackcloth and ashes under you.‖ הלזה תקרא צום ויום רצון לה' "Can you call this a fast and an acceptable day to the Lord?" The fast that I demand consists of charity, abnegation, justice, honesty, sincerity and truth. What is the use of theory without practice, of appearance without substance, of words without the facts that give them life? The Talmud properly says that

* Isaiah i. 13. § Isaiah i. 15. ‖ Isaiah lviii. 5.

"a man who studies the Law and does no good actions, is like a horse nicely caparisoned, but without bit, so that it will cast its rider violently to the earth" * אדם שאין בו מעשים טובים ולמד תורה חרבה דומה לסוס שאין לו רסן לבלום כיון שאדם רוצה לרוכבו זורקו בבת אחת: Piety without good actions shines sometimes in the eyes of inexperienced men, but it soon shows what it really is: a false splendour, a light without heat, like the brilliancy of the fire-fly; it is that which men call hypocrisy and deception, therefore our sages compared it to an unbridled horse. The imprudent rider is thrown over by that unrestrained animal; so men, easily deceived by appearance, are often the victims of pretended piety and observances which they had mistaken for religion.

But, my brethren, the worst has still to come. Even the willow, says the Medrash, signifies Israel, for as the willow has neither taste nor smell, so there are in Israel men who cannot boast either of religious science or of good qualities and virtues. Yes, we must confess it to our shame, there are those who are at the same time irreligious and immoral who, disregarding Divine and human laws, live the life of brutes, useless to themselves and to their brethren. Their heart is stone-like, it does not beat with pity at the sight of the sufferings of their fellow creatures. Their hand, never open to the relief of the indigent, is stretched out to order or accomplish iniquity. Their lips, unable to utter the praises of the Lord, or to pronounce kind words towards those who need consolation, are open to blaspheme, to foul, abominable language. The path of man's life is often traced between two precipices: but it has on each side a breast work, a solid rampart of

* Abot. R. Nathan, xxiv.

defence. When both of them are preserved, safety is assured, when one of them is missing, safety is uncertain, but it may still be obtained ; but if both ramparts are thrown down, how can the passenger's life have a chance of preservation ? The two walls represent religion and virtue : when neither exists, what chance is left to men? Can they hope for success when, as Solomon said, " the way of the wicked, their way is as darkness, they know not at what they stumble"* דרך רשעים כאפלה לא ידעו במה יכשלו: They may have fallen into that state of degradation through their inability to control their bad instincts; then they will be absolutely accountable for their faults ; they may also have been the victims of careless or bad education ; then their punishment will be shared by their parents who with unpardonable indifference have let their children go their own way, and have neglected to exercise that strong authority, which should remain in the hands of a good father, at least until he sees his offspring fairly engaged on the right path. These men, "without smell and without taste," without religion and without virtue, do not generally appear at the celebration of our religious rites ; but they are well represented by the useless willow and, compared with their good brethren, they appear as insignificant as the branch of willow compared with the verdant myrtle, the sweet date, and the odorous citron. Of the four classes of Israelites, symbolized by the four species, the ד' מינים, the first alone is according to the wish of the Lord, the first alone deserves His favour, and will earn His protection. And how will the Lord act towards the second and the third, which are scarcely tolerable ? What will He do to the fourth which seems to

* Prov. iv. 19.

deserve no pardon? Will He destroy them, will He annihilate that chosen race which He bore on eagles' wings and brought unto himself, which He carried in His bosom as a nurse carries a child? "No," says the Medrash, "God cannot destroy the children of His love:" "ומה הקב״ה עושה להן לאבדן אי אפישר *׃ What then will the Lord do? He will say: Let all of them come together before me, and they will atone for, they will protect, each other" אלא אמר הקב״ה יוקשרו כלם אגודה אחת ואלו מכפרים על אלו§: Oh my brethren, what a grand, what a sublime idea! What a consoling doctrine of the mercy of our heavenly Father who envelops the innocent and the guilty in the garment of his love! What a law of brotherhood and affection! Happy, happy the people ruled by such a religion! blessed is the race which adores the Eternal! You see it, the Lord regards us all with the same mercy, with the same tenderness.

Oh! let us imitate Him, let us be united, let us be responsible for each other, and we shall be strong, invincible! Let us appear in the house of worship, before the Lord, with the intention of praying for each other, even for sinners, even for our own enemies; but let us be united by a strong and noble brotherhood, always and everywhere. Let us show that, though represented by these four opposite classes, the Israelites are always closely attached to each other, that they form only one, as the branch of palm tree, the citron, the myrtle, and the branch of willow are united in one bundle in our hands. We may delight in the beautiful signification of this symbol, but we must also avail ourselves of the warning which it gives us, we must strive in order to

* Vaikra Rabbah, 30. § Ibid.

THE LULAB.

belong to the first class, to the number of those who cherish alike religion and virtue, who always mindful of God, never forget their duty to man. Then our ceremonies and the words of our lips will really be equivalent to our sacrifices in the Temple in the days of old, to our three pilgrimages in the time of our greatness and independence; then we shall have really offered to God all that is in our power, as it is written in Deuteronomy: "Everyone shall give as he is able, according to the blessing of the Lord thy God, which He hath given thee" איש כמתנת ידו כברכת ה׳ אלהיך אשר נתן לך:* May the Almighty look upon our religious observances with an eye of satisfaction! May He, as we have prayed this morning in the additional service, have mercy on us, as well as on His sanctuary of old! May He rebuild it, and restore to it its ancient splendour! May He guide us back to Zion with singing, and to Jerusalem, His residence, with uninterrupted joy, so that we may again morally or materially re-establish our obligatory sacrifices, the daily sacrifices according to their order, and the additional sacrifices according to their institution § והביאנו לציון עירך ברנה ולירושלים בית מקדשך בשמחת עולם ושם נעשה לפניך את קרבנות חובותינו תמידין כסדרן ומוספין כהלכתן:

AMEN.

* Deut. xvi. 17.   § Ritual.

WOMAN AND PASSOVER.

ולא יראה לך חמץ ולא יראה לך שאר בכל גבולך :

"And there shall no leavened bread be seen with thee, neither shall there be leaven seen with thee in all thy quarters."

EXODUS xiii. 7.

בשכר נשים צדקניות נגאלו ישראל ממצרים :

"It is for the sake of virtuous women that Israel was redeemed from Egypt."

TALMUD SOTAH, 11.

MY DEAR BRETHREN,—The day has nearly elapsed. The sun is declining towards the horizon, and the moment of sacred rest draws nearer and nearer. Noise and confusion have given place in the house to quiet and order. The walls of our rooms are shining with fresh cleanliness, the table is covered with a splendidly white cloth, and over it hangs a gilt lamp. A young woman has presided over this work of arranging and purifying; she is neatly dressed, and her face breathes happiness. Her husband arrives; he is tired with his weekly work, but scarcely feels now his fatigue because repose is coming. "My beloved one," he says unto her, "have you thought of the poor?" "I have." "Have you performed the preparatory ceremonies which the Sabbath imposes?" "I have." "Then it is time

to light the sacred lamp" *עשרתן ערבתן הדליקו את הנר:
And while her husband attends the Divine service,
while he and his children pray in the place of worship
for themselves and for her, she lights the lamp, and
alone, in intimate communion with God, she says:
"O Lord, bestow thy blessing upon my husband, and
my growing children, and preserve their dear existence. Protect the development of my little darlings,
and let them grow up good, religious, and intelligent.
O grant my supplication, as Thou didst grant the supplication of the wives of the Patriarchs, and never let
Thy Divine light depart from my house." Thus she
makes a temple of her house; and will God refuse
His blessing to a family when an adorable creature
asks it?

Upon the Jewish wife and the Jewish mother depend the preparation for, and the celebration of, our
weekly festival. But is that all? We are now com-
memorating the great event to which we owe our political and religious existence as well as the most precious
gift which a nation or a man can possess—liberty. We
celebrate, at the same time, the transition of nature
from a wintry sleep to a delightful spring, and the
passage of our ancestors from darkness to light, from
dejection and humiliation, to hope and triumph. Upon
the activity, the diligence, the religious zeal of the
Jewish women devolves the care of working for the
solemnity of Passover, of preparing our families for the
performance of our home worship, of purifying our house
from any leaven or anything that is leavened, in order
to raise it to the beauty and delicacy of those pious acts
which constitute one of the most marked characteristics

* Talmud, Shabat, 34.

of our religion. That is woman's mission, and no office more adapted to her powers and tendencies ever was or ever could be found.

I.

And this I emphatically declare, for I know that there are some people prompted by prejudice, and many more by ignorance, who persistently accuse Judaism, as they accuse all ancient nations and religions, of disregarding woman and, as though she were inferior to man, of depriving her of all importance in the State or the family, of considering her as a slave, as a being incapable of noble ideas and generous actions. The Bible, the book of truth, studied in the original tongue, would dispel this and many other erroneous opinions. But the sacred language, which ought to be familiar to all the followers of Monotheistic religions, is known but to few scholars, and the Bible is generally studied only through commentaries which often strip it of all its beauty, and oftener still, misinterpret its noble words and elevating doctrines. "Had not woman been held," they say, "by the Hebrews to be an inferior being, would polygamy have been permitted by the Mosaic law? Would not the daughters have been allotted a part in their father's inheritance? Would the parents have sold their daughters on the occasion of their marriage? Would authority have been bestowed upon a father, or a husband, unscrupulously to break a woman's vows, as if her words were childish utterances, and her self-imposed privations foolish exaggerations? And does Jewish tradition give reparation to the wronged woman and call her to a higher place? No, the Hebrews, in that respect, were no better than their contemporaries. It was in their eastern nature to undervalue woman, and even their subsequent writings exhibit the same tendency. She was only valued because she could bring forth children, slightly appreciated when she had many, cruelly rejected when she had none. For a later creed was reserved the glory of raising woman to her true station, to her dignity and nobility."—This is the mass of accusation heaped upon us, upon the most equitable legislation. But it is surely like the Tower of Babel, the completion of which was prevented by the confusion of tongues; it is like those castles which children build and which a puff of wind throws to the ground. It might be easily proved that modern society does not pay much respect to woman, that all laws enacted in her favour are taken from the ancient code of the Hebrews. But that would carry me too far. It will be enough for the present to clear Judaism of the injustice attributed to it by its adversaries. It was not only Moses's intention to assign to woman a noble place in his Constitution, but as a more striking contrast with the laws and customs of the nations by which the Hebrews would be surrounded, he proclaimed it in the first pages of the Pentateuch, and declared it intimately connected with the event of Creation. Can woman be thought inferior to man, when she is a part of his being, of the same nature, taken from him? Can there be any difference in their essence, since both were made of the same flesh, animated by the same eternal spirit, since in order to be united to woman and to form with her, "one flesh," והיו לבשר אחד * man was allowed to abandon his parents, his natural protectors, and the objects of his respect? This great declaration, which shows how much Moses

---

* Gen. ii. 24.

valued woman, is also a proof that polygamy was opposed to his principles. He did not forbid it, as he did not forbid slavery, in consequence of the peculiar condition of the people with whom he had to deal, but when he said: ודבק באשתו "he shall cleave unto his wife,"* not unto *his wives*, he morally proscribed polygamy, implicitly showing that it was an obstacle to the happiness of man. Had Isaac more than one wife ? And would Jacob have had more than one wife if, instead of the lovely Rachel, his cunning father-in-law had not given him the tender-eyed Leah ? Were not the kings forbidden from keeping a large harem, and were not Solomon's sins and misfortunes attributed to his numerous wives ? As it is written, § ויטו נשיו את לבו "And his wives turned away his heart." It is true that the principal part of a man's inheritance was bequeathed unto his sons, especially the firstborn son. But that regarded landed property only ; and it was inevitable in a nation constituted like the Hebrews, whose tribes were to preserve the territory allotted to them. But when there were no sons, the daughters inherited, as it happened for the daughters of Zelophehad." ‖ Does not the same system prevail in many modern civilised nations ? And are we to go so far in order to find one of them ? The Hebrews are accused of selling their daughters to their husbands. This fact which is certainly opposed to modern views, was one of the customs rooted in the ancient nations ; but it did not constitute a general rule among our ancestors. We do not see that Abraham bought Sarah or Keturah, nor did Isaac buy Rebecca ; he was a wealthy man, and made unto her wealthy presents. And can we say that Jacob bought Rachel ?

* Gen. ii. 24.   § 1 Kings xi. 3.   ‖ Numb. xxvii. 1.

Can we call a regular contract, the long labour to which he submitted through his ardent love? A seller indeed there was, but it was the Aramean Laban, the type of a father whose feelings are stifled by cupidity. But even consenting that women in ancient times were sold, no degradation was thus inflicted upon them, just as no degradation is now inflicted, as an acute writer has said, upon young men who seem to be bought by their brides.

No proof of lack of respect to woman is to be found in the fact that Moses gave authority to a father and a husband to break the vows of their daughter and wife. It was, on the contrary, a tribute paid to the generous ideas which a woman conceives under the exaltation of the moment, to the self-sacrifice which she pronounces too easily, when her noble heart is deeply moved. But it was an obstacle raised to the facility with which she binds herself, and for which she after a time repents; and can a law of true wisdom and protection be considered as a proof of indifference or contempt? Had not the Hebrew woman been highly appreciated, would there have been a woman at the head of government like Deborah, or a prophetess like Huldah? Would Moses have commanded father and mother to be equally honoured? Would he have even given precedence to woman, as when he said: איש אמו ואביו תיראו.* " Ye shall fear every man his mother and his father." Would Malachi have uttered bitter reproach against him who has "dealt treacherously with the wife of his youth?"§ But the Jewish tradition exhibits even greater respect towards woman, and in the Talmud innumerable are the sentences recommending man to respect his wife, defending

* Lev. xix. 3.   § Mal. ii. 14.

her rights and upholding her dignity. "He who loves his wife as himself, and honours her more than himself," says one of the sages, "he who puts his sons and his daughters on the good way, shall have the peace which God has promised to the righteous" * כל האוהב את אישתו והמכבדה יותר מגופו והמדריך את בניו ואת בנותיו בדרך ישרה עליו הכתוב אומר וידעת כי שלום אהלך: "Woe unto him who wrongs his own wife; the Divine vengeance will be as ready as the lament of the betrayed woman." "If thy wife be short, bend down over her and speak to her" § איתתך גוצא נחון ותלחוש לה: . "Why," said a doctor to Rabbi Keyah, "why so much kindness to thy wife who, by her temper, embitters thy existence?" "Is it not already a great merit for our women," he answered, "that they educate our children and save us from sin?" ‖ דיינו שמגדלות את בנינו ומצילות אותנו מן החטא: Much greater is the reward God promised to women, than that promised to men." ¶ So the Talmud, which is nothing but the extensive commentary on the words, the expressions, and the doctrines of the Bible, follows the noble example of its hallowed text. Both of them assign to woman a position as reserved as her instincts prompt her to be, as modest as her virtues ask to remain; but they assign to her at the same time a mission of love, by which she may become a source of blessing to society, for she makes her family a school, capable of furnishing to society its most useful and generous elements. The following legend places in a still more prominent light the high idea which the sages of tradition had of women: ** Alexander the Great arrived with his victorious army before a town inhabited only

---

* Talmud Jebamot, 62.   § Talmud Baba Meziha, 59.   ‖ Ib. 63.
¶ Talmud Berachot, 17.   ** Talmud Tamid, 4.

by women, and prepared for the attack. The women sent him this message: "Why dost thou wage war against us? If thou vanquishest, thou wilt have no glory, for the world will say: 'This great hero has conquered women.' And if the battle end in our triumph, then thy shame will be greater, since thou wilt have fallen by the hand of women." Alexander offered unto them an honourable peace, and asked for provisions. The women brought unto him gold bread in gold plates. "Why," said the king, "do they eat gold in this country?" "Certainly not," answered the shrewd women, "but is there no bread in thy empire that thou hast come to seek bread in our land?" Then Alexander departed with his soldiers; but before starting, he wrote these words upon the gate of that town: "I, Alexander of Macedonia, was heedless and without prudence, until I came to this African country and learnt wisdom from the women" אנא אלכסנדרוס מוקדון הויתי שטיא עד דאתיתי למדינת אפריקי דנשיא וילפת עצה מן נשיא:

II.

Having summarily answered the assertions of our opponents, it is not my intention to plunge into controversy on this interesting subject. Our Law defends itself. It stands at equal distance from the two extremes. Concerning woman, it adopts neither unbounded liberty nor seclusion. It does not bestow upon her the solemn functions of priesthood which exclusively belong to men; but on the other hand, it does not allow her to live a life of asceticism, to live apart from the world, in a grave though in the midst of society, with the object of meditating upon heavenly things, while she is upon the earth, and subject to earthly wants and feelings. Judaism does not violate the laws of nature. So among the Jews woman has no public religious office, and she will have none, as long as Judaism is not undermined by rash and unreasonable changes. But a graceful office, as I said, is reserved for her. When I asserted that she prepares our dwellings for the celebration of Passover, that she purifies them from every leavened substance, I meant that the Jewish woman is the priestess of her home, that upon her alone it depends for the Jewish houses to become houses of prayer, houses in which our religious observances are performed thoroughly, exactly, sincerely, houses of practical morality and real virtue.

You must reflect, my good sisters, for it is to you especially that I address myself on this sacred day, that the obnoxious leaven, against which you are to direct your efforts is not to return into our houses when it has once been banished from them. You must reflect also that it is not easily banished, for it is sometimes deeply rooted in the very foundations of our homes; your exertions must, therefore, be the more energetic and incessant if they are to triumph. You understand that I do not refer only to material leaven, and that this is one of the symbols of our religion which admits of a two-fold interpretation. The leaven which I mean, symbolises the moral imperfections which often deface our families, those imperfections which are one of the causes of their misery, just as physical disease destroys the health of a body, or as revolutions undermine the existence of empires. Those moral imperfections must therefore disappear; that leaven ought no longer to be seen, but neither ought it to remain hidden, for even if

it is not seen, it works destruction* ולא יראה ולא ימצא
And you have the power of performing such a task,
however difficult it may be, provided you employ the
four ways which the Book of Proverbs points out to
you.

You are not weak, my sisters, your weakness is only
apparent. You are the "faint" to whom God gives power,
and those who have no might to whom the Lord increas-
eth strength § : נתן ליעף כח ולאין אונים עצמה ירבה
Your husband's authority is over you, but the government
of your house is in your hands, and upon you the responsibility for it rests. Pharaoh, in making Joseph ruler over
all the land of Egypt, gave him his royal ring and said
unto him : אתה תהיה על ביתי ‖ "Thou shalt be over
my house." And so it has been with you since the day
on which you received the nuptial ring. You can
and you do exercise great influence. Take care then,
that this influence should be good and beneficial.
Exercise it first of all over your husbands themselves ; be
good wives, true Jewish wives. Constantly struggling
against the foaming stream of society, unsuccessful in
their transactions, deceived in their expectations, de-
frauded by friends, stung by calumny, they bring home
the leaven of bad temper, of irritation, gloom, and
dejection. Sometimes they threaten vengeance, sometimes they despair. It is your duty to soften what is
hard, to make smooth what is rough, it is your duty to
send a ray of light through that cloudy sky. Like the
illustrious Beruriah of the Talmud who, though inexpressibly grieved for the sudden loss of her two children,
yet had the courage to console the partner of her life,
and to utter such words of wisdom as impressed upon

* Exodus xiii. 7.   § Isaiah xl. 29.   ‖ Genesis xli. 40.

him the duty of resignation; be always unto your husbands the advocates of kindness, indulgence, forgiveness and patience. Remind your husbands of resignation, but do not forget religion. A gay or agitated youth has perhaps taught them to believe little, and to practise less. Banish, for God's sake, banish that leaven, and by your smile, which is a reflection of the smile of heaven, by your charming manners which are the secret of your power, bring, oh, bring back to religion and worship that spirit which only needs a soft and graceful guide. Then, you will be the woman of whom Solomon said: "The heart of her husband will safely trust in her, so that he shall have no need of spoil. She will do him good and not evil all the days of her life"* בטח בה לב בעלה ושלל לא יחסר: גמלתהו טוב ולא רע כל ימי חייה: Be good wives, my sisters, Passover has come, and that is the first way of destroying all leaven.

The second way is that you should be good mothers. And this dear name recalls to the mind of everyone, (those excepted who have become forlorn orphans in their childhood) ideas of sweetness, piety, and unbounded love. Providence is always symbolised by a mother. It seems, in fact, as if the Lord had made woman a reflection of His attribute of kindness, when He placed into her graceful hands the key of the human heart. Remember, my sisters, that the love which you have for your children, the love of Jewish mothers, that is, an ardent and unconquerable love, will be inefficient if you do not prove it by educating your darlings' hearts as you educate their minds. The neglect of this duty would be such leaven as would produce the bitterest fruits. King Solomon said: "My son, forsake not the law of thy

* Prov. xxxi. 11, 12.

mother" * ואל תטש תורת אמך   This *Law* probably means religious instruction. But a mother must give it, if it is to be listened to. She alone can give it, because it consists of truths that speak to the heart: and who, better than a mother, can touch the children's heart? Oh, if you begin to speak to your children of God, the very day on which they can lisp the word God, if, while you give them religious knowledge, you accustom them to religious acts, if you labour every day and devote to your work the time given by others to out-of-door amusements, your exertions will not be vain, you will reap a harvest of blessings. Your sons will be such Jews as our religion needs, enlightened, strong in their faith, unshaken in their observances; they will be at the same time such members of society as modern progress demands: instructed, industrious, moral, ready to sacrifice everything for the country and the sovereign. They will love, honour and venerate you, and their affection will be a most precious, but also a most glorious, crown around your brow. But if you neglect your sacred duty, you will be punished by the indifference, and perhaps by the disrespect of your offspring. If later in life, grieved to find themselves without any religious knowledge, your children say with regret: "It is our mother's fault; she taught us nothing;" these words will be a reproach that will torment and follow you to your grave. My sisters, Passover has come, the leaven of irreligion ought to have departed from your children's heart.

The Talmud says that "women are merciful" § נשים רחמניות הן: It adds that "woman remains at home and gives bread to the poor" ‖ איתתא שכיחא בביתא

* Prov. i. 8.   § Meghilah 14.   ‖ Tahanit 23.

SERMON VI.

וִיהַבָא רִיפְתָא לְעָנְיָא : And by these expressions it refers to the leaven of unkindness that exists in a house wherein no charitable action is done. And you, my sisters, are again called upon to banish that leaven; you must be the angels of charity; you, whose sensitive heart feels more than the heart of man does, you who, subject to hard sufferings, feel the whole depth of the sufferings of the poor, of the distress of a wife who has no bread for her sick husband, of the despair of a mother who has no food for her starving children—you must be the friend of the poor and make your dwelling the storehouse of Providence. You must give bread to the hungry; you must not wait till it is asked for, you must offer it and force it into the hand of those who struggle between the stings of hunger and the shame of begging. Woman's heart treasures true charity, and the benevolence of the Jewish woman is known: innumerable blessings are invoked upon those noble hearted ladies among you, to whom the way to the poorest houses is familiar, who delight the needy by their presence, and console them by their words, while their hand offers substantial relief. Oh, let your houses be graced every day by an act of charity; away, away with the leaven of unkindness; it ought never, never to exist, either during Passover or after Passover, wherever a Jewish woman dwells.

But, my beloved sisters, it is impossible for you to be good wives and good mothers according to the spirit of Judaism, to be charitable, if you are not at the same time religious, if the fear of God is not deep in your heart. It is not my opinion that you should be theologians, that you should plunge into the intricate labyrinth of philosophical discussions. That is not your department. I do not ask that your mind should possess a deep knowledge of our dogmas; but I do ask that your heart should be warmed by ardent faith. To your feelings as well as to your reason I make an appeal. You must know the God of Israel, that God who preserved our nation amidst the hardest trials. You must know the deeds of that God who is the father of all creatures, but who has chosen our race, from the midst of all races, to be His own people. Fear Him, love Him, and never forget that dishonest, immoral, immodest or unchaste actions are opposed to His will. Pray unto Him in your grief, hope in His assistance when you are unhappy, and you will feel ineffably relieved and consoled. That is the result of faith. But when the moment comes of performing the observances of religion, the true Jewish woman who can be pious without bigotry, practises them with punctuality and devotion. The poetical symbols of our religion are acceptable to her poetical and loving heart, and she must carry them out with fondness; then she will exercise around her such irresistible attraction, that she will succeed in winning her whole family over to her ideas and convictions. Her example becomes their guide. Then all leaven really disappears, and for ever, from her house, which she has thoroughly purified.

She will preserve a strong link between the Judaism of the past and of the present; between Sarah, Rebecca and Rachel of old, and the Rachels, Rebeccas and Sarahs of modern times. A wise adviser of her husband, an affectionate teacher of her children, a Providence to the poor, a faithful servant to the God of Israel, by preserving Judaism at home she will preserve it everywhere. And if our sages attributed to the virtues of the Hebrew women in Egypt the deliverance of Israel, בשכר נשים

SERMON VI.

צדקניות נגאלו ישראל ממצרים * future generations will in their turn bless the memory of the Hebrew woman of the present, and attribute to her the safety of our religion. " Give her," they will say, " the fruit of her hands, and let her own works praise her in the gates "§ תנו לה מפרי ידיה
ויהללוה בשערים מעשיה :

AMEN.

* Talmud Sotah, 11. § Prov. xxxi. 31.

THE MESSIAH.

A PASSOVER SERMON.

לא ירעו ולא ישחיתו בכל הר קדשי כי מלאה הארץ דעה את ה
כמים לים מכסים :

"They shall not hurt nor destroy in all My holy mountain: for the earth shall be full of the knowledge of the Lord, as the waters cover the sea."
ISAIAH xi. 9.

זכו אחישנה לא זכו בעתה :

"If they are righteous I will hasten the moment of redemption; if they are not righteous, it shall take place in its own time."
TALMUD SANHEDRIM 98.

MY DEAR BRETHREN,—Since the day when the terrible sentence of defeat, humiliation and dispersion, pronounced against us by the supreme Judge, was carried out, none of the sacrifices prescribed by the Law have been offered up to the Lord. Our temple, our altar, our high priest, have long disappeared and are almost lost in the mist of centuries. Yet a ceremony which may be called a real sacrifice, has been preserved, and wherever the Jew lives is solemnly performed. It is the paschal sacrifice. No blood is shed, no lamb is slaughtered, no column of smoke rises from its smouldering remains. It is a domestic sacrifice—all peace and joy. The father, who is the real priest, and the mother the real priestess of the family, surrounded by a charming group of young worshippers, accomplish the simple and touching rites; they relate the miseries of the past, while as a symbol, they eat the bread of poverty, and express in immortal songs of praise, their gratitude unto the Lord for His visible protection and repeated wonders resulting in the Hebrews' triumphant redemption. The characteristics of the Passover service do not consist in earnest words of thanks unto the Lord for His gracious favours in the past, and for His unceasing blessings in the present only; but also in our fervent hope for the accomplishment of His great promise in the future. When we sing the enthusiastic words of David: * " blessed be he that cometh in the name of the Lord," ברוך הבא בשם ה׳, we involuntarily hasten to the door and open it. Whom do we expect? Why, when the ceremony is over, do we exclaim, before parting: " This year here, next year in the land of redemption?" We expect him, who will be the bearer, for the first time, of real peace, of more stable happiness and splendour than we can now enjoy; and our aspirations are directed towards the city which the Lord has chosen to be the place wherein Israel and all other nations will join in praying unto the One God. This is the reason why we exclaim לשנה הבאה בירושלים " Next year in Jerusalem," § while a gleam of sweet hope gladdens our hearts. Both the Bible and tradition have established a mysterious link between the triumph of our ancestors over Egypt, and the final triumph of our race over a moral but more dangerous enemy. "Therefore, behold, the days come, saith the Lord, that it shall no more be said, The Lord liveth that brought up the children of Israel out of the land of Egypt, but, the Lord

* Psalm cxviii. 26. § Passover Service.

liveth that brought up the children of Israel from the land of the North, and from the land whither he had driven them; and I will bring them again into their land that I gave unto their fathers."* According to the Talmud, "it was in spring, the auspicious period of the revival of nature, that the Hebrews were rescued, and in spring they shall again be redeemed"§ בניסן נגאלו ובניסן עתידין ליגאל: These are the thoughts with which our mind is unconsciously occupied during this solemn but most charming festival. Let me therefore, this morning, dwell briefly on the personification of the future redemption, that is, on the Messiah. In choosing this subject I do not intend to raise any controversy whatever; but I think it my duty to explain to you, my brethren, one of the principal dogmas of our faith, and to foster a hope which may be the source of generous ideas and noble deeds. The time is most appropriate. This is the last day of our Passover, which cannot be better closed than by meditating on the forthcoming Passover, both of Israel and of mankind. For this purpose we have, this morning, read the celebrated eleventh chapter of Isaiah, which may be called a glowing description of the Messianic times.

I.

It is a recognised and visible fact that Israel is a race distinct from all other human races, and endowed, physically and morally, with different characteristics. But even his history and destiny are unlike the history and destiny both of ancient nations, which we know through their monuments, and of modern peoples among whom we live; exactly as Moses said: "So shall we be separated, I and this people, from all the people that are

* Jerem. xvi. 14, 15. § Roshashana, 11.

upon the face of the earth "* ונפלינו אני ועמך מכל העם אשר על פני האדמה: The existence of ancient nations, as is that of plants, is generally divided into three distinct periods: the period of their bloom, of their full growth, and their decay. The beginning of a nation is always humble, and sometimes even unworthy, like that of the Romans, whose direct ancestors were a gang of robbers, the terror of Latium. The second period is one of power, extensive conquests and glory, when the nation has reached its highest point of prosperity. The third period is that of decay, followed by utter destruction and, for more than one empire, by the loss of its very name and of all traces of its existence upon the earth. But nothing of the kind is to be observed respecting the Hebrew race. At its very beginning it was great and noble, it attained to a spiritual grandeur that no other race has ever approached. As soon as they began to exist, the Hebrews achieved their deliverance from a state of subjection and slavery, and were raised, a few days after, to the glorious condition of God's chosen people, and received from Him, in a direct manner, those divine laws which must ever rule the destiny of man. The earthly glory of the Hebrews, on the other hand, was nothing compared with the glory of Babylon, Greece or Rome. Their number was small, their land was not extensive, and as conquerors they very seldom spread terror among their neighbours. They had their period of decline, but in spite of the loss of their nationality and freedom, in spite of their dispersion, they were not destroyed; and, what is more, they were promised and will have that which was denied to their great conquerors—a splendid future.

* Exod. xxxiii. 16.

THE MESSIAH.

Yes, a splendid future. Scattered by the Romans on the three great continents of Europe, Asia, and Africa, deprived of all material power and influence, condemned to the most demoralising abjection, the Jews never renounced their patriotism, their enthusiastic love for Palestine! Could they have had any hope of calling it again their own when they saw it seized by the powerful arm of the Roman emperors, and after them by the successors of Mahomet, by the Western States leagued together, and again by the warlike Turks? No, they could not have nourished that hope; and yet their love for their fatherland became almost a worship. Although dispersed over the surface of the earth, they would keep a colony of their brethren in the Holy Land, as a proof that they had not renounced its possession. At the cost of immense sacrifices, of intolerable humiliation, they would dwell in it, so that a few among them, at least, might pray by the remains of the Temple, for they would not give up their sacred right of possession. But whence this perseverance? Whence? They looked to the great man who was the first leader of their ancestors and their inspired liberator, Moses. From Moses they urned their eyes to future ages, and saw another great deliverer. They were, and they are sure that the Moses of the future will reunite their scattered members and animate them with new life, so that the great wrongs of the past may meet with a great reparation. This idea of the Messiah, the king of the era of justice, gave them the power of suffering in silence, and of bearing patiently such persecution as would have crushed any other race. The doctrine of the Messiah made them heroes and martyrs, an object of admiration even to their tormentors.

The advent of that great time was predicted first by Moses who, knowing that the morning can indicate the brilliancy or the gloom of the day, could, from the tendencies of the Hebrews, perceive their future rebellions and punishment; but relying upon the Divine mercy, he announced at the same time their future redemption. His words are unmistakable, and can only refer to events which are still to happen, to that which no human eye has as yet seen. "If any of thine be driven out unto the utmost parts of heaven, from thence will the Lord thy God gather thee, and from thence will He fetch thee" *אם יהיה נדחך בקצה השמים משם יקבצך ה' אלהיך ומשם יקחך: The prophets declared its certainty in beautiful and glorious language, which cannot be adequately translated. The Talmud teaches that "all the predictions of our inspired seers concern the advent of the Messiah" § כל הנביאים לא נתנבאו אלא לימות המשיה: But although all had the same aim in view, they expressed themselves by different images and poetical figures! Zachariah and Malachi, both of whom lived in a time of deadly struggle, saw the restoration of the Hebrew nation as the effect of bloody and fiery battles and of terrible convulsions of nature, when the heavens will open, and the stars will stay their course, the rivers will return to their fountains, the valleys will become mountains, and the mountains valleys. Ezekiel represented the blessed epoch as a time of purification and revival, when uncleanness and iniquity shall vanish, when desolation and destruction shall no longer be seen upon the earth. Isaiah, with the unrivalled sweetness of his words, described it by saying that the ruins and waste places of Jerusalem shall break forth into joy, and shall celebrate

* Deut. xxx. 4. § Berachot, 34.

together the redemption of Israel; and by announcing that the "watchmen shall see with rapturous joy, eye to eye, when the Lord shall return to Zion." Joel prophesied that in those blessed days the Lord will pour His Spirit upon all flesh, when our sons and daughters shall have Divine visions. The Talmud, in its turn, expresses the idea of the Messiah's advent with a profound thought. "The re-assembling of the exiled Hebrews will be as great as the day on which heaven and earth were created": *גדול קבוץ גליות כיום שנבראו שמים וארץ "That time, teaches the Medrash,—making use, as usual, of bold metaphors and picturesque language,—will be remarkable through ten great events: the light of the sun will be stronger and more brilliant in the world; manifold sources of limpid water will spring forth in Jerusalem and will restore strength and health to all creatures; the trees will be wonderfully productive and their fruit will cure the sick; all the ruins of the world will resume their former shape, even Sodom will be rebuilt; Jerusalem shall be restored to greater beauty, and will become more than formerly the object of universal admiration; the most ferocious animals shall be tamed; a covenant of peace shall be established between Israel and all created beings; groaning and weeping shall no longer be heard in the world; death shall be mastered; joy shall reign everywhere." §

II.

All Jews agree that this period of wonderful regeneration will come; they all firmly believe in this which constitutes one of the principal dogmas of our faith. Yet they often differ from each other when they seek to define both the Messiah and his mission; and the

* Pesachim, 88.   § Shemot Rabbah, xv.

opinions that are sometimes expressed do not greatly enhance the value of our doctrines in the eyes of our neighbours. They cause the Jewish nation to be deemed selfish, and indifferent to the happiness of mankind. According to some, the Messiah is simply a powerful man, who will lead back Israel to the land of his ancestors, and exercise a cruel vengeance against the tormentors of our race. According to others, the Messiah is simply a myth, not a person, but only a symbol of a period of prosperity for all nations, so that not even the material restoration of Israel will be required. In this divergence of ideas, we see how extremes meet in the human mind even on the most important points and on spiritual subjects. Both opinions are fallacious. The Messiah, according to the true teachings of our religion, will surely be a man, a descendant of the royal house of David. A man who, endowed with supernatural power, will reconstitute the nationality of the Hebrew race. The Mosaic edifice will be reconstructed, and the inheritance of Jacob will no longer be in the hands of the stranger; but the Messiah will, according to the Talmud, cause the fall of all tyranny and oppression * אין בין העולם הזה לימות המשיח כי אם שעבוד מלכיות בלבד: Thus Israel's happiness will be the source of the happiness of all other human families. Will there, however, be great miracles? Will astounding events take place? Will the universe break through its laws and exhibit unheard-of phenomena? It is true that many of our prophets and Talmudical sages have clearly foretold the accomplishment of marvellous facts. But if we turn to the simple words of Moses, we see that he announced no miracles, nothing but the recall

* Berachot, 28.

of Israel from his secular exile and the advent of the time when he will be the people of God, and God his heavenly Father. And so Isaiah who, after Moses, was surely the greatest among the Hebrew seers, predicted no other miracles but those which are wrought by the triumph of truth, justice and reconciliation. In the glorious 11th chapter he described the character of the great anointed King who will stay the horrible effects of injustice, iniquity, violence and war. Then the mighty will not conspire against the safety of the weak, the great and the small will dwell peacefully together; ferocity will no longer have adherents. Then "the wolf shall dwell with the lamb, and the leopard shall lie down with the kid; and the calf, and the young lion, and the fatling together; and a little child shall lead them."* When the earth is full of the knowledge of God, who will arise to hurt or destroy in all the holy mountain, who will damage the temple of the universal God?§ Maimonides, justly termed the eagle of Israel, rejected, in his turn, all ideas of miraculous deeds. The wonders foretold by the prophets, he said, are mysterious parables, which will in the Messiah's time be explained by great events. The world will follow its normal course, but in the moral order great changes will take place, and all men will return to the law of truth. There will be no famine, no hostility, no envy, no hatred, for abundance and wealth will be shared by all men, who will thus be able to devote their mind to the knowledge of God. "The true mission of the Messiah will be to cause all the world to worship the Lord together" : ויתקן את העולם כלו לעבוד את ה' ביחד ||

* Isaiah xi. 6. § Ib.
|| Maimonides Treatise on Kings, xi., xii.

A mission of religious truth can neither be efficient, nor salutary nor honourable, if it does not foster at the same time social virtue, and above all a spirit of reconciliation. There arose in former times founders of new religions, but their leading principle was not toleration. They were afraid lest their mission should fail; they were incensed by the resistance which men opposed to their new dogmas: therefore, while they preached love, they practised violence and war. They would compel their neighbours to adopt their creeds, and were thus the cause of bitterness and discord, dividing the father from the son, the brother from the sister, the mother from the children of her blood. But the Messiah who will really derive his inspiration from the Lord, will be the bearer of peace, concord and mutual brotherhood. Not only he will not separate those beings who ought to be united with each other by the sweetest ties, but, as Malachi feelingly said,* "He shall turn the heart of the fathers to the children and the heart of the children to their fathers" והשיב לב אבות על בנים ולב בנים על אבותם: The success of a human task is generally sought by means of anger and struggle. But the mission that is really divine, triumphs through love alone. The triumph of Israel's glorious undertaking through the Messiah will not confer upon him any material grandeur, any supremacy or power. Israel cannot aspire to universal domination. He will be "unto the Lord a kingdom of priests," § not those priests who exercise sovereign authority, who receive the substantial tribute of the submission of nations, who need earthly wealth in order to shine with earthly splendour; but such priests as teach, and

* Mal. iii. 6. § Exod. xix. 6.

THE MESSIAH.

consider their duty done only when the hearts of men are filled with truth and the earth with the knowledge of God. Our religion, as tradition teaches, will doubtless become the universal religion, but only so far as dogmas are concerned; our worship, our ceremonies always binding upon us, will not be obligatory on the whole of mankind; Israel may again offer the fat of bulls and rams in the sanctuary of Mount Moriah, but the Lord's house will be a house of prayer for the other nations. "Their burnt offerings and their sacrifices shall be accepted upon Mine altar; for My house shall be called a house of prayer for all people"* עולתיהם וזבחיהם לרצון על מזבחי כי ביתי בית תפלה יקרא לכל העמים: Oh, the Jew ought to be aware of the beauty of his doctrines, he ought to be able to answer when questioned on religious subjects. He ought to be able to show the contrast which, concerning salvation, exists between our religion which admits all *pious men of other nations* to the enjoyment of future felicity, and those creeds which teach that out of them there is no possible redemption.

This noble doctrine of the Messiah, thus understood, can be the subject of long and consoling meditation. There are moments when we feel irresistibly inclined to be alone with ourselves, our reason, our faith, our conscience. There are moments when all men, even those who are entirely devoted to material pursuits and sensual pleasures, feel hunger, yet not for bread; and thirst, yet not for water; but for something higher and purer which may better interest our souls, in accordance with the prophet: "I will send a famine in the land, not a famine of bread, nor a thirst for water, but of

* Isaiah lvi. 7.

hearing the words of the Lord"* לא רעב ללחם ולא
צמא למים כי אם לשמוע את דברי ה' : And our longing for
spiritual musing will be satisfied, our heart will be
refreshed and our hope restored, if we meditate on the
Messiah, the nature of his mission, and the probable
time of his advent.

III.

But when, when shall we see this blessed epoch
which will open to mankind new paths towards virtue
and its reward? When shall we see this Messiah, whose
name has become the symbol of ardent, but unsatisfied
hope? Daniel has alone among all the prophets, answered
this all-absorbing question, but he expressed his ideas
so enigmatically that a satisfactory solution cannot be
obtained, and tradition—probably to signify the impossibility and perhaps the inadvisability of the attempt
—relates the legend of that commentator who "found
the explanation of Daniel's prophecy, and was about to
write it down, when his pen was arrested by a mysterious hand." But Moses who, while always sublime, is
nevertheless simple and clear, fixes the condition for,
instead of the time of, the announced redemption.
"Thou shalt return to the Lord thy God, and shalt obey
His voice" § ושבת עד ה' אלהיך ושמעת בקלו : Then,
"the Lord thy God will turn thy captivity and have
compassion upon thee" ║ ושב ה' אלהיך את שבותך ורחמך :
The advent of the Messiah cannot be abrupt. Great
changes upon the earth can only take place by slow
gradation. Twilight is the necessary transition between
night and day; spring is the transition between the
season of decay and the season of revival; so labour
only can be the bridge that will carry us to the shore of

* Amos viii. 11. § Deut. xxx. 2. ║ Ibid. 3.

rest. The coming of the Messiah must be brought about by proper preparation, and must be made possible by religious and moral progress. Our thorough regeneration, accomplished with all our heart and our soul, is the true precursor and harbinger of the object of our ardent hope. The Lord promised that the great fact shall take place, and said:* אני ה' בעתה אחישנה "I, the Lord will hasten it in its own time." But how, observes the Talmud,§ how can these two opposite ideas of *hastening* it, and of doing it in *its own time* be reconciled? The first part of that verse is probably a promise, the second a threat : זכו אחישנה לא זכו בעתה "If they are righteous, I will hasten the moment of their redemption; if they are not righteous, it shall take place in its own time." This idea is beautifully illustrated by a legendary tale of the Talmud. ‖ "Rabbi Joshua ben Levi met the prophet Elijah and said unto him : 'Master, when is the Messiah coming?' 'Ask him, and he will tell you.' 'But where can I find him?' 'At the gate of the city.' 'How shall I recognise him?' 'By this sign, that he lives in the midst of the poor and the sick. They try to cure their wounds all at once, but he cures them successively.' The sage hastened to the gate of the city, found the Messiah, and said : 'Master, when are you coming?' 'Even to-day.' But the hope of the Rabbi was disappointed. He went again to Elijah, and complained of the deception which the Messiah had practised on him. 'He has not deceived you,' answered Elijah. 'He is ready to come even *this day* היום, but on condition that you deserve it ; in accordance with David's warning,¶ *To-day*, if ye will hear his voice,'"

---

* Isaiah lx. 22.   § Sanhedrin, 98.   ‖ Ibid.
¶ Psalm xcv. 7.

היום אם בקלו תשמעו : "The Messiah will not come," continue our sages,* "until the proud are banished from Israel" אין בן דוד בא עד שיכלו גסי הרוח מישראל : "Jerusalem can be saved only through the influence of charity" אין ירושלים נפדית אלא בצדקה : "If Israel is truly repentant, he will be redeemed, otherwise he will not be redeemed" אם ישראל עושין תשובה נגאלין ואם לאו אין נגאלין :

And is not this object worthy our attempt? Is not the reward more than adequate to the labour which ought to prepare it? When Isaiah said that the "Law shall come out of Zion, and the word of God from Jerusalem," he did not utter a prophecy, but he gave a lesson. We must strive in order that it may become a fact. We must study and teach, observe and perform the holy precepts of the Law. If the earth is to be "full of the knowledge of the Lord as the waters cover the sea," it must be through our agency. We must infuse that knowledge; we possess the best materials for that instruction, and we must make it a duty and a glory to enlighten the world. We can, by our marvellous vitality, bear witness to the Lord's rigorous fidelity to His promises of the past. And we must, by our religious and moral conduct, hasten the time when He will keep His word concerning the future, that is, when all men, animated by feelings of peace and charity, will form only one united family.

It is not without reason that tradition has closely associated our deliverance from Egypt with the final

* Talmud, Ibidem.

deliverance of mankind from all tyranny. Our rescue from Egypt gave us the existence and independence of a nation, the crown of the Law, and the privilege of being led by God. Our future rescue will give to mankind, made one nation, the religion of truth, and the law of love. The defeat of the Egyptians checked the despotism of one king, the ferocity of one race. The future redemption will exercise its beneficial influence over all the earth; it will cause the voice of justice to echo in every heart. Our deliverance from Egypt gave us possession of Palestine: our future deliverance will give us possession of all countries, for our principles and laws shall become the wisdom of every king, the guidance of every state, and the Temple that received the sacrifices of the Hebrews shall hear the prayers of all nations. Every one among us can work for that great end. The men, by their steadfastness in religion, by the purity of their hearts, by the honesty of their actions; the women, by making their houses the dwellings of decency, dignity, charity, and religious education; even children, by learning the lessons of Judaism, and by walking early on the path of religious observance. Then we shall feel convinced that we have worked for the Messiah's advent, that we have hastened it, and that we shall soon have to celebrate another Passover, much greater than the present, both in its origin and signification. Then we shall have full cause to repeat Isaiah's hymn of gratitude: "O Lord, I will praise thee: though Thou wast angry with me, Thine anger is turned away, and Thou comfortedst me. Behold God is my salvation; I will trust and not be afraid: for the Lord is my strength and my song; He also is become my salvation. Therefore with joy shall ye draw water out of the wells of salvation.

And in that day shall ye say : Praise the Lord, call upon His name, declare His doings among the people, make mention that His name is exalted. Sing unto the Lord; for He hath done excellent things : this is known in all the earth. Cry out and shout, thou inhabitant of Zion : for great is the Holy One of Israel in the midst of thee " * : צהלי ורני ישבת ציון כי גדול בקרבך קדוש ישראל

AMEN.

* Isaiah xii.

# THE ANSWER OF ISRAEL.

A FEAST OF WEEKS SERMON.

ועתה אם שמוע תשמעו בקלי ושמרתם את בריתי והייתם לי סגלה מכל העמים כי לי כל הארץ :

"Now, therefore, if ye will obey my voice indeed, and keep my covenant, then ye shall be a peculiar treasure unto me above all people: for all the earth is mine."   EXODUS xix. 5.

חביבין ישראל שניתן להם כלי חמדה שבו נברא העולם :

"The proof that the Israelites are dear unto the Lord, is that unto them was given a precious jewel, the Law, for the accomplishment of which the world was created."   TALMUD ABOT, iii. 18.

MY DEAR BRETHREN,—When the sixth day of Sivan approaches, and the Feast of Weeks arrives, accompanied by all the beauties of Nature then in her greatest splendour, it is impossible for an Israelite not to recall the past, the youth of the daughter of Zion, the day of her wedding with the Lord, when the heavens and the earth were the witnesses, the blue vault of the sky was the canopy, the brilliant sun and the flashes of lightning piercing the cloud which enveloped Mount Sinai, were the nuptial torches. He still sees the mount trembling and convulsed, and the sounds of the invisible trumpet, of the voice of the Lord and of Moses, still ring in his ears. His heart is moved, his lips unconsciously utter the words of the Decalogue, and irresistibly convinced, he exclaims, "The Lord He is the God; the Lord He is the God!"* ה׳ הוא האלהים ה׳ הוא האלהים :

* 1 Kings xviii. 39.

But other words reach my ear. They are not the words of past ages, they do not come from Sinai. They come from a distant country, from a city which has existed twenty-five centuries, and which has seen, more than any other spot in the world, the constant alternation of prosperity and misery, of greatness and humiliation. They are words addressed unto Israel by mighty and numerous priests, in order that we may bid farewell to our ancient religion and become the followers of a different creed, the believers in an opposite doctrine.* The announcement is so strange, the intelligence is so unexpected, that we may really apply to ourselves Habakkuk's words, which have just been read, שמעתי ותרגז בטני לקול צללו שפתי : "When I heard, my belly trembled, my lips quivered at the voice."§ Yes, our astonishment is great. Yet no indignation is mixed with it. That a man possessed of comfort and ease, with the treasure of a large fortune may offer his help to a man surrounded with the horrors of poverty, is natural and generous; but it becomes ridiculous if the offer is made unto him who is possessed of unlimited wealth. Pity may equally be felt for a man whose health is shattered, whose death is unmistakably approaching. But that commiseration becomes absurd if it be shown to him who is still endowed with all the strength of manhood, and in whom nothing foretells the decrease of physical power. Now, is Israel really so unfortunate a nation as to need the compassion of his neighbours?

---

* In April, 1870, 506 bishops petitioned the Œcumenical Council sitting at Rome, and of which they were members, "to address a paternal invitation to the *unfortunate* nation of Israel, in order that they, fatigued with a long and vain expectation, may recognise Jesus as the Messiah promised unto Abraham and announced by Moses."

§ Habakkuk iii. 16.

THE ANSWER OF ISRAEL.

Is his religion so inefficient, so fallacious, that he can feel it necessary to abandon it? Has his creed, his system of dogmas, or his moral legislation, any vulnerable side which may make it desirable for him to follow a new path?

No questions could be better adapted than these to the religious solemnity which we are now celebrating. No subject could be more appropriate than this to the commemoration of Revelation. All over the surface of the earth Israel is this day assembled in his houses of prayer, in order to assert the greatness, the stability of his religion, and yet we are asked to forsake it! Oh, what sacrifice could we offer up unto the Lord on this sacred day, which could be more agreeable unto Him, than to answer our officious advisers, to expound that Law with which He has proved His love unto us, and to assert our fidelity to its precepts, our firmness in its belief, whatever may be done to estrange and detach us from it? Our profession of faith on this occasion will be the renewal of Israel's allegiance unto the Lord; it will constitute that obedience, which, according to Samuel, is better than sacrifice, and that hearkening which is preferable to the fat of rams *
הנה שמע מזבח טוב להקשיב מחלב אילים :

I.

How can the greatness of a religion be proved? Are we to seek it in the number of its followers, or in the power of the countries which it influences, in its long existence, or in the martyrdom suffered in its behalf by generous men? There are religions which possess these

* 1 Samuel xv. 22.

four characteristics and which yet are manifestly weakened by organic defects, that is, by erroneous doctrines, so that their power and secular life are but the result of hazard. This is a rule, the truth of which could be proved by more than one striking instance. But can it be applied to Judaism, to the dogmas which form its immovable basis? Is its astonishing vitality to be attributed to mere chance, or to the undeniable truth of its teachings? Their simple enunciation will be the most eloquent answer.

The dogmas of Judaism are these: the existence of God; His unity; His incorporeity; His eternity; Revelation; the divinity and immutability of the Law; Providence; the mercy and justice of God; the free will of man; the regeneration of the human family; the immortality of the Soul. The nobility, the divinity of these principles is proved from the age in which they were proclaimed, as well as from their intrinsic value. Who does not know the condition of the world at the time of revelation? Athens, Rome and many of the greatest cities now considered to belong to the remotest antiquity had not yet been founded. In Assyria the immoral and monstrous laws of Semiramis were still in vigor. Babylon was splendid, yet barbarous. In Egypt an ephemeral civilization imperfectly concealed the degraded state of society. Men recognized the existence of divine beings; but what beings! Idols which represented physical strength and sensuality. Idols, infinite in number, subject to the meanest among human passions, and represented in their turn under hideous forms, polluted every day with the blood of human sacrifices. That was darkness in all its horrible aspect. But light suddenly appeared in the shape of wise and humane laws, of principles answering the claims alike of the heart and the mind, satisfying the aspiration of the human soul towards spiritual life and ideal purity. And could the mind of a man have imagined such perfect dogmas, at a time when human reason was still in its infancy?

There is a God, said Judaism. There is the necessary Being who possesses existence in its reality and fulness. He is sufficient to Himself, and all creatures are in need of His assistance. He lives by His own power, keeps all creatures alive, and gives them their food in due season* : ואתה נותן להם את אכלם בעתו That God is one, absolutely one, one so as to exclude not only the monstrous Polytheism of idolatry, but also the mystical plurality which, strange to say, is considered by millions of human beings as the symbol of unity. That God is incorporeal, and would never assume any material form, because He cannot be subjected to the accidents of material beings. "To whom then," said the Prophet, "will ye liken God? or what likeness will ye compare unto Him?"§ ואל מי תדמיון אל ומה דמות תערכו לו "Remember," said Moses unto the Hebrews, "remember that on the day that the Lord spoke unto you, ye saw the similitude of no figure"|| : כי לא ראיתם כל תמונה That God is eternal, and according to His own words, He is the first, and also is the last : אני ראשון אף אני אחרון ¶ He had no beginning and will have no end. The Creator of everything, He is above space, above time, which He regulates for the limited existence of His creatures. That God we must adore, and no one but Him, for He is the One God. We must not worship any of the forces of nature, for they are His tools and have no power.

* Psalm cxlv. 15.   § Isaiah xl. 18. || Deut. iv 15.
¶ Isaiah xlviii. 12.

Unto Him we must raise our heart and address our prayer, for if as severe as a judge, He is as loving as a father. "He is nigh to all those that call upon Him." * ״קרוב ה׳ לכל קראיו״ "Whosoever shall call on the name of the Lord shall be delivered" § ״כל אשר יקרא בשם ה׳ ימלט״: Therefore no mediator is necessary. "A man," say our sages, "has a noble protector. When in distress, he addresses himself to his patron's agent in order that he may intercede on his behalf. Then he may or may not be admitted into the great man's presence. But with the Lord it is not so. If a man is unhappy, he must not pray either to Michael or to Gabriel. He must turn unto the Lord and he will be relieved" ‖ ״אם באת על אדם צרה לא יצווח לא למיכאל ולא לגבריאל אלא לי יצווח ואני עונה לו מיד״: No one can be a mediator between us and God; not even the prophets, not even the martyrs; for their virtues cannot make atonement for our sins. We must pray unto the Lord and obtain His mercy by virtuous deeds. That God is merciful. He saw the insufficiency of man's intellect to secure happiness; therefore He revealed Himself unto those who by the purity of their heart and the elevation of their mind had deserved to be the teachers of mankind. First among them was Moses who remained virtuous amidst the corruption, and monotheistic amidst the idolatry, of Egypt, and who, though endowed with the highest prophetic power, never assumed divine attributes; though the greatest of men, he was worthy to be called the humblest of all. The Law of which Moses was the bearer, was the work of God, and is necessarily perfect. And since what is perfect can need no change, so that Law shall remain unaltered

---

* Psalm cxlv. 18.   § Joel iii. 5.
‖ Talmud Jerusalmi, Berachot, ix.

for ever; it will witness the progressive modification, and even the disappearance of erroneous doctrines, but will not be affected by time. It has been given for all generations to come, it will be unto Israel an everlasting covenant * : לישראל ברית עולם Great is the value of every man before the Lord, for every man has within himself an immortal soul, a true reflection of the divine light. He has the power of calling down upon himself either good or evil, according to the right or wrong direction which he gives to his faculties. He has therefore a free will, without which neither vice nor virtue can exist. But God who cannot be omnipotent if He is not omniscient, knows both the thoughts and the actions of man. He pronounces on them and is infallible in His decisions. "He shall judge the world with righteousness, and the people with His truth" ישפט תבל בצדק ועמים באמונתו § And on such a day as is known unto Him alone, the Lord will raise mankind from its immoral state, destroy vice, war, wickedness, and religious error, restore the ruined nationality of Zion, and after having revived all those who have departed from us, He will bestow upon the regenerated human race endless peace and ineffable delight.

These are the dogmas written in the code of Judaism; these are the Divine rules which ought to constitute the guidance of our existence. They are like the geometrical point which ceases to be a point if anything is added to, or taken from, it. "Thou shalt not add thereto," said Moses, "nor diminish therefrom" ‖ לא תסף עליו ולא תגרע ממנו : Do we not assign unto God all the attributes that belong unto Him? Do we not raise the dignity and importance of human individuality? Do we not

* Psalm cv. 10.   § Psalm xcvi. 13.   ‖ Deut. xiii. 1.

glorify justice? Do we not feel a strong hope for the gradual amelioration and final perfection of mankind? Are not these dogmas all that human reason can believe? Should we add other dogmas to these, or exchange them for better ones? And where are they? We seek, but we cannot find. We examine the creeds of ancient nations, we investigate modern religions, but although we see in them some excellent principles, yet they contain what betrays a human origin, "the work of man's hand" : מעשה ידי אדם * We therefore repudiate the dualism of the ancient Persians, which divided the universe into two opposite kingdoms, that of Good, and that of Evil. We repudiate the fatalism of the Mahomedans, which makes man the slave of a blind destiny and deprives him of all liberty. We repudiate the doctrine of the unity of God when that unity is not absolute and perfect. We repudiate the dogma which teaches that man is born in a state of sin; for we cannot believe that the immortal spirit created by God, is already corrupt in the moment of its creation. That principle is contrary to the Law which declares the innocence of man, and says unto him: "Sin lies at the door. Unto thee shall be his desire, and thou shalt rule over him" § לפתח חטאת רבץ ואליך תשוקתו ואתה תמשל בו : We repudiate the idea that the Lord has come to alter the Law which He Himself had proclaimed and declared eternal. We repudiate the belief that the Lord has sent to earth the Messiah, the Redeemer of mankind, when we see the human race still the prey of struggles and sorrows, of error and iniquity. We repudiate anything that is opposed to the Mosaic code. Israel's dogmas are then sufficient unto him. He is not unhappy, he is not

* Psalm cxv. 4. § Genesis iv. 7.

subjected to misery by following the Law of his forefathers. On the contrary, we are proud of that Law. We are happy by that religion, which is for us a title of glory and wisdom in the eyes of all nations* כי היא חכמתכם ובינתכם לעיני העמים: We are not willing to "forsake the fountain of living waters, to hew *us* out cisterns, broken cisterns that can hold no water" §
לחצב להם בארות בארות נשברים אשר לא יכילו המים:

II.

It is thus proved that the dogmas of our religion are in no way inferior to those of any other creed, for they are complete in whatever aspect they may be studied. Perhaps it is in the other cardinal division of our Law, in the moral section, that some deficiency may be found, or a gap discovered. And is it true ? Are the morals of Judaism to be proclaimed inferior to the morals of any other faith ?

There is in the heart of man something innate which prompts him to act kindly and mercifully, and to avoid that which might result in the suffering of others. It is a blessed spring with which God has endowed the moral mechanism of men of all races, and all ages. It is therefore not surprising to find in the writings of Pagan philosophers such noble and beautiful sentences on kindness and generosity as would honour any legislation. But these excellent lessons are like a small oasis, which is lost in the midst of a vast desert; so the good that they might have done was stifled under a burden of immoral laws, cruel ceremonies, or corrupting customs. The founder of a more modern creed may have placed before his followers moral precepts of a

* Deut. iv. 6.   § Jeremiah ii. 13.

very elevating description. But did he assert anything new, anything that had not been taught among the nations from which he sprang? No, for his noblest sentences have a parallel either in the Bible or the Talmud. Has Christianity, which we are invited to adopt, proclaimed one single moral principle which had not repeatedly been preached by Moses, the prophets, or the first sages of Tradition? No, it has not. There are however, two doctrines which it may claim as its own, and for the authorship of which we shall never feel eager. The first is that signified by the words *compelle intrare* (proselytism by violence) which may be held as the real source of intolerance, fanaticism and all the horrors that they created. The second is the eternity of punishment, which we consider to be thoroughly opposed to the will of the Lord, the Father of mercy.

No one can dispute to Judaism the honor of having first announced that men are all the children of the same father, and of having proclaimed universal brotherhood. Judaism is a law of love which by the precepts of justice, prevents men from hating each other, and by the precepts of charity, induces them to contribute to their mutual welfare. The laws given to Israel immediately after revelation, regarded justice and benevolence. Those that concerned the Lord's Tabernacle and sacrifices came only in the rear, thus unmistakably declaring the superiority of virtue over ceremonial acts. It is in this manner that Judaism had spiritualised morality long before Christianity had arisen to boast of having first given the noblest ethics to the world. "Moses," say our sages,* "proclaimed 613 precepts, and David

* Talmud, Macot, 24.

reduced them to eleven: that is, to practise honesty, to act with justice, to tell the truth in our heart, never to calumniate, never to hurt our fellow-creatures, never to humiliate our neighbours, never to lay usury upon any one, never to receive bribery in order to condemn an innocent man, to be modest, to honour the pious, to be unselfish. Isaiah reduced them to six: to walk in the path of virtue, to speak honestly, to reject illicit profit, to refuse the present of corruption, not to listen to sanguinary words, not to look at evil things. Micah reduced them to three: to do justice, to love benevolence, to walk humbly before the Lord. Isaiah again reduced them to two: to observe justice, and to act with judgment. Habakkuk came and reduced them to one: בא חבקוק והעמידן אל אחת שנאמר צדיק באמונתו " Faith יחיה: " Why," asked a sage, " did Moses command us to walk after the Lord? Can we follow a spirit, a devouring flame and fire? Certainly not, but it means that we should imitate the qualities of the Lord, that we should do as He does: clothe the naked, visit the sick, console the afflicted, bury the dead."* " The beginning of the Law is charity, the end of the Law is charity§ : תורה תחילתה גמילות חסדים וסופה גמילות חסדים It is thus that morals were closely bound to religion, so that they are indispensable to each other.

There is no corner in the field of morals that Judaism has not tilled and made fruitful. Just like the rainbow which, while it exhibits to the human eye the seven prismatic colours, contains really sixty-six different but harmonious gradations, so Judaism after having rigorously prescribed justice and hinted that charity is above worship and religious performance, descends to its various

---

* Talmud Sotah, 14. § Ibidem.

parts, to its minutest details, to its most delicate gradations. Well acquainted with human nature, it takes the utmost care to make a great distinction between alms-giving and charity, which are so often mistaken for each other, a mistake which leads the wealthy to believe that they have complied with the claims of charity when they have distributed abundant alms. "Charity," says Tradition, "is superior to alms in three things: first, the latter is practised only by means of property; the former by all that man possesses, property, body and soul: second, the latter is practised only in behalf of the poor, the former in behalf of the poor and the rich, whose tears charity can wipe, and whose sorrows it can soothe: third, the latter is practised in behalf of the living, and the former in behalf of the living and the dead" צדקה לחיים גמילות חסדים בין לחיים בין למתים: * We have no temple, no altar, we can no longer show repentance by sacrifices. But there is something that can be equivalent for all these,—Charity. All social and individual duties are strongly recommended by Judaism, whether they refer to benevolent hospitality, to respect for our parents, to strict probity or to obedience to constituted authority. At the head of our duties towards ourselves are placed modesty, reserve, chastity, purity of habits and thoughts. "The idea of vice is considered as worse than vice itself." הרהורי עבירה קשין מעבירה: § Guided by the loftiest principles of tolerance, Judaism teaches that *the followers of other creeds may enjoy eternal felicity, provided they live a righteous life.* "*Charity can atone for all their errors*" הצדקה מכפרת על הגויים: ||

And the world can see the wholesome effect of these

---

* Talmud Succah, 49.   § Talmud Jebamot, 29.
‖ Talmud B. Batra, 10.

sublime lessons. To them we owe our astonishing preservation as a nation, and the vitality with which we are still endowed. To their vivifying power we owe that great aptitude for civilization and progress which surprises the most enlightened philosophers. To their moralizing influence we are indebted for the virtues which adorn every Jewish family: union, harmony, sobriety, purity and sanctity. How many are the Jewish women whose names have been dragged into the mire before the judges, and before the unforgiving tribunal of public opinion? They are good wives, good mothers, and know how to respect themselves. Our moral laws are their safeguard. How many are the Jews who have attempted to take the life of their neighbours? When has a Jewish hand wrought such tragic deeds as frequently disgrace modern society? How often has a Jewish name been registered in the records of justice with a note of undying infamy? Our moral laws have always been our guardian angel.

And yet we are solicited to forsake that religion which has done so much for us. We are asked to give up that decoration of nobility, that we may share the distinctions of the multitudes of the earth. But who entreats us to do so? Those who, as can be easily proved, have taken from our immortal documents all the good doctrines which their religion contains. Are then the rules of the world inverted? Is it no longer the mother who offers her breast for the nourishment of her child, but is it the child who pretends to feed the still young and vigorous mother? No, let us answer, we cannot abandon our religion. And may the wind which, by its undulations, brings to our ears the most distant sounds, carry this answer to the Œcumenical Council in Rome, as well as to would-be conversionists throughout the world. Misery and discouragement are only for those who live in doubt concerning the noble truths of religion. Israel is neither miserable, nor unfortunate, because in his sacred code he finds the best guarantees for his mission and for the future destiny of his soul. We cannot give up our faith for, in accordance with King Solomon, "it is an ornament of grace unto our head, and chains about our neck. It is health to our navel and marrow to our bones. It is a tree of life to them that lay hold upon it, and happy is every one that retains it" * עץ חיים היא למחזיקים בה ותמכיה מאשר: We cannot abandon our religion because we find in it freedom of thought, freedom of inquiry, freedom of conscience, that moral liberty which, allied to reason, constitutes the immense superiority of man over the animals, of civilized and well-governed nations over the unhappy populations who labour under the intolerable yoke of tyranny, of civil and religious oppression. We cannot forsake our religion, because Moses said: "This commandment, which I command thee this day, it is not hidden from thee, neither is it far off: it is not in heaven, that thou shouldest say, Who shall go up for us to heaven, and bring it unto us, that we may hear it and do it? Neither is it beyond the sea, that thou shouldest say, Who shall go over the sea for us, and bring it unto us, that we may hear it and do it? But the word is very nigh unto thee, in thy mouth and in thy heart, that thou mayest do it" § כי קרוב אליך הדבר מאד בפיך ובלבבך לעשתו:

* Prov. iii. 18.   § Deut. xxx. 11, 12, 13, 14.

THE ANSWER OF ISRAEL.

Prayer.

Almighty God, who by Thy infinite wisdom didst raise our forefathers to the noble height of revelation, and who, by Thy unbounded mercy, didst receive with favour their unanimous promise of obedience ושמענו ועשינו "We will hear it, we will do it,"* accept with the same graciousness the solemn acknowledgment of devotion to Judaism which, on this anniversary of the proclamation of the Decalogue, we make before Thee with enthusiasm and conviction. For Thou who canst read in our heart, seest that all the solicitations of our neighbours, all their repeated attempts to allure us away from Thy Law, only increase our attachment to, our love and zeal for, that religion, which we hold as the best teacher of men, the safest rule for society, the richest source of peace, joy and salvation. We forgive the exertions of their misunderstood piety, as we have long forgiven all the harm which they did to us, all the cruel persecutions, banishment, plunder and torture, with which for many centuries they embittered the existence of our unfortunate ancestors, under the cover of false accusations and abominable calumnies. But we hope that at last the truth will be known, that the religion which is free from erroneous doctrines, will shine in the midst of all other creeds, as the sun shines triumphantly among the planets. We earnestly pray unto Thee that Thou mayest shorten the day of darkness and gloom, the day of indecision and doubt concerning heaven and earth, material and spiritual life, the fall of man by sin and his redemp-

* Deut. v. 27.

tion by means of an inspired deliverer. We devoutly entreat Thee, O Lord, to hasten the approach of that evening which, according to the prophet, will be marked by a fresh dawn : " At evening time it shall be light " * והיה לעת ערב יהיה אור: Yes, light that will not fade, that will shine and glitter without dazzling; that will warm the heart, delight the soul of all men ; for it will announce the union of all human creatures under one flag, the fusion of all creeds in one religion, the submission of all the states of the earth to one king, God. " And the Lord shall be king over all the earth : in that day shall there be one Lord, and His name one " § והיה ה׳ למלך על כל הארץ ביום ההוא יהיה ה׳ אחד ושמו אחד:

AMEN.

---

* Zechariah xiv. 7. § Ib. 9.

JACOB'S DEATH.

ויקרא יעקב אל בניו ויאמר האספו ואגידה לכם את אשר יקר
אתכם באחרית הימים :

"And Jacob called unto his sons and said: Gather yourselves together that I may tell you that which shall befall you in the last days." GENESIS xlix. 1.

בשעה שהצדיקים נפטרים מן העולם אינן מצוין לבניהם לא ע״י ממון
ולא על ידי נכסים אלא בשביל יראתו של הק״בה :

"When the righteous die, their last recommendations to their children do not refer to wealth or material inheritance, but only to moral ideas, to the fear of God." AGADAT BERESHIT.

MY BRETHREN,—A touching spectacle appears before our eyes. A man is on his death bed, and his offspring, his numerous sons surround him in silence. The old man looks venerable; more than that, he seems inspired. The white flowing beard falls on his breast, and on his face we can read the age of 147 years, a great and wonderful age. His sons, twelve powerful stalwart men, look at him with respect, almost with fear, and are silent, ready to listen to those words which they know will be the last. And ye, men, who are so irresistibly fond of moving, exciting spectacles, who run in such large crowds to witness the coronation of a sovereign or the execution of a culprit, to look at the appalling flames of a destructive fire, or the rich retinue of a royal wedding, come, come, I convene you to this scene, the scene of death; come, here you will be moved, here you will have something to learn; in fact, as the prophet says,* " It is better to go to the house of mourning than to go to the house of feasting, for that is the end of all men, and the living will lay it to his heart."

Old men generally shudder at the idea of death; in their last illness they are visited with terrors of all kinds, with an inexpressible fear, especially when their conscience is not reproachless. All that they had valued so highly during their lifetime now appears contemptible and useless. Truly, as one of the greatest doctors of the Mishna said, " Every man has three friends while he lives: his children and his relations, his property, and his good actions; when death approaches, he addresses himself to each of them for help and rescue. " Will you let me depart so miserably," he says to his children, " will you not save your father from the grave?" " We cannot," they answer, " knowest thou not that no man has power in the day of death?" * ואין שלטון ביום המות " And wilt thou not, O wealth, for which I have laboured and striven so hard, wilt thou not assist me in this supreme moment?" " No, I cannot, for riches profit not in the day of wrath "§ : לא יועיל הון ביום עברה " And will ye, good actions that I have achieved, do nothing for me?" " Fear not," they alone answer, " fear not, for we will precede thee before the throne of the Almighty." ||

On the face of that old man, of Jacob, when he is about to bid farewell to what is dearest unto him, to the earth, I see nothing of the sort; I see, on the contrary, something bright on his brow, something that is the mark of his inward thoughts, faith and hope in the

* Eccles. vii. 2.　　　　§ Prov. xi. 4.
 || Pirke R. Eliezer, chap. xxxiv.

future. The future! If there is an idea that can powerfully strike our heart it is that of the future; it is for the future that we labour, think and hope, it is the mover of our actions, it is the aim of all our exertions. We begin in our childhood to labour under the influence of that idea, and we obey its rule when we are men; it is like a distant and brilliant horizon; we advance towards it as if to seize it, but it recedes and escapes our reach: it thus remains the constant object of our efforts, both when we strive for the satisfaction of our immediate wants, and when we meditate on that which will constitute the monument of our glory. But this thought appears greater and greater when our life is on the decline, when the future that stands before us is no longer a limited earthly existence, but an everlasting life, immortality. To that point, and not to worldly possessions, did the old man turn his mind, and his movements were in that moment so solemn, his face was so majestic, that he looked more like an august prince, surrounded by his lords, than like a father about to take leave of his children and of the earth. Like Jacob were all the patriarchs and pious men in Israel. When, before the separation of their soul from their body, they bestowed upon their children their last blessing, and bequeathed to them the inheritance of revelation, they all uttered the word of a consoling future, repeating with Jeremiah; "And there is hope in thine end, saith the Lord" * : ויש תקוה לאחריתך נאם ה׳ Jacob showed in his last utterances, that the thought of the future was predominant in his mind, but he showed also that his faith and his hope in the future were firm, unshaken; and he tried to inspire with the same noble

* Jeremiah xxxi. 17.

principles, not only his sons but his sons' sons, and the numerous posterity that was to descend from them, and inherit the mission of communicating those principles to mankind. When the patriarch, feeling his end approach, began by blessing his dear Joseph's children, he said, "The angel which redeemed me from all evil bless the lads" * המלאך הגואל אותי מכל רע יברך את הנערים: But what can this mean? We find angels repeatedly mentioned in connection with Jacob's eventful life; the vision of angels ascending and descending on the gigantic ladder graced the first night of his journey towards Mesopotamia. Again, the angels of God met him on his return to his native land; an angel wrestled with him during the darkness of the night, but his object was to prostrate him. No angel therefore, can be said to have redeemed him from all evil. Yet it is true; something like an angel was a constant shield to Jacob; something like an angel was with him from his childhood and assisted him in the hardest trials, as it was with all the great men of our nation, as well as with every pious man upon the earth. By that angel, he meant the strong faith which always had followed him, which had never abandoned him, not even in his saddest vicissitudes, that strong faith which had supported him in all circumstances and all struggles, in the joys and in the sorrows of his long career. Four times he had been in the greatest danger; in danger of losing his life when Esau, embittered by the consequence of his own imprudence, wished to see his father die, that he might be able to take his revenge; in danger of being deprived of his property and of the beings dearest to his heart, when the ungrateful and envious Laban, after having deceived him *ten times*, pursued him with even

* Genesis xlviii. 16.

JACOB'S DEATH.

more hostile intentions; again, in a terrible danger when the mysterious being came suddenly to struggle with him as he was crossing the stream Jabok; and in equal peril again, when Esau, who could be calmed only by costly presents, appeared before him in a threatening attitude and followed by four hundred armed men. By inspiration he saw that his descendants would also be subjected four times to horrible sufferings, and be in danger of utter destruction; he saw them enslaved and treated as brutes in Egypt during two centuries; he saw them conquered, decimated and led to bitter exile by the wild ruler of Babylon; he saw them tortured by the cruel Antiochus, who was perhaps the first to show to the world of what ferocity religious fanaticism is capable; he saw them the victims of the Roman sword, of the Roman flames. But he saw at the same time that the powerful angel that had redeemed him would redeem them; that the faith which had supported him would support them; a faith that nothing could break or shake. A consoling angel would lessen all the misfortunes that Israel was to endure for many, many a century. That angel could be nothing but faith, love of God, faithfulness to the religion of their fathers, to the law given to Israel as a sacred deposit never to be surrendered. Therefore keeping his eyes fixed on the distant future, Jacob said to his sons: "Fear not; the torments which the nation will have to undergo shall be long but not eternal, they shall at last pass away; ye shall not always be the timid lamb, ye shall in due time be the lion's whelp that comes up from his prey."* גור אריה יהודה מטרף בני עלית "Ye must bear patiently the time of misery, ye must obey for a

---
* Genesis xlix. 9.

season the other nations, but the sceptre shall at last belong to Judah, when *Shiloh* shall come; Shiloh, that is he to whom shall belong the kingdom, to whom the nations shall bring the tribute of devotion "* לא יסור שבט מיהודה ומחוקק מבין רגליו עד כי יבא שילה ולו יקהת עמים: But night will come before day and, alas! the persecutions will unfortunately be cruel, the innocent will not be spared, and the earth will be watered with their blood and with their tears. "The archers will sorely grieve him, and shoot at him, and torment him. But his bow shall abide in a strong impregnable rock, and the time of rescue shall come" § וימררוהו ורבו וישטמוהו בעלי חצים: ותשב באיתן קשתו וכול׳

This faith of which Abraham was the first example when he believed in God, as it is written in Genesis: "And he believed in God, and He counted it to him for righteousness,"|| והאמן בה׳ ויחשבה לו צדקה, this faith, which Jacob again so strongly asserted, was a seed the grains of which were not scattered about and destroyed by the wind; it was deeply rooted in the noble soil of the Jewish heart and constantly bore rich fruit; it gave Judaism the power of crossing a stormy sea without great loss, of passing almost unhurt through times of relentless agitation that cost the life of more than one great empire; it gave to our religious doctrines a strength which could not be broken, either by all the united efforts of our enemies or by the implacable hatred of the Inquisition, or by an adversary not less dangerous, if meeker in appearance, I mean a deleterious

---

* Gen. xlix. 10. Our sages have explained the Hebrew word שילה, *Shilo*, as שי לו, *shy lo, a tribute unto him* who is the Messiah, and whom the nations shall obey.

§ Gen. xlix. 24. || Gen. xv. 6.

philosophy of doubt and scepticism. After so many victories over persons and things, victories which may be considered really wonderful when it is remembered that we have always preserved a passive attitude, if we still doubt the imperishable vitality of our religion and our race, if we still doubt their final triumph; if we have no faith in our destiny, it is because our heart is dry, because our heart is incapable of noble feelings, because a thick cover of materialism envelops us on all sides, and reduces us, as it were, to the condition of the brutes that care for nothing but their daily food. That cannot be said of the Jew. Faith is for him the fire that shall ever be burning upon the altar of his heart; it shall never be quenched. Faith is, according to our sages, the best course that a man can choose. "Which is the right way that a man should prefer? It is faith; steady and unconquerable faith"* איזה דרך ישרה יחזיק באמונה: And this sentence acquires a double value when pronounced by those great champions, the warriors of the spirit, who proved by facts which admiring history has rendered immortal—that faith has the power of saving individuals from despair and nations from destruction. Jacob had faith in the future of the Jewish nation, then still in its cradle; but he had faith in his own future, in the future of his sons, because the belief in the immortality of the soul was deeply rooted in the heart of the founders of our race. He foretold in glowing terms, the military achievements of the serpent-like, shrewd, and courageous Dan; but before speaking of the warlike Gad, that is, while hinting at the political struggles to which Israel would be exposed, he exclaimed: "But it is in Thy salvation, O Lord, that I

* Talmud Tamid, 28.

trust"* : לישועתך קויתי ה׳ Why did he utter this exclamation at that last moment? What danger was then threatening him? Enemies? Poverty? Illness? Why then did those few words of stirring prayer interrupt his blessings? Could he have referred to an earthly rescue, since he knew that he was to live only a few minutes longer, and Death stood already before him? The very thought of the struggles which Dan and all his sons were to encounter, of the ceaseless griefs which torment mankind, of the iron circle which encompasses the life of the children of Adam, reminded him of that existence of the spirit in which salvation is ineffable and eternal, and caused him to long more and more ardently for the land of immortal life, the land which David meant when he said: "I will walk before the Lord in the land of the living"§ : אתהלך לפני ה׳ בארצות החיים After his prophetic blessing was over, Jacob said, "I am to be gathered unto my people; bury me with my fathers, in the cave of Machpelah"‖ אני נאסף אל עמי קברו אותי אל אבותי אל המערה וכו׳: Can there be any connection between these two expressions—to be gathered unto his people, and to be buried with his fathers? Are they dependent upon one another, or are they equivalent? No, they are not, for Abraham was, in accordance with the promise of the Lord, gathered unto his people, and yet his tomb was far away from that of his father or his ancestors. To be gathered unto his people means, according to the Jewish doctrines, to ascend to the region of immortality; it means to return to our ancestors—to our father, mother, wife, husband, children, brothers—to all those to whom the link of love had bound us upon the earth; it means to return to the country wherefrom we

* Genesis xlix. 18.   § Psalm cxvi. 9.   ‖ Genesis xlix. 29.

were sent in the moment of our birth : it means not to die, but to live.

The Bible never makes use of that expression "and he was gathered unto his people" ויאסף אל עמיו when the wicked die; he died, says the Bible in that case; and it seems that with death everything is over for the impious. How can the wicked hope for such sweet consolations as the future life reserves for the righteous? When the soul is separated from her garment of clay, however painful the separation may be, it soars towards the place of its aspirations, towards Him that is the God of all spirits, towards the region where it shall live an endless life, free from the control of what is material and perishable. It is impossible to be present at the death of a virtuous man, and not to think of immortality; it is impossible to see the close of the life of the pious father of a family, when he stretches his trembling hand over the head of his weeping children, when he utters almost inspired words of advice and benediction, and not believe in the doctrine of a future existence. Should that man who has lived a praiseworthy life, who has achieved so much in behalf of his fellow-creatures, who has ever been animated by a powerful, benevolent and really divine spirit, vanish in a few moments, like a spiral column of smoke, like a cloud dissipated by the wind, like a small flame extinguished by a passing breath? No, it is impossible. His death is not destruction, but the beginning of another existence. This is what we think in keeping the eyes of our imagination fixed on the scene of Jacob's death; and in spite of our tendency towards incredulity, we are obliged, fully convinced, to bow to the doctrine of immortality; we feel some internal power that forces us to proclaim it loudly and strenuously in spite of the specious arguments raised against it, in spite of the triumphant declaration of its opponents that no distinct mention of it is to be found in the Law. In a former sermon, I have dealt, I trust victoriously, with this argument. Now I only ask one question. What but this belief could have given the Jews that wonderful strength by which they successfully resisted all attacks? The hard exile of Babylon regenerated the heart of the Jews. From that moment, they felt themselves capable of dying for their God and their faith, for those sublime principles which, till then, had been weakened by idolatry. Then they learnt how to endure tortures, how to be martyrs. That idea of immortality inspired the nation with heroic courage; they fought desperately with the Syrian kings, and when vanquished, they scorned the tyrant that slew their wives and children, but they remained firm in their belief. They opposed to Vespasian, Titus, and Hadrian such heroism as no other nation had before displayed, and when they saw their city and Temple burnt and destroyed, when they were thrown, an easy prey, to the beasts of the circus, they repeated the *Shemang*, and died faithful to their religion; they felt certain that the glory of immortality and everlasting beatitude would be their reward; that infinite joy would compensate them for their short, though cruel, miseries. The life of a Jew was then an uninterrupted series of sufferings and hard battles, as well as an existence of exclusion and contempt. But he willingly renounced the good of this life for that of the future world. When David, the sweet singer of the religion of the heart, said: " Thou wilt show me the path of life; in Thy presence is fulness of joy, at Thy right hand there are pleasures for evermore " * תודיעני ארח חיים

* Psalm xvi. 2.

שבע שמחות את פניך נעימות מימינך נצח: could he refer to the path of earthly life? Could he refer to those joys which pass away as soon as they come, to those pleasures which are even followed by regret? Could he apply the word "evermore" to that which, to show how transitory it is, could be compared to nothing better than a flower which one day glows in beauty, and the next lies faded and lifeless upon the ground? David, then, did more than hint at, he proclaimed that the immortality of the soul was essentially the belief of the Hebrews. Oh, those who have read this morning's lesson of the Law with due attention, and have not merely gone through an impatiently accepted duty, must have felt their heart moved and their mind agitated by serious thoughts. Their imagination must have anticipated the day when they too will be called upon to restore their body to the dust, and the spirit to heaven. "Oh, may we die," they must have said, remembering Jacob, "may we die the death of the righteous, may our end be like his"* תמות נפשי מות ישרים ותהי אחריתי כמוהו: But shall we die with the same serenity, without sufferings, with the same fearlessness, with the same faith, with the same certainty about a forthcoming spiritual reward? Shall we see our children, grown up and prosperous, surround our death-bed in an attitude of veneration? Shall we be able to foretell to them, as Jacob did to his children, happiness and glory? And can the reply be doubtful? Oh, my brethren, your own conscience will answer you; it will tell you that this will depend upon yourselves alone. This life, as Jacob himself defined it when speaking to Pharaoh, is nothing but a short stay on our long journey, so to speak, from

* Numbers xxiii. 10.

the world of spirits to the world of spirits again. But even this short station has a programme: a long succession of struggles, anxieties, temptations to be gone through, and we must carry it out, on the one hand performing its conditions, on the other, always keeping our eyes fixed on the moment when our sojourn on the earth will be over. In a word, we shall have well employed the time of our abiding, if we occupy it in preparing ourselves for the moment of our departure, in accordance with the great sentence of our sages*
מה יעבר איניש ויחיה ימית עצמו וימות יחיה עצמו: "What should a man do in order to live? He should cause himself to die. What should he do in order to die? He should cause himself to live." It would be impossible to express in a more concise and powerful manner the whole programme of life. The man who aspires to an existence really pure, calm and happy, a reflection of the everlasting happiness of the future one, should be "dead," that is, invulnerable to the attacks of the passions and the depraved inclinations that constantly urge him to what is reprehensible, unlawful and fatal. He should be "dead," that is, absolutely deaf to the sweet and enchanting voice of seduction, which lulls the weak-minded creatures who lend their ear to its first melodious notes to the sleep of vice and corruption. On the other hand, he who wishes to "die" the death of the righteous, the death which is the painless transition to the spiritual land of beatitude, he should "live." He should accomplish with unremitting activity, the three-fold life of duty towards the Creator, towards our neighbour and towards ourselves; he should be a useful and productive agent of society by the noble exercise of

* Talmud Tamid, 32.

the precious qualities which are the best gift of Providence to man; he should raise himself to the sublime heights of virtue by humility in the day of joy, by courage in the day of grief, by bending the heart to the law of what is beautiful, good and true. In conclusion, if your earthly existence is from beginning to end a chain of good actions and well-performed duties, if we enjoy its transitory pleasures with moderation, always remembering, in order that we may not love them too much, the day when we shall abandon them; if our heart be strengthened by unconquerable faith in Him that disposes of everything, and by a firm hope in the spiritual future; if we work steadily in order to prepare a valuable inheritance for our offspring, not only of ease and comfort, but of good counsel and noble example, then our death-bed will not be a mournful scene, not a heart-rending struggle, but a peaceful separation from life and from the beloved beings whom we shall one day see again. "Then," as Isaiah said,* "and thy righteousness shall go before thee: the glory of the Lord shall be thy reward" והלך לפניך צדקך כבוד ה׳ יאספך:

PRAYER.

Almighty God! Nothing is so appalling as the aspect of death, nothing so painful as the sight of the dissolution and decomposition of man. The idea that this corporeal frame in which I prided myself will become cold, and stiff, and still; the thought that this countenance, the beauty of which flattered my vanity, will become lifeless, ash-coloured, and distorted, forces me

* lviii. 8.

to shudder in spite of courage and energy. Horror overpowers all my being, and the instant of death appears unto me irresistibly terrifying. Yet, by reflecting on the last moments of Jacob, I see that there is a death which is not so frightful; that the separation between soul and body can happen without terror, overcoming pain and cruel agony, and that is the death of the righteous. O Lord! oh, let my mortal career and the mortal career of my brethren end as that of the Patriarch; let my death be like his, a peaceful extinction of life, without struggle and without torture. Let my mind face with calmness and serenity the unknown existence of spirits. Let me be, when on my deathbed, not only free from regret and remorse, but comforted by the recollection of a spotless life, of a life nobly and usefully spent. Let my mind, in that moment of a departure that has no return, be filled with holy thoughts, with the sweet hope that I shall soon begin a life of uninterrupted happiness. In Thee alone, O Lord, I place my trust and expectations. I may say of Thee, with Job: הן יקטלני לו איחל: "Though He slay me, yet will I trust in Him; but I will maintain my own ways before Him."* For this is the belief which I devoutly express every morning when I open my eyes to the light.§ "O Lord, the soul that resides in me is nothing earthly, or corruptible, but a pure flame, a heavenly essence, which Thou hast breathed into me. It is not an increated spirit, nor an emanation of Thine. It is a work of Thine omnipotence. Thou hast created it, Thou hast formed it, Thou keepest it within my body. When the time comes, Thou wilt take it away from me, but not for ever, and in a distant future Thou wilt restore it unto me. All the time that

* Job xiii. 15.   § Morning prayers.

JACOB'S DEATH.

this divine breath shall animate my frame of dust, I will praise Thee; O Lord, my God, and the God of my fathers, I will acknowledge Thee as the Ruler of Creation, the Master of all souls, the King of all creatures. Blessed be Thou, O Lord, who wilt restore the soul unto the dead bodies."

כל זמן שהנשמה בקרבי מודה אני לפניך ה׳ אלהי ואלהי אבותי שאתה הוא רבון כל המעשים אדון כל הנשמות מושל בכל הבריות ברוך אתה ה׳ המחזיר נשמות לפגרים מתים:

AMEN.

THE WAR.

הבה לנו עזרת מצר ושוא תשועת אדם : באלהים נעשה חיל והוא
יבוס צרינו :

"Give us help from trouble, for vain is the help of man. Through God we shall do valiantly; for He it is that shall tread down our enemies."
PSALM cviii. 12, 13.

חרב בא לעולם על ענוי הדין ועל עוות הדין :ועל המורים בתורה
שלא כהלכה :

"War is sent to desolate the earth when iniquity prevails, when justice is not done, when the law is erroneously explained."
TALMUD, ABOT v. 11.

MY DEAR BRETHREN,—Everything decays, passes away, vanishes, and falls to pieces before our eyes; a new world insensibly arises in the place of that which we saw in our childhood : the scene is quite changed, new personages appear on the stage of life; everything departs from us, and plunges into that abyss which is called nothingness; and in the midst of these eternal revolutions, God alone stands for ever and appears majestic in His omnipotence; God alone, while He changes the face of the universe, remains what He was, what He is, and what He will be.

"Athenian sage," said Crœsus to Solon who, while travelling in order to study the laws and customs of foreign nations, had visited the court of Lydia, and to whom the king had shown with a proud complacency the unrivalled splendour of his wealth, "Athenian sage, who can be more fortunate and happy than myself? What can be wanting to my perfect joy? Is not my position, both as a man and as a king, the most enviable upon the earth?" "O Crœsus," answered Solon, simply and tranquilly, "wait, wait until the last day of thy life;" אל תאמן בעצמך עד יום מותך: "Rely not upon thyself till the day of thy death."* Solon's words were prophetic, and Crœsus lost his wealth and his glory, his kingdom and his liberty, and to the mercy of his enemy he was indebted for the preservation of his life.—Nearly at the same time, another king was almost insane through his haughtiness and pride, and thought himself invulnerable, unassailable in his greatness. He was walking on a beautiful terrace at the top of his splendid palace, and looking around him at the city which stood at his feet, "Is not this," he said in his unconquerable vanity, "great Babylon, that I have built for the house of the kingdom, by the might of my power, and for the honour of my majesty?"§ הלא דא היא בבל רבתא די אנא בניתה לבית מלכו בתקף חסני וליקר הדרי But in that moment, a tremendous voice was heard from heaven, saying: "O King Nebuchadnezzar, to thee it is spoken, thy kingdom is departed from thee," ‖ that thou mayest know that the Most High ruleth in the kingdom of men, and gives it to whomsoever He chooses." And the Lord's will was instantly carried out. Nebuchadnezzar lost more than his kingdom: he was deprived of his reason; he fled to the woods; he lived for seven years amidst the brutes, the grass was his food, the open sky his roof.—O kings, O princes, do not

* Talmud Abot, ii. 3. § Daniel iv. 27. ‖ Ib. 28.

rely too much upon your thrones, they are vacillating; seek not security in your stately palaces, their basis is weak and fragile; a certain wind blows, they fall to the ground, they are dust, they are no more, even their traces disappear. The events of ancient times are now repeated. Every day we see monarchs deprived of their thrones: we see them take up the staff of a pilgrim and quit their country, not as kings, but as exiles, as fugitives, seldom accompanied by the pity of their subjects, but often followed by hatred and execration.

Is not the greatness of nations as transitory as that of their monarchs? And are the empires more secure than their rulers? Oh, my brethren, were it so, we should not see so many vicissitudes. Look at that country which a narrow channel divides from us; half a century ago it suffered from great disasters, but it recovered. The country, the towns offered the aspect of prosperity. Its population was increasing, its commerce was flourishing. Oh, it is so pleasing, so refreshing to see the blessed effects of industry and activity! to see the people enjoy the produce of their work and be delighted and happy, "practise the great law of labor, and enjoy its reward.* It is refreshing to see in the towns, all busy in the exercise of their arts and professions; the fathers carefully bring up their children to their hereditary industry, and prepare the future welfare of their family; to see wealth acquired by means of honest transactions. It is consoling to see in the country the wonders that human exertions create, to see the invaluable treasures that the hand of man obliges nature to bring forth out of her bosom: to see the labourer together with his family well rewarded for his hard work,

* Psalm cxxviii. 2.

happily seated, according to the biblical expression, איש תחת גפנו ותחת תאנתו "under his vine or under his fig tree;* to see the joy of the peasant when he reaps his harvest, or when he is gathering in the grapes! That was a happy state of things, but it was not to last.

Suddenly the cursed cry of war is heard, and all that welfare, and all those blessings are gradually blighted. The inhabitants are frightened. All repair with confusion into the fortified towns. The songs of the labourer have ceased, the roads are deserted and silent. No, they are not silent; frightful sounds echo everywhere—in the plains, on the hills, and among the mountains. The sound of drums and of trumpets, of guns and of cannons, the engines of death and destruction. The roads are no longer solitary; masses of men approach, but they are soldiers, animated with fury, ready for a deadly struggle, prepared to kill or to be killed. "The snorting of his horses," says Jeremiah, almost describing modern events, "is heard from Dan; the whole land trembled at the noise of the neighing of his strong ones, for they have come and have devoured the land and all that is in it; the cities, and those that dwell therein" § מדן נשמע נהרת סוסיו מקול מצהלות אביריו רעשה כל הארץ ויבאו ויאכלו ארץ ומלואה תבל ויושבי בה: Terrible battles are fought, whole ranks, whole battalions, whole regiments fall to the ground, and vanish for ever from the stage of life. A thick smoke envelops the scene of disorder and horror, but out of it mingled cries arise: they are the cries of the wounded and of the dying; the touching lament of the fallen that ask for mercy; the brutal voice of the conqueror that answers: "No quarter." They form the chorus of war, which is the

* 1 Kings v. 5. § Jeremiah viii. 16.

curse of mankind. After the ranged battles on the field, there are desperate fights around the fortified towns, and sieges and bombardments, the destruction of the best monuments of art, and the slaughter of peaceful and unarmed citizens, of women and of children, the ruin of whole cities. And can the conqueror derive joy from his victory? Has he not lost the best of his soldiers, the promising youths of the fatherland? Oh, in both countries, among the victors and the vanquished, only mourning and desolation are seen, there is not one family that has not lost one of its dearest members; "there is not a house where there is not one dead" * אין בית אשר אין שם מת: Yes, Jeremiah spoke truly when he said—"A cry of distress is heard upon the hills, lamentations and bitter weeping: there are the mothers who weep for their children, who refuse to be comforted for their children who are no more" § קול ברמה נשמע נהי בכי תמרורים רחל מבכה על בניה מאנה להנחם על בניה כי איננו: Even when successful, war is a fearful calamity. It creates ruin and misery, and leaves behind a track of blood and of tears. It extinguishes the living forces of nations. It destroys all the treasures that peace had carefully and slowly accumulated for their welfare. It destroys the work of many generations. It precipitates a people from the height of power and prosperity to the depths of humiliation, weakness and distress; it wrests from their hand the sceptre of influence which had formerly been their pride.

This description of the evils which now afflict two generous nations is far from exaggerated, and hour after hour the telegraph brings us gloomier and gloomier tidings with heart-rending details. Our first movement

* Exodus xi. 30.   § Jeremiah xxxi. 15.

THE WAR.

is to address ourselves to the Almighty for commiseration; but we immediately after ask ourselves: do we deserve the mercy of the Lord? Is the present state of society so good that its terrible sufferings should surprise us? When we look at war in a religious point of view, the words of complaint about to be uttered die on our lips, for we see that men have given cause for it. What is the opinion of our sages, who had so high a sense of the duties of man? בעון עינוי הדין ועוות הדין וקלקול הדין חרב וביזה רבה ודבר ובצורת בא לעולם ובני אדם אוכלין ואינן שבעין ואוכלין לחמם במשקל: "Through the sin of neglect of justice, of violation of each other's rights, through neglect of religious instruction and misrepresentation of the Law, war, and plunder, and slaughter, and famine come upon the earth; men eat but are not satisfied, their bread is insufficient."*

And does justice prevail among men? Why the numerous array of legions that each state musters, by which the youths, the vigorous part of the nation, are withdrawn from the fields, from useful professions, from the seats of learning, by which heavy sacrifices out of proportion to his power are imposed upon the citizen? Why? It is because there is general mistrust between nation and nation, because each knows that the sacred voice of justice would not be listened to. Great empires will be ready, at the first opportunity, to extend their limits at the expense of a weak neighbour, and small states which know that the fable of the wolf and the lamb may at any moment become at their cost an historical fact, strive to erect a feeble dyke which may stay for a time the fury of the flood. Treaties

* Talmud Shabat, 32.

are signed with solemn promises and oaths, but they have no greater strength than the parchment on which they are drawn. Instead of justice, brutal force prevails.

Nor are the claims of justice better regarded within each state. Wherever despotism rules, everything depends upon the will of one man, the whole machinery of government is put into motion by one lever, the master,—just as a watch is wound up by one key. And whenever the interest, or even the caprice of the master is at stake, then the people demand their due in vain, the balance trembles in the hand of the magistrate, and inclines on the side which the sovereign finger points out. Ask Siberia, and Siberia will speak; question the tears of the wretched exiles, and they will answer, Between man and man the strict rules of justice are equally disregarded; otherwise would the places of punishment be so crowded? Would the criminal courts be, horrible to say, every day engaged in judging acts of dishonesty and deceit, fraud or burglary, rape or homicide? Should we hear so often of crimes against the honour, the property, the life of our fellow creatures? And yet this is a time when excellent institutions are founded; when the convention of Geneva for the assistance of the wounded, the league of peace, and an association for the suppression of vice are established. It is true that the human mind during these few centuries, has achieved wonders; civilisation has put itself at the head of mankind: yet what does all that progress regard? It regards the increase of wealth, it regards the creation of new comforts, it regards a larger and more refined enjoyment of life. But have the advocates of progress done anything for the morality, the education, the edification of the people? Have they tried to improve the heart, in the same measure as they have tried to develop the mind? No, they have not, and it may be truly said that as long as civilisation does not go hand in hand with morality, its effects are not only not good, but hurtful, poisonous and fatal. Tell me the discoveries that have recently been made in order to root in the human heart love for our neighbours, in order to inspire a deeper fondness for labour and economy, in order to prevent poverty? Instead of that, you will have to announce that fearful implements of death have been invented; the mitrailleuse, which spreads destruction by manifold mouths at the same moment; the chassepots which throw bullets that tear the poor flesh into which they penetrate; the needle and rifle guns which fire with astounding rapidity and kill without a moment of respite;—these are some of the results of civilisation when it is not prompted by morality. And is it for such inventions that God has bestowed upon men an immortal soul and a creative intellect? There is a society for the suppression of vice; but what are they doing? Do they strive to prevent vice? Do they study the means of teaching the people of the lowest classes how to like and appreciate sobriety, to shun intemperance and vice, and consequently how to avert misery and misfortune, disease and untimely death? Oh no, they are content with punishing those that have fallen low into the depth of vice. They are not the protectors of society; they are only its avengers.

But the neglect of religious instruction and the misrepresentation of the Law are also assigned as the causes of war * המורים בתורה שלא כהלכה: Society is

* Talmud Abot, v. 11.

like a great school with an immense number of children. The multitude consists indeed of a great many childish beings. But just as it happens that if unsound instruction is given, the children will soon grow up into vicious young men, so if the literature of a country is immoral, and even if, though condemning vice, it describes its excess with glowing colours, so as to make it almost alluring, the people will be corrupted; they will say: "The cup of pleasure is enervating, yet it is so sweet that we cannot help approaching our lips thereto, were it only for one moment." If the people are not taught the sound principles of religion and morality which is its result, then sensuality, self-interest and ambition will be their sole advisers; and are not these defects the indirect sources of war? But besides that, there are those who expound the Law erroneously, who, instead of ministering to the people the spiritual food of the divine precepts, employ their ingenuity and their learning in throwing doubt upon that which is divine; in teaching men not to believe; in emptying the human heart of all religious feelings. When these are totally banished, will not immoral tendencies, by a natural consequence, take their place? We ought not to be surprised if, when society has descended to that degree of corruption, the Lord inflicts upon it severe sufferings, as he said through the Prophet: הנני צורפם ובחנתים "I will melt them and try them."* And these incisive and threatening words of the prophet can only mean war, because the heart of man is not easily moved; if a warning is to affect it, it must be a warning of death, an awful crisis, a catastrophe like that which just now fills us with horror. The just hand of God who punishes

* Jeremiah ix. 6.

the wickedness of men by the means of the folly and ambition of men is clearly discernible.

And yet this great event, the war, in spite of its mournful effects, which many amongst us, though not engaged in it, feel so deeply, will not be for us without utility if only we are disposed to learn the lessons that it conveys to men. It teaches us that ambition and an immoderate desire of acquiring, of conquering, and of extending our dominion at the expense of our neighbours are always fatal, but that its final victims will be the ambitious themselves. It teaches us that the real welfare of nations does not depend upon military glory, the basis of which is a sea of blood and heaps of human corpses, but upon peace, labour, industry, and commerce; upon the development of the natural resources of the country; upon sound instruction, by which the people may learn and practise what they owe to God, to society, and to themselves; I mean their rights and their duties. It teaches us the necessity of concord, which is as valuable among nations as among individuals; it teaches us that each nation has received its lot from the Lord, in accordance with the words of Moses : * בהנחל עליון גויים בהפרידו בני אדם יצב גבולות עמים and it is such a lot as can satisfy its wants; cursed is the nation that attempts to usurp the lot of a sister nation, as it is written in Deuteronomy § ארור מסיג גבול "Cursed be he that removes his neighbour's landmark," but cursed is also the nation that from cowardice or exhaustion, lets its inheritance be stolen away. It teaches us that kings are not the despotic masters of the lives of their subjects. They are raised to the throne, in order that they may work for the happiness of the millions of human beings placed under their sway, not in order that

* Deuteronomy xxxii. 8.   § xxvii. 17.

when it suits their caprice or their selfishness, they may drag whole hosts to a struggle of destruction, thus exposing their country to devastation and ruin. It teaches us that human life is short enough, that consequently we ought not to make it shorter, but that we ought to employ it in deserving the protection of the Almighty, an invaluable protection, which will cover us upon the earth and still shelter us after death, and which we shall be able to obtain, if we act righteously, if we do justice and charity, the real foundation of all religions. In accordance with the words of Isaiah * שמרו משפט ועשו צדקה כי קרובה ישועתי לבא וצדקתי להגלות "Thus saith the Lord, keep ye judgment, and do justice; for my salvation is near to come, and my righteousness to be revealed." But there is another lesson therein which we ought to take to heart. At the sight of the indescribable miseries to which men are subjected, at the sight of the rapidity with which human life passes away, ought not our heart to be softened and moved by generous emotions? Ought we not to feel our love for our fellow creatures increased, our eagerness to lend them assistance made greater and greater. Oh, my dear brethren, there has never been a time more adapted than this to works of charity, whether it assumes the aspect of liberal contributions, of kind offices, or of prayer. When we represent to ourselves that many more than a hundred thousand human creatures lie down cruelly wounded and are in need of untiring assistance, is it not a duty for us to offer what it is in our power to give, in order that we may have the consolation of knowing that we have at least contributed to the comfort, perhaps to the recovery of one sick man? When we

* lvi. 1.

THE WAR.

see around us so many wretched strangers who have fled from the advancing legions, from the bearers of fresh devastation and bloodshed, ought we not to feel eager to lend our service by advice or by consolation to these foreigners, to whom Moses recommends us to show kindness, because we have in our wanderings acquired the experience of that which strangers must have to suffer? Is it not written, ואוהב גר לתת לו לחם ושמלה: The Lord "loveth the stranger in giving him food and raiment?"* And when we see that the plague of war has not yet quenched its fury, that the struggling parties are prepared for fresh fights, ought we not to raise our supplications to the Father of all creatures, that He may in His mercy stop the fiery and bloody quarrel, that He may inspire the warriors and their leaders with more humane feelings, that He may prevent this year from closing amidst blood, and the new year from opening amidst slaughter?

Are these lessons to be useless to us? Ah no! I hope not. The heart of an Israelite is naturally prone to mercy. Yes, the children of Israel who during the past have suffered so much, have learnt how to pity and assist the sufferers, and through their inexhaustible charity are deservedly called the descendants of Abraham, המרחם על הבריות בידוע שהוא מזרעו של אברהם אבינו: § I am sure, therefore, that I shall not have spoken in vain; I am sure that some assistance will be given, some kindness shown; that every heart will now pray with me for the restoration of peace unto Him who, as the Talmud says,‖ אפילו בשעת כעסו הק״בה זוכר את הרחמים: "even in the moment of His wrath remembers mercy." I am sure that every soul will raise itself with mine unto Him who never

* Deut. x. 18. § Talmud Bezah, 32. ‖ Pesachim, 87.

rejects a prayer prompted by charity and uttered with sincerity, and Who formally promised unto Moses,* ונתתי שלום בארץ   " And I will give peace in the land."

PRAYER.§

Almighty God! Omnipotent and Invisible King of all created things, before whom the greatness of those who dwell in a house of clay is as nothing, their strength and valour are as vanity; we fall upon our face with emotion and fear, because sad intelligence has reached us that has made both our ears tingle. Two noble and powerful nations have mustered their numerous legions, and have begun a deadly conflict with each other, armed with fearful implements of death for their mutual destruction; their land is desolate, terror prevails all around; they have already cast down thousands of wounded; yea, a multitude of strong men have already been slain.

O Eternal, Thou art the God of armies, but Thou art also the Father of mercy and the Master of peace. Oh, listen to our supplication, say unto the war: Spread no further, here shall thy proud waves be stayed. Prevent war from entering our land, prevent sword and shield from being seen in our cities, for much dearer unto us are the results of peace than all the glory and laurels of warriors. Inspire the two nations, their armies and their leaders with love of peace, with mercy and humanity, so that they may cease their work of destruction; stay the

---

* Leviticus xxvi. 6.

§ This prayer, of which the original Hebrew follows, was recited for many weeks, during the Franco-Prussian war, in the Synagogues under the supervision of the author.

shedding of blood, and spare the unarmed and the innocent, old men, women, and children, so that they may be convinced that upon their union depends their prosperity; that their struggle is for both of them a curse and a crime. Remove hatred from their hearts, and make them remember that all men are brethren, and Thou art their Father, loving and merciful; then they will not lift up sword against each other, neither learn war any more!

Oh, our Lord, who art in heaven, look mercifully at the present crisis! Our Lord, who art in heaven, oh, send peace upon the earth, send peace upon this kingdom! Let it be Thy will that we may live and see days of calm and concord, of quiet and security; the day when Thou, O Lord, wilt ordain peace for us, and bless Thy people with peace, Amen!

תְּפִלָּה

רבון כל העולמים מלך נורא ונשגב אשר שמת השמים כסאך והארץ הדום רגליך ּ אשר לפניך גדל שוכני בתי חמר כאין וכל כחם ומעוזם כאפס נחשבו ּ הנה אנחנו נופלים לפניך ארצה באימה וברעדה כי באה עדינו שמועה רעה אשר כל שומעה תצלינה שתי אזניו ּ שני גויים גדולים ורמים אספו את מחניהם מערכה לקראת מערכה וכלי זעמם בידם לחבל זה את זה ביום קרב ּ הנה ארצם שממה מגור מסביב ּ רבים חללים הפילו ועצומים כל הרוגיהם:

שוכן מרומים אתה אלהי צבאות אמנם אב הרחמים ואדון השלום נקראת ּ ועתה שמע נא אל קול תחנתנו ּ אמר למלחמה עד פה תבאי ולא תוסיפי ופה תשיתי בגאון גליך ּ חרחק מלחמה בארצנו וחרב ומגן אל יראו ברחובותינו כי טוב לנו מעשה השלום מכל שלל גבורי החיל ּ תן רחמים בלב השרים

SERMON X.

ובלב צבאותיהם למען יחסו על זקנים ועל נערים על בחורים ועל יונקי שדים ולא ישפכו עוד דם נקי · וידעו ויבינו כי בהתחברם
ייטיבו איש אל אחיו וכי מריבתם תהיה להם מקור קללה ועון · העבר שנאה מתוך לבם ויזכרו כי כל בני אדם אחים ואתה אביהם אוהב ומרחם ולא ישאו עוד איש אל אחיו חרב ולא ילמדו עוד מלחמה:

אלהינו שבשמים ראה בדחק השעה · תן שלום בארץ · תן שלום במלכות הזאת · יהי רצון מלפניך שתכתבנו בספר חיים ברכה ושלום ונזכה ונראה ימי שובה ונחת והשקט ובטח כאשר אתה ה׳ תשפות לנו שלום וברכת את עמך ישראל בשלום · אמן:

THE BURNING BUSH.

וירא והנה הסנה בוער באש והסנה איננו אוכל:

"And he looked, and, behold, the bush burned with fire, and the bush was not consumed."
EXODUS iii. 2.

הראה הק״בה למשה איש בוערת ואיננו אוכל ואמר לו כשם שהסנה
בוער באש ואיננו אוכל כך המצריים אינן יכולין לכלות את ישראל:

"God showed unto Moses a fire that burnt and caused no destruction, and said, 'Behold as the bush is burned with fire, and is not consumed, so Israel cannot be destroyed by his enemies.'"
SHEMOT RABBAH, chap. ii.

MY DEAR BRETHREN,—Three years ago, on this very day, I made the burning bush the subject of a religious meditation; and although both religion and morals place before a preacher an immense but yet not wholly unexplored field, although the beautiful section of the law which we have just read, and the words of which are still ringing in my ears, present more than one great and soul-stirring subject, I turn again my attention to the burning bush, which I shall consider under a different aspect, and from which I can derive new, profitable lessons: it is upon the burning bush that I intend briefly to dwell this morning, for I think that it was the first step that led to Israel's deliverance, of which we are this day so solemnly reminded, and that it ought to be held by the Israelites of all countries and all ages as a serious warning. Can there be a more fitting subject? A bush that had caught fire and yet was not consumed was doubtless so wonderful an apparition as to amaze Moses. The fire which so easily destroys dry branches and prickles did not consume the bush. The flame crept through it, yet the bush remained untouched; it was defended by no bark, and yet it was not devoured. * "And why," said Moses, "why is the bush not burned?" מדוע לא יבער הסנה§ הסנה בוער באש והסנה איננו אוכל: But when he heard the mysterious voice speak out of the midst of the bush, when he heard that that was the voice of the God of his fathers, then he felt that it was a great and terrible sight; he hid his face, and in that moment the most distant future was made known unto him. In that bush, apparently so weak and frail, he saw the people of Israel;—Judaism, in the fire which enveloped it and ran through it without destroying it; he saw the horrible persecutions which were to torment Israel, and the furious attacks which were to be made against his religion, yet without their destroying the one, or annihilating the other. And we Israelites who see ourselves so clearly symbolised by the burning bush, who see ourselves alive after an eventful and rude career of thirty-two centuries, can we help repeating with deep gratitude those words which, perhaps without due reflection, we recite in our Morning Prayers?—"We are happy: how good is our lot, how beautiful our inheritance, how great our destiny" ‖ אשרנו מה טוב חלקנו מה נעים גורלנו מה יפה מאוד ירושתנו:

---

* Exodus iii. 2.　　　§ Exodus iii. 3.
‖ Ritual, Morning Prayers.

THE BURNING BUSH.

I.

Israel is symbolised by the bush which burns and is not consumed. This is a truth which cannot be doubted, either by those who study the development of man's mind, or by those who record human events. No great keenness of intellect is needed for us to know that the human mind is constantly progressing and moving from darkness to light, and if possible from light to splendour. Yet in consequence of this constant movement, human opinions undergo continuous modifications. Speculative ideas cannot remain immutable; and the doctrines which to-day are the object of man's admiration and even worship, will in a few years appear defective, less commendable, and will become a source of dispute and bitter controversy. So religions are at first adopted with enthusiasm, but sooner or later their truth begins to be doubted, their superhuman origin is denied, and at last they either are abandoned, or give rise to a number of sects which, after their development, come to have little in common with the primitive theories. Nations, in their turn, exhibit even in a more striking manner that they are subject to changes, infirmities, decay and death; that is, either complete destruction, or amalgamation and fusion with a predominant race. They live, so to say, the four ages of human life; they are unconsciously growing in their childhood, wild but vigorous in their youth, powerful and absorbing in their manhood, enervated in their old age, until they vanish not to reappear. They are like man, whose days are as grass, and who flourishes as a flower of the field; but the "wind passes over it and it is gone; and the place thereof

shall know it no more " * כי רוח עברה בו ואיננו ולא יכירנו
עוד מקומו: They perish without leaving even a trace
behind. What has become of the four empires so
graphically symbolised by the great image of Nebuchadnezzar's dream, "the head of which was of fine gold, its
breast and its arms of silver, its belly and its thighs of
brass, its legs of iron, and its feet part of iron and part
of clay?" § That statue, although so strongly built, had
no duration. "A stone smote it upon its feet, and it
fell and was broken into pieces " || חזי הוית עד די התגזרת
אבן דלא בידין ומחת לצלמא על רגלוהי די פרזלא וחספא והדקת
המון: Babylon and Persia, Greece and Rome are the
four empires alluded to by Daniel, each of which exercised a powerful influence over a large part of mankind.
But where are they? Where is Babylon with its gigantic
walls and stately palaces? Where is Shushan with its
indescribable and inexhaustible wealth? Where is
Athens, with its innumerable temples, statues, and
paintings? Where is Rome, with its seven hills covered
with gorgeous temples, basilicas, statues and triumphal
arches? Of those four great empires, the first was
destroyed by the second, the second by the third, the
third by the fourth; "they swallowed up each other
quickly" : איש את רעהו חיים בלעו ¶ And the fourth,
Rome,—so well represented by the image's feet, "part of
iron and part of clay," for in consequence of its great extent
it was weak though apparently so powerful,—was smitten
and broken into pieces by a rough stone. It was par-
celled by seven nations of barbarians into a thousand
minute fragments. Each of those empires lived and
died. "It passed away, it is no more; I sought it, but

* Psalm ciii. 15, 16.   § Daniel ii. 32, 33. || Ib. 34.
¶ Talmud Abot, iii. 2.

it cannot be found"* ויעבור והנה איננו ואבקשנו ולא
נמצא:

The fate of the ancient religions of mankind was not dissimilar from that of the various nations. Where are you, ancient idols? Where are you, terrible Jupiter, wise Minerva, charming Venus, bull-headed Osiris, blazing Mitra, powerful Odin, and wild Thor? What does there remain of all your temples and rites? Naught save what a few ruined monuments, and often incomprehensible papyri can show? It is true that in Asia some hundred millions of men still adore such gods as Brahma, or Buddha, or Fo. But the third, Fo, the Chinese idol, is scarcely eighteen centuries old, and its religion is already in the period of weakness and decay. The religions of India and Thibet are really ancient, their origin is lost in the darkness of antiquity. But can there be any doubt that, as soon as a glimpse of true instruction, of true progress can penetrate through the mist of the sluggish and idle Asiatic spirit, all those monstrous idols will be shattered as unworthy of adoration, as the cause of the degradation of man? Some of the ancient mythologies are still appreciated for their artistic value, and not for the doctrines that they can teach, but all of them, as adopted religions, have perished for ever, because, as Samuel said,§ "they could not profit nor deliver, for they were vain" אשר לא יועילו ולא יצילו כי תהו המה: But can we find, at least in the religions which still exist and are followed by millions of human creatures, any elements of durability? No, for the people no longer agree on the most important dogmas, on the basis of their doctrine; from the main body of the faithful, dissenters constantly withdraw and, almost

* Psalm xxxviii. 36. § 1 Samuel xii. 21.

every day, new sects arise. Ought we to be surprised at these ever recurrent results? Innumerable men still unfortunately worship the work of their own hands. "Their gods," as David said, "are silver and gold, the produce of material labour"* עצביהם כסף וזהב מעשה ידי אדם : "They bow," says the Talmud, "to the very dust of their feet"§ משתחוים לאבק שברגליהם : The religions that are the invention of the human mind, even of a gigantic mind, are sure, sooner or later, to be modified, altered, and perhaps rejected. Only one religion can be true, that which is the fruit of revelation, the word of God; and the Talmud teaches that "divine revelation does not rest with the other nations of the world" : לא תשרה שכינה על אומות העולם ‖

There is, therefore, a law of destruction against everything that is human and that, being imperfect, contains within itself the elements of its death; in accordance with the pathetic exclamation of the Prophet: "What man is he that lives and shall not see death? ¶ מי גבר יחיה ולא יראה מות : There is a law of dissolution that operates on every nation, every religion. Yet there is one nation, one religion which seems to be an exception, and to which the general rule does not apparently apply. It is an astounding fact, but it is a fact and cannot be denied. One people among the peoples of antiquity has not perished, one of the most ancient religions has not disappeared. 'A small people it is; it has lost its independence and territory, it is scattered all over the world, but no fusion with any conquering race has taken place, and it still exists with the type, the characteristics, the customs, that pertained to its forefathers four thousand

---

* Psalm cxv. 4.   § Talm. B. Megillah, 86.
‖ Talmud Berachot, 7.   ¶ Psalm lxxxix. 49.

years ago. Judaism traversed with Israel the period of ancient civilisation, and afterwards a long period of darkness; it has again entered the period of progress, but it has not undergone the changes brought into all human organisations, it has remained unaltered. Time, the great destroyer of all earthly things, has passed over Israel and his religion, and has not affected them. והסנה איננו אכל "And the bush was not consumed." That people is not numerous, it is weak; rather than the cedar of Lebanon, it resembles the frail bush of the mountain, which nothing can defend from the storm. Yet Israel exists. והסנה איננו אכל But look there is FIRE IN THE BUSH, a devouring flame envelops it. The earth has often been reddened with the blood of thousands of victims; it has been a battle-field on which the fire consumed everything it met; the kings of the world conspired against that people, they invented calumny, employed persecution, and attempted to efface it from the number of the living; all the enemies united by one bond, hatred, cried in the moment of the struggle: ' No mercy, no quarter; ravage, ravage, until destruction is complete'* האמרים ערו ערו עד היסוד בה and yet Israel exists: והסנה איננו אוכל And that is natural, for God said of Israel: " Touch not mine anointed, and do my prophets no harm " § : אל תגעו במשיחי ובנביאי אל תרעו So it is natural that our religion should not have perished, for it is the expression of the Lord's will, it is His own word, "and the word of our God shall stand for ever " § ודבר אלהינו יקום לעולם : Let us therefore, contemplate with unbounded gratitude the effects of a promise which has not failed through centuries. In spite of the bitterest trials, Israel is still full of life. He rests amidst the

* Psalm cxxxvii. 7.   § Psalm cv. 15.   ‖ Isaiah xl. 8.

storms, and while confusion seems to prevail in every mind, while some doubt, many fear, and few hope, he is what he was, he feels secure and is not afraid of coming events. Can there be a better proof of the vitality of our race? Can there be a better proof of the mercy of God, who has done as He said:* "For the mountains shall depart, and the hills be removed; but my kindness shall not depart from thee, neither shall the covenant of my peace be removed, saith the Lord that hath mercy on thee?" וחסדי מאתך לא ימוש וברית שלומי לא תמוט אמר מרחמך ה' :

II.

My brethren, I have shown you that both our religion and our race possess great vitality, or in other words, that they have obtained a most glorious victory, the victory over time and events. But what is the first thought of a man who perceives that a most precious jewel is in his possession? It is certainly to place it under proper care, to preserve it. Our vitality is really an invaluable jewel. It was handed down to us by our ancestors, from the time of the Patriarchs. But shall we be able to preserve it? To have safeguarded it during many centuries of unparalleled difficulties constitutes our immortal glory. But to lose it at a time when no danger threatens, when the way is comparatively smooth and easy, would mark us with imperishable shame. What then are we to do in order to preserve our inheritance in its integrity?

Are we to remain inactive and silent according to the law, and to let the Lord fight for us? ה' ילחם לכם ואתם תחרשון § Are we to think that the Lord who saved us

---

* Isaiah liv. 10.   § Exodus xiv. 14.

in the past, will save us in the future? Are we allowed to ask for wonders constantly, and thus to tempt the Lord? He performs miracles when necessity demands them, when no other way is left, when both the safety of His people and the glorification of His name are at stake. He gave heavenly bread to the Hebrews in the wilderness, because nothing else could be had: but "the manna ceased on the morrow after they had eaten the old corn of the land"* וישבת המן ממחרת מאכלם מעבור הארץ: The events of ancient times were such as to cause our forefathers to deserve miracles, as the Talmud says, §ראויים היו לעשות להם נס yet our ancestors did not remain idle. They worked with all their power for the preservation of their race and religion. On behalf of these they sacrificed all their property, all that was dearest unto them, even their life. Though it is declared by God that Judaism shall be preserved, yet we can, by our ardour or our lukewarmness, hasten or delay its triumph. And if it is in our power to shorten the time of transition between the reign of error and the reign of truth by our exertions, it would be unpardonable in us not to enter the field of action at once.

We ought to be active, but our activity should never assume a hostile character; it should never constitute an attack against other religions and their followers, it should never impose our religion by violence. No, that was never the object of our noble doctrines, and could not be the means of their preservation. Mahomet put a sword into the hands of his followers and ordered them to go forth and conquer adherents to

---

* Joshua v. 12. § Talmud Berachot, 4.

his cause. They went, they conquered, and for two centuries streams of human blood flowed in the name of religion, which ought to mean kindness and charity. Moses put the law only, into the hands of the Hebrews, and ordered them to study and learn it, so that it might be constantly in their mouth and in their heart, so that it might be the anchor of their safety, and the source of their glory. Instead of making conversions we are bound to defend our camp, our homes, our children from the audacious attempts of conversionists because we are responsible before God for each soul that we lose through our carelessness.

Nor should we try to maintain our strength by adapting our religion to the ever-varying exigencies of different epochs. We live in a time when war is waged against all forms; are we to make our religion a mere collection of dogmas, of spiritual doctrines, of vague lessons, and to deprive it of those rites and ceremonies which embody its precepts and history, and make it possible for man to carry them into practice? Are we to proclaim a complete separation between the principle and its application? But then, religion would be an impossibility; it would abandon the earth, as the soul does when separated from the body. For religion is like vapour which cannot be prevented from vanishing if it is not confined within a solid vessel. But if the alterations demanded do not go so far, if we are merely asked to limit the number of our religious acts, should we seek in that operation the preservation of our vitality? Should we remove one day a line, another day a precept, and clear the religious ground "here a little, and there a little"* ׃ זעיר שם זעיר שם But which are

---

* Isaiah xxviii. 13.

the religious laws or ceremonies that we should abolish? Shall we declare prayer to be superfluous, and prevent the multitude either from paying to God the only homage that is in the power of men to give, or from seeking relief in sorrow by addressing the Father of all creatures, the healer of all diseases? Or are we to abandon, as useless, that feeling of brotherhood which leads us to the bed of the sick, to the hovel of the poor, to the house of mourning? Or are we to omit the merciful obligation of performing on behalf of the dead those duties which constitute a real merit, for they are accomplished without any hope of reward, as Rashi, commenting on Jacob's words, says:* חסד שעושים עם המתים הוא חסד של אמת שאינו מצפה לתשלום גמול: "The acts of benevolence done to the dead are true mercy, for no recompense is awarded for them?" Are we to abolish those dietetic laws which may be minute, but which secure our bodily health, and alleviate the effects of all contagious diseases and ravaging plagues? Are we to abandon those rules which rigorously establish the duties between relations and relations, between husband and wife, father and son, brother and brother, and which have made the Jewish families an example of morality and love? And should we give up with such thoughtlessness and levity that which caused us to be called a clever and prudent nation? For there is no doubt that when men said of Israel§ : רק עם חכם ונבון הגוי הגדול הזה "Surely this great nation is a wise and understanding people," they did not refer only to the law which was in his possession, but to the manner with which he carried it out.

No, it is not by inaction, nor by a warlike policy, nor

* Comment. on Genesis xlvii. 29.   § Deut. iv. 6.

by stripping our religion of its necessary garment that we can increase, or even keep, our strength. The secret of Samson's physical power lay in the length of his hair, the secret of the greatness of the Romans lay in their discipline, and the secret of our prolonged existence lies in our religion, as Moses said : *
כי הוא חייך וארך ימיך "For it is thy life, and the length of thy days." In the past we did not take part in the events that happened around us; we remained aloof, and sought relief from our sufferings in our union, in our brotherhood, in being responsible for each other, in a religious life, in the performance of our ceremonies. And we shall be able still to retain our vitality, which all men observe with respect and admiration, if we place it under the same safeguard—union, brotherhood, mutual responsibility, and religious observance; if we do not renounce our characteristics, our individuality; if we refrain from forming family alliances with other races. For it is not true that we need new elements of vigour; it is not true that Israel is a diseased body. The Jewish stock is healthy, young, and vigorous, and does not require an infusion of fresh blood. We must remain true Jews, we must remain a distinct race; but we must at the same time obey the duties of citizens. Our religion is not opposed to progress. When I say this, I do not mean that we should subject our religion to the scissors and caprices of fashion. But the truth of which I wish to convince you is this, that we may do all that progress demands of modern society, that is to acquire knowledge, to enlighten our minds, to avail ourselves of the wonderful discoveries of science, while at the same time we abide by the tenets of

* Deut. xxx. 20.

THE BURNING BUSH.

our faith which is not only not opposed to instruction, but rigorously commands it.

Finally, the vitality of our race and religious doctrines may be considered as a wonderful monument, resting upon a threefold basis, upon three great pillars. All of them must be preserved, for all of them are equally indispensable. "Dogmas, religious acts, and morals" are the three pillars which we are called upon to preserve and defend at any cost. By their means the little bush will be saved from destruction, by whatever fire it may be enveloped; by their means we shall enable ourselves to accomplish our mission, which consists in spreading all over the earth the pure and true knowledge of the One God. The conversion of the world to our ideas is not a light work, it cannot be done all in one day. We must then labour with constancy and perseverance and teach our creed silently, by our example, by a noble and pure life which will assuredly be more persuasive than the most powerful eloquence; it will master all resistance and lead the nations to truth. "And many people shall go and say: Come ye, and let us go up to the mountain of the Lord, to the house of the God of Israel, to the house of the God of Jacob; and He will teach us of His ways, and we will walk in His paths"* והלכו עמים רבים ואמרו לכו ונלכה אל הר ה' אל בית אלהי יעקב ויורנו מדרכיו ונלכה בארחותיו: Let us consider our religion as a flaming beacon and seek our salvation in its light; let us call it our polar star, our guide in the darkness of life, let us carry through centuries and generations, ביד רמה "with a high hand," the distinctive marks of our emprise, the ensigns of our commission,—our religious customs, our

* Isaiah ii. 3.

sacred language, our poetical and elevating traditions. And our exertions will have only one result, but it will be glorious and worthy of our past, it will be that which Isaiah announced unto us in manifold passages and glowing language. "Yes," he exclaims, "one shall say, I am the Lord's; and another shall call himself by the name of Jacob, and another shall subscribe with his hand unto the Lord, and surname himself by the name of Israel"* זה יאמר לה׳ אני וזה יקרא בשם יעקב וזה יכתוב ידו לה׳ ובשם ישראל יכנה :

PRAYER.

Almighty God, in this morning's meditation we have applied the bush which burned and was not consumed to the striking vitality which has long animated and still animates, both our race and our religion. But if we raise our minds to the higher task of reflecting upon Thine essence, we see in the fire of the bush another signification, we see Thine unbounded mercy. Yes, Thy mercy which in spite of the growing corruption of man, promised that a wholesale destruction should no more come upon the earth, that "seed time, and harvest, and cold and heat, and summer and winter, and day and night, shall not cease;"§ Thy mercy, which after the abominable rebellion of Israel on the occasion of the exploration of the Holy Land, pronounced the word, Pardon : ‖ סלחתי כדברך Thy wrath has always been, in fact, like the fire in the bush, which enveloped it without consuming it. "In wrath Thou hast remembered mercy" ¶ ברגז רחם תזכור : Thou didst inflict upon us

---

* Isaiah xliv. 5.   § Genesis x. 22.   ‖ Numbers xiv. 20.
¶ Hab. iii. 2.

THE BURNING BUSH.

severe punishment at various times, but in the moment of real danger, Thine hand has always been unto us the shield of preservation. For it is true that "He that keepeth Israel shall neither slumber nor sleep."* Though we feel convinced of the final triumph of our cause, yet the great moment may be very distant, we may still have to traverse periods of grief and suffering, like a traveller who perceives at a distance the object of his aspirations, but the way which leads to it is yet long and beset with perils. We may again be forgetful of our mission, we may go astray as our forefathers did, we may deserve correction and forfeit Thine assistance. But we have faith in Thy mercy, in that fire which warms without burning, which animates and does not destroy; and we earnestly pray unto Thee that our way may be smooth, that all stumbling-blocks may be removed from it, and that we may be preserved from the crises which come from time to time to afflict mankind. So that what Thou didst say unto Moses may be gloriously accomplished. "I will put none of these diseases upon thee which I have brought upon the Egyptians, for I am the Lord that healeth thee" § כל המחלה אשר שמתי במצרים לא אשים עליך כי אני ה' רפאך:

AMEN.

* Psalm cxxi. 4.   § Exodus xv. 26.

KNOWLEDGE OF GOD.

וִידַעְתֶּם כִּי אֲנִי יְיָ אֱלֹהֵיכֶם :
"And ye shall know that I am the Lord your God."

EXODUS vi. 7.

שָׁאַל פַּרְעֹה לְמֹשֶׁה וּלְאַהֲרֹן מִי ה' אָמְרוּ לוֹ אֱלֹהֵינוּ הוּא אֱלֹהִים חַיִּים וּמֶלֶךְ עוֹלָם, אָמַר לָהֶם כַּמָּה שְׁנוֹתָיו כַּמָּה עֲיָירוֹת כָּבַשׁ אָמַר לוֹ אֱלֹהֵינוּ כֹּחוֹ וּגְבוּרָתוֹ מָלֵא עוֹלָם וְכוּ' :

"'Who is your God?' said Pharaoh unto Moses and Aaron. 'Our God is the living God, and the King of the universe.' 'How old is He? what has He achieved? How many cities has He conquered?' 'Our God fills the universe with His power, He existed before the creation of the world, and will exist when the world shall end; He created thee, and breathed into thee the breath of life.'"

MEDRASH SHEMOT RABBAH, ch. v.

MY DEAR BRETHREN,—There are few events in the whole Bible as highly important as the oppression, the rising and the deliverance of a whole nation, as well as the obduracy and the exemplary punishment of all its tormentors: of the king, his ministers, his people, and even the land in which tyranny had been pitilessly exercised. Throughout the history of ancient nations there are few narratives which possess the characteristics of impressiveness and interest, which are as dramatic as that contained in the first four sections of Exodus. Yet infinitely more significant are the moral lessons which we may derive from each phase of that startling event,

KNOWLEDGE OF GOD.

from each page and each line of that wonderful narration. From them we may deduce religious and moral improvement, and it becomes our sacred duty to master them by constant study and untiring reflection. For this object alone it was said: "This book of the Law shall not depart out of thy mouth, but thou shalt meditate therein day and night."* לא ימוש ספר התורה הזה מפיך והגית בו יומם ולילה: For this object alone, wherever there has been a Jew, during two thousand years, a section of the Pentateuch has been read every Sabbath with solemnity and devotion.

Let us now briefly dwell upon the most salient principle to be learnt from the chapters which we have read this morning, and which can be summarised by these words: *the knowledge of God*.

God created man in His own image, and from that man whom He made out of the dust, and whom He animated by an immortal spirit, from that source alone descended all mankind. Of this great truth, proclaimed in the very first pages of the Law, we are often reminded, so that men reflecting upon the oneness of their origin may learn to love each other. No one human family can claim to spring from a nobler source than another; and no nation can have the right of enslaving another nation. Slavery is an insult to that Providence which made all human races equal to each other, whatever the physical modifications may be to which they have been subjected by the influence of climate. When therefore the Egyptians, trampling upon all the laws of justice and hospitality, turned into slaves those whom they had willingly received as guests, when they treated

---

* Joshua i. 8.

them barbarously, and not content with condemning them to the hardest labour, attempted to prevent their increase by throwing those unfortunate little beings into the depths of the Nile, whose only crime was to be of Jewish parentage, then the wrath of the Lord broke forth, then He stretched out His arm and lifted His hand, in order to punish those who had refused to believe in His existence and acknowledge His power, and who had rejected His command to give liberty to the race which He had chosen; in order to punish those who had dared to say: * "Who is the Eternal, whose voice I am to obey to let Israel go? I know not the Eternal, nor will I let Israel go" מי ה' אשר אשמע בקולו לא ידעתי את ה' וגם את ישראל לא אשלח: We know the ten plagues which infected the elements and which arose in terrific gradation, afflicting all classes of society, from the king down to the wretched prisoner, but afflicting especially the priests, in order to show the impotence of the idols in whose name they spoke and acted.

Here I must ask a question. What was the object of the Lord in performing so many miracles, that is, so many alterations of the laws of nature? Some say that the object of the Lord was the deliverance of the descendants of the Patriarchs from their secular chains, the deliverance of the people in whom all the families of the earth were to be blessed. As it is written,§ "And I have come down to deliver them out of the hand of Egypt, and to bring them out of that land" וארד להצילו מיד מצרים ולהעלתו מן הארץ ההיא: And this was doubtless a noble aim, for it proves the mercy of the Almighty towards all those who suffer, whether they be nations or individuals. Others believe that the Lord's

* Exodus v. 2.   § Exodus iii. 8.

intention was to take revenge on those who had set His power at defiance, and to inflict upon Pharaoh and his people so severe a punishment as to render them an ever memorable warning unto all those who should follow in their footsteps. As it is written, "And I will stretch out my hand, and smite Egypt with all my wonders that I will do in the midst thereof"* ושלחתי את ידי והכיתי את מצרים בכל נפלאתי אשר אעשה בקרבו: This again proves the justice of the Lord, who cannot suffer to see iniquity remain unpunished, and who, holding all men who do wrong, whatever their fortune and position, to be equally guilty, always bestows a punishment corresponding to the crime committed. The Lord, however, could have easily obtained these two objects without any great display of His divine power. One moment, one word would have sufficed for the carrying out of His all-potent will. But the object of the Lord was even grander and more elevating, as the Scriptures clearly assert: "And ye shall know that I am the Lord your God, who bringeth you out from under the burden of the Egyptians" § וידעתם כי אני ה' אלהיכם המוציא אתכם מתחת סבלות מצרים: During their two hundred and ten years of slavery, the Hebrews had almost forgotten the pure idea of the Divinity as bequeathed unto them by the Patriarchs; they had almost learnt from their oppressors to worship that which is visible, manifest to our senses and material. And yet Israel, whom God had already called "my son, even my first born" בני בכורי ישראל was, as such, to exercise a decisive influence in the future over the whole human family; he was to become "the witness of the Lord" ואתם עדי and the depositary of His law, of

* Exodus iii. 20. § Exodus vi. 7.

the eternal truths which are indispensable to the very existence of the world. He would therefore make Himself known to both nations, the faithful and the idolaters. He would perform before them such wonders as would oblige them to acknowledge Him as the true, the One God, the absolute Master of heaven and earth. "All this I have done and more will I do, that ye, Israelites, my children, may recognise that I am the Lord"* וידעתם כי אני ה': "All this have I done, and more will I do, that Pharaoh, and all heathens may know that none is like the Lord God"§ למען תדע כי אין כה' אלהינו: And it is so. The object which the Lord had in performing for Israel's glory and preservation, both in Egypt and in the wilderness, in Palestine and in the land of exile, so many great deeds which are engraven in the immortal pages of history, was that we should acknowledge Him as the Perfect Being to whom alone worship and adoration are due. And the object which He has still in achieving the marvels which we witness every day and every moment, is to force us to know His greatness and immensity, compared with which we are much less than the worm which creeps upon the earth is, compared with us.

Moses had failed in his first attempt to soften the heart of Pharaoh on behalf of the Hebrews. Severely rebuked by the tyrant, Moses saw the previously gloomy condition of his brethren become ever worse and intolerable. Then yielding to his impatience and to a feeling of despair, he addressed a complaint to the Lord. "Wherefore," he said, "hast Thou so evil entreated this people? Why is it that Thou hast sent me? for since I came to speak to Pharaoh in Thy name, he has done

* Exodus vi. 7. § Exodus viii. 10.

KNOWLEDGE OF GOD.

evil to this people, neither hast Thou delivered this people at all"* : והצל לא הצלת את עמך Moses lacked faith for a moment, and in him that was a great fault. The Lord, in His answer, made him aware of his condemnable short-coming, for in a few words He mentioned His three cardinal attributes, which Moses ought never to have forgotten. "I am the Lord," He said unto Moses, "and I appeared unto Abraham, unto Isaac, and unto Jacob by the name of God Almighty, but by my name *Adonai* was I not known unto them"§ אני ה': וארא אל אברהם אל יצחק ואל יעקב באל שדי ושמי ה' שדי *Elohim*, אלהים The three words לא נודעתי להם: *Shaddai*, 'ה *Adonai*, imply the three great qualities which characterise the Lord, and by which He ought to be known and adored. They signify Justice, Omnipotence, Eternity.

By the word אלהים *Elohim*, which is often applied in the Bible to human judges, God reminded Moses that He was the essence of justice. The patriarchs had known Him by this attribute, for He had repeatedly commanded them "to do justice and judgment." Abraham saw that He was the upright "judge of all the earth," when He punished the four cities stained with the most abominable vices, and poured upon them His divine fire, dooming them to utter destruction. In all their vicissitudes the patriarchs could clearly see the effects of the Divine justice; and either the victory obtained by the 318 servants of Abraham against the four armies headed by Kedorlaomer, or the protection afforded to Isaac from the envious Philistines, or the final triumph of the unjustly tormented Joseph, were palpable proofs that the laws of justice cannot be trodden upon with impunity, and that the moral order established by the Creator

* Exodus v. 22, 23.   § Exodus vi. 2, 3.

between man and man cannot be broken without fatal results to the unscrupulous transgressors. Jeremiah explained this Divine quality in the right manner, when he said,* "For Thine eyes are open on the ways of the sons of men, to give every one according to his ways, and according to the fruit of his doings" אשר עיניך פקחות על כל דרכי בני אדם לתת לאיש כדרכיו וכפרי מעלליו: His eye sees the torments of those who are unjustly oppressed, the blood unjustly spilt, the property unjustly usurped. With His ever-open ear He hears the complaint of the innocent, as He heard "the groaning of the children of Israel, whom the Egyptians kept in bondage" § וגם אני שמעתי את נאקת בני ישראל אשר מצרים מעבדים אותם: From whatever part of the earth the cry for help may come, from the palace or from the cottage, whether uttered by a widow or by an orphan, by a king or by a beggar, if it is really the complaint of innocence against iniquity, it will surely reach the ear of the Almighty "who," as our sages teach, "is always ready to bestow a good reward upon those who walk before Him" ‖ נאמן לשלם שכר טוב למתהלכים לפניו:

But the Lord could not exercise the quality of justice if He did not possess the attribute of omnipotence. If His power was limited, how could He dispense full punishment or full reward? But then the Lord is omnipotent; therefore He called Himself *El Shaddai*, and "as such, He made Himself known unto the patriarchs." In all the visions which He granted to them, in all the words which He addressed unto them, in all the circumstances in which He acted on their behalf, He always impressed them with the idea of His omnipotence.

* xxxii. 19.   § Exodus vi. 5.
‖ Rashi on Exodus vi. 3.

KNOWLEDGE OF GOD.

Oh, my dear brethren, God is great, God is immense; and who can doubt it? Is it necessary to reflect so profoundly in order to know that the Lord wields unlimited power? Look at His works. Raise your eyes and observe the majesty of the heavens, those stars which in their greatness move so regularly above our heads, and compared with which, the earth is but an imperceptible atom. What magnificence! Who is the artist who said: Let the sun be created and preside over the day; let the moon appear in the firmament and be the gentle queen of night? Who gave both existence and movement to that multitude of stars, which are as many suns, surrounded by their planets, followed by their satellites, on which they spread a softened reflection of their light? Who can be the author of so many marvels which our feeble mind can scarcely comprehend? And who but God can be the Creator, the Omnipotent Sovereign of the universe? "No one but God," said Isaiah,* "bringeth out their host by number: He calleth them all by names, by the greatness of His might, for that He is strong in power: no one fails" המוציא במספר צבאם לכלם בשם יקרא מרב אונים ואמיץ כח איש לא נעדר:

God is invisible; yet we can see Him in His works, which on the one hand are governed by laws too regular to be ascribed to casualty; on the other, they are too far above mortal power to be attributed to man.—A Roman Emperor was one day speaking with a Hebrew sage of the practices which constitute an almost impassable barrier between our nation and all other races, when he suddenly exclaimed: "Since, as thou sayest, thy God is so powerful and the master of all

* xl. 26.

created beings, I order thee to show Him unto me." An open disobedience to the order of a Roman Emperor would have been a sentence of death. Therefore, the sage answered : " Oh, my sovereign, I will do thy pleasure, if thou wilt only meet me to-morrow at noon, beyond the town in the open plain." When on the following day the emperor met the sage, he said, "Wilt thou point out to me at last this God of thine?" "Raise thine eyes, O sire, and fix them upon that burning sun." The emperor was soon overpowered by the dazzling splendour of that great source of light. "Thou canst not," said the sage, "bear for one moment the light of the sun, which is one, and not even the greatest, of the manifold works of my God, and how wouldst thou gaze with thy mortal eyes at the omnipotent God Himself, of whom the angels, all human creatures, all animated beings constantly say : ' Holy, holy, holy is the Lord of hosts; the whole earth is full of His glory ' "* קדוש קדוש קדוש ה׳ צבאות מלא כל הארץ כבודו :

And it is true : the universe is an open book which announces the omnipotence of its author. Not to learn how to read therein is already highly condemnable in man, whom God made the ruler of the earth ; but to disbelieve it and boldly to exhibit our scepticism by our actions, would be always a foolish and sometimes a dangerous undertaking.—Canute the Second, king of England and Denmark, who lived some eight hundred years ago, was one of the most powerful and, what is better, one of the wisest kings. As it happens with princes and sovereigns, with the rich and the great, he was surrounded with courtiers who, foolish in their praises and exaggerated in their flattery, attributed to him those high qualities

* Isaiah vi. 3.

KNOWLEDGE OF GOD.

which belong only unto the Almighty. Unable to put a stop to their senseless adulation, he resolved to give them a severe but useful lesson. He assembled them one stormy day, on the sea shore; the wind rose higher and higher, the billows appeared agitated by internal convulsions. "It is your opinion," said Canute to his courtiers, "that even the elements would obey my orders; I command the sea, therefore, to resume its calmness, and no longer to disturb our sports." But in that moment the gale became furious, and a wave as huge as a mountain fell upon the king and his courtiers and nearly swept them all into the sea. "God, not man," said the king to his terrified followers, "God, not man, is omnipotent; God let us praise, God let us adore, for 'His kingdom rules over all'" * ומלכותו בכל משלה: The sea and its innumerable inhabitants, the mountains and their eternal snow, the cedar of Lebanon as well as the humblest flower, the regular phenomena which we see renewed every day, and the phenomena which, like the plagues of Egypt, seem to break the order of nature, and the cause of which we vainly attempt to discover, are so many trumpets by which God causes these words to sound in the ear of man וידעתם כי אני ה': "Ye shall know that I am the Lord," the only one God, and that "beside me there is no Saviour" § ואין מבלעדי מושיע:

The point, however, on which the Lord laid more stress in His kind rebuke to Moses, was this third attribute, Eternity; without which both justice and Omnipotence would become inefficient, useless. That is the quality which is so beautifully expressed by the ineffable name, that holy name which we are forbidden to utter as it is written, and which, in token of our awe,

* Psalm ciii. 19.   § Isaiah xliii. 11.

veneration and even terror, we merely pronounce *Adonai*. In the Hebrew language alone there is one word which possesses the most comprehensive meaning, since it signifies eternity in its three parts: past, present, and future; it means, that the Lord is not limited by time, since He Himself is time. We perishable creatures can look back to the time which has passed since our life began. We can look forward to the time which will elapse till our end comes; but our present consists merely of one atom, that in which we mention it. The Lord had no beginning, He will have no end; and His existence is, so to say, an everlasting present, because He does not change, and as He was, so He is and will be. "Thou art the same, and Thy years shall have no end."* ואתה הוא ושנותיך לא יתמו: When He said to Moses: אני ה' "I am the Lord," He meant that time is nothing unto Him, that His promise shall never fail, for the future is under His power, and His will is immutable. Reasons known to Him alone may delay His interference, but He will doubtlessly bestow His protection upon the weak against the strong, upon the innocent against the guilty, upon the oppressed against the oppressors, until justice is done. "He is the faithful God which keeps covenant and mercy with them that love Him and keep His commandments to a thousand generations. § האל הנאמן שמר הברית והחסד לאהביו ולשמרי מצותיו לאלף דור:

So the object of the Lord's acts is that we should know Him in His essence and in His attributes. And surely, when we see ourselves surrounded by the marvels of God's creation, when we observe the order and harmony which prevail in the wonderful mechanism of

* Psalm cii. 28.   § Deuteronomy vii. 9.

the universe, we are forced to recognise that there is a God. But will that knowledge exercise no influence over us, over our mind and our character? How! when we are really and deeply convinced that the Lord is just and omnipotent, can we ever indulge in wicked actions, or even in wicked thoughts? At the idea of a judge whose will finds no obstacles, whose power is unlimited, a judge who is upright but inexorable, shall we not be deterred from walking in the path of vice, dishonesty, or crime? When we really understand what the eternity of God means, shall we, if tried by failure, or oppressed by misfortune, ever murmur against Him, exhibit impatience, or want of faith? No; we shall hope in Him who rules time, who promises and is sure to keep His word, who knows the right moment to give assistance, to bring about the rescue of those that are unjustly oppressed, that suffer for the good cause, the cause of the Lord. This knowledge of the Almighty is necessary to man, to whatever creed he may belong; it is as indispensable to his intellect as light is indispensable to his eyes; and just as a tender mother obliges her child to take the food which, from caprice, he sometimes rejects, so the Lord enforces His knowledge upon all the sons of men. When He has to deal with the good and the righteous, it is by His favors, by the deeds of His mercy, by bestowing upon them protection and untiring assistance, that He leads them to acquire the knowledge of His existence and omnipotence. He acted thus with Israel, to whom He said:* "And ye shall know that I am the Lord your God, who bringeth you out from under the burden of the Egyptians." But those that are naturally wicked, whose evil disposition prompts them to

* Exodus vi. 7.

transgress even the laws of natural religion, are differently treated. It is by the means of hard blows, of terrific plagues, of heart-rending misfortunes, that the Lord enforces upon them the knowledge of His attributes, His justice, His omnipotence and His eternity, as it is written : * כי בפעם הזאת אני שלח את כל מגפתי אל לבך ובעבדיך ובעמך בעבור תדע כי אין כמני בכל הארץ: "For I will this time send all my plagues upon thine heart, and upon thy servants, and upon thy people, that thou mayest know that there is none like me in all the earth."

Our sages said that "a precious jewel hung around the neck of Abraham" אבן טובה היתה תלויה בצוארו של אברהם אבינו: § It was not a talisman, an amulet, supposed by the superstitious to keep away the consequence of envy, of evil eye; the jewel was the knowledge of the Lord, of the one God, of the Omnipotent Being, that knowledge which Abraham disseminated among men; it was the spiritual jewel which ought to be treasured in the heart of every good man, of every true Israelite. We have inherited that jewel, we have it still. Oh, let us wear it with pride, for it is the noblest decoration. Let us preserve the knowledge of the Lord, let us teach it to our fellow creatures, and our mind will be elevated, our heart ennobled, our path enlightened, and our actions will bear the stamp of justice, we shall then be able to perform our mission, our destiny upon the earth in accordance with the words of Moses : ‖ "Ye shall walk after the Lord your God and fear Him, and keep His commandments, and obey His voice, and ye shall serve Him, and cleave unto Him" אחרי ה׳ אלהיכם תלכו ואתו תיראו ואת מצותיו תשמרו ובקלו תשמעו ואתו תעבדו ובו תדבקון:

---

* Exodus ix. 14.   § Talm. B. Batra, xvi. 6.   ‖ Deut. xiii. 5.

PRAYER.

O Lord! according to Thy word the heaven is Thy throne, and the earth Thy footstool; where can we build a house worthy of Thee, what can we call on earth the place of Thy rest? We must confess Thy greatness, Thine immensity, and our insignificance when compared to Thine omnipotence; no temple can we erect, the splendour of which may even approach Thy splendour, and of which we may say: "there is the resting place of the Divinity;" for a voice directly arises and exclaims: "Behold, heaven, and the heaven of heavens cannot contain Thee, how much less this house which I have built" * הנה השמים ושמי השמים לא יכלכלוך אף כי הבית הזה אשר בניתי: Yet in Thy mercy, Thou art satisfied if we build unto Thee a temple within ourselves. Thou art satisfied if we unclose our eyes and bid them gaze on Thy beautiful works, from the grain of sand to the mountain, from the microscopic insect to the gigantic whale. Thou art satisfied if we open our ears and listen to the harmonious voices which, throughout the universe, constantly sing Thy glory. Thou askest from us nothing more than we can give, nothing more than the heart, for the heart alone can feel the effects of Thy wisdom and power, the heart alone can offer unto Thee the sacrifice which Thou preferrest. O Lord, make it not fat, for then it would be unable to understand; subject it not to hard trials and alluring temptations: if it be soiled, purify it; if it be corrupted, renew it in us. By this means alone we shall be able to know Thee, Thy qualities, and Thine attributes which

* 1 Kings viii. 27.

make Thee the essence of everlasting perfection ; by this means alone, we shall be able truly to serve Thee ; we shall long for Thee, we shall aspire towards Thee. " As the hart panteth after the water-brooks, so panteth my soul after Thee, O Lord : "§ כאיל תערג על אפיקי מים כן נפשי תערג אליך אלהים :

AMEN.

* Psalm xlii. 2.

EDUCATION.

רוּחִי אֲשֶׁר עָלֶיךָ וּדְבָרַי אֲשֶׁר שַׂמְתִּי בְּפִיךָ לֹא יָמוּשׁוּ מִפִּיךָ וּמִפִּי זַרְעֲךָ
וּמִפִּי זֶרַע זַרְעֲךָ אָמַר ה׳ מֵעַתָּה וְעַד עוֹלָם:

"My spirit that is upon thee, and my words which I have put in thy mouth, shall not depart out of thy mouth, nor out of the mouth of thy seed, nor out of the mouth of thy seed's seed, saith the Lord, from henceforth and for ever."
 ISAIAH lix. 21.

דברים שאדם אוכל פירותיהם בעולם הזה המגדל בניו לתלמוד
תורה:

"A man who gives his children a religious education, possesses a capital, the interest of which he begins to enjoy in this world."
 TALMUD SHABBAT, 126.

MY DEAR BRETHREN,—Among the qualities which place the Bible so high in the esteem of all men is this, that the inspired writers never flatter their heroes, never attribute to the greatest among the Hebrews any impossible virtue, never call them infallible. Even Moses, whose five books may be termed his autobiography, related his own greatness, but did not conceal his own short-comings; and when he spoke of the founders of our race, of the Patriarchs, he judged them with equal impartiality. For instance, in the lesson of the Law which we have read this morning, Moses gives us an account of Isaac's family, and of the youth of his two sons.

His picture is truly life-like, and he places before us both sides of the medal, the good and the reprehensible qualities; the simple virtue of Isaac and Rebecca, but also their favoritism, the partiality of the former for Esau, and that of the latter for Jacob * ויאהב יצחק את עשו וכול׳ ורבקה אוהבת את יעקב: He plainly describes the effects of that system of education which made Jacob a wretched wanderer and a servant, and Esau very nearly a murderer. Although the attentive study of the historical part of the Law can be eminently useful, it is not now my intention to examine the Patriarchs' eventful lives. Everything that happened to them seems to have been extraordinary, and directed by the hand of God, whose will was to be fulfilled in its minutest details. But I cannot help referring to modern times, to our actual life, what the Bible says of Isaac and his family. I cannot help thinking of the condition of many children who are allowed to grow up without proper education, or without education at all, and of the miserable existence which will probably be their lot. Contradiction and disagreement between parents concerning the manner in which they are to act towards their offspring, the preference of one parent for this child, the open predilection of the other parent for that child, insignificant but constant acts of partiality and injustice are things of every day's occurrence. They are the remote cause of the discord and unhappiness of many a family, as well as an eloquent proof that domestic education is either defective or thoroughly neglected. Let me therefore deal briefly with "home training," which is of capital importance, and a rigorous precept of Judaism. Let me explain who are to be the workers in this sacred

* Genesis xxv. 28.

cause and the system which they should follow. No subject could be more adapted to the nature of current ideas, since education has now become the general topic, so that it is in the mouth of every orator, and falls from the pen of every writer; in it philanthropists generally seek the themes of their addresses, and tribunes become popular by proclaiming it the imprescriptible right of all classes of citizens.

I.

Education, that especially which parents ought to bestow, has always been the object of all the solicitude of Judaism. We cannot peruse the fundamental laws of the various religions without meeting with frequent exhortation that men should exert themselves for the acquisition of religious science. But it is given more in the form of advice than of precept, and sometimes is very exclusive. In fact the codes of India and Egypt place the study of religion within the reach of no one but the priests. "I am a treasure," says science to the Brahmin, "with the guard of which thou alone art entrusted." "The sacred books are an efficient remedy for all moral diseases," taught the priests of Osiris, but the priests alone knew how to understand those books. "It is not enough to read the precepts of religion," wrote Zoroaster, "but they must be studied, and engraven in man's memory." "Wisdom," asserted Manu, "is the first thing to be learnt, and it consists of the knowledge of the duties prescribed by religion." But the doctrine of Judaism, regarding study and education, is anything but vague and undecided, and its positive, rigorous precepts on that cardinal point are certainly one of the reasons why it contains the con-

ditions of human progress, and why it will in future be the universal religion. While the houses of legislature, as well as the country resound with endless orations and desultory discussions about education and the necessity of making it compulsory, or leaving it voluntary; about ordering religion to be a part of, or to be excluded from, public instruction; Judaism, like Alexander, cuts the Gordian knot and resolutely solves the difficult problem. It makes no distinction between secular and religious education, proclaims instruction a sacred duty, and declares ignorance a sin,—a sin which prevents man from realising his resemblance to the Almighty, since that resemblance results from the education and elevation of the heart, and the development of the precious faculties of the intellect. The Hebrews were suffering under the Egyptian yoke, and all their thoughts and hopes were directed towards the announced deliverance. Yet, even before demanding obedience to His commandments, even before ordering them to bind His words upon their hands, and to place them as frontlets between their eyes, the Lord said: "And thou shalt show thy son" : והגדת לבנך *
By these simple words He laid the foundation of the great law of education. The immortal Lawgiver seemed as anxious to impose gratitude towards God upon the Hebrews as to urge on them the task of narrating the divine graciousness to future generations. He thus taught how dependent these two duties are upon each other. When in the last month of his life he repeated the contents of the Law to the assembled nation, and laid stress upon the great vision of Sinai, the covenant between God and man, he entreated the Hebrews never to grow

---

* Exodus xiii. 8.

indifferent to the marvellous events which they had witnessed; and he pointed out to them, as the only way of averting that evil, the care of revealing those wonders unto their children. "Only take heed to thyself, and keep thy soul diligently, lest thou forget the things which thine eyes have seen, and lest they depart from thy heart all the days of thy life, but teach them thy sons and thy sons' sons."* והודעתם לבניך ולבני בניך Thus home education was unmistakably provided for. But Moses referred with equal clearness to public education, to the education of the people, when he commanded that "at the end of every seven years, in the solemnity of the year of release, in the feast of tabernacles, when all Israel is come to appear before the Lord in the place which He shall choose, this Law shall be read before all Israel in their hearing"§ תקרא את התורה הזאת באזניהם: The year of repose from agricultural labour was to be given to the cultivation of the mind, the spiritual soil. The sages of tradition, faithful to the spirit of the written Law, were not content with recommending only, but they rigorously prescribed that "it is a duty for a man to give his son instruction"|| חייב אדם ללמד בנו תורה: And the fulfilment of that duty must begin early in the child's life. "As soon as he can speak, his father must initiate him to the study of the Law"¶ קטן היודע לדבר אביו חייב ללמדו תורה: This education, which is so urgently demanded, and in which the secular and the religious element must be thoroughly blended together, is to consist of something much higher than those insignificant and often little understood recitations which materialism generally suggests. It takes every

---

* Deuteronomy iv. 9. § Deuteronomy xxxi. 10, 11.
|| Talmud Kidushin, 29. ¶ Talmud, Baba Batra, 14.

SERMON XIII.

opportunity of teaching what God is, shews Him in His works and the phenomena of nature, and knows how to infuse into the heart of the child the idea of duty, justice, and charity, but simply, comprehensibly, causing him to find in himself the application of every lesson. Moses instituted no schools; therefore he meant that this work should be done at home, and by those who have given life to the tender beings. Wise and affectionate parents consider that work a labour of love, while it is called intolerably heavy by mercenaries, and often remains barren of good results in their hands. Every moment, every indifferent circumstance in life affords opportunity for the best lessons, to those parents who are willing to make use of it. And when the child is grown, when his mind is prepared and his heart formed by the affectionate teachings of his parents who, by means of simple and familiar conversation, have been able to give instruction, while they divested it of that solemnity which so often frightens a young mind; then the time has come to speak of Judaism, a religion all simplicity and without mystery. The idea of one God, invisible yet as loving as a parent, will appear almost clear to the mind of the boy and take root in his heart. Our excellent moral principles will seem a matter of course to the child who is generously disposed by nature, and our touching ceremonies will make a profound impression upon him. The natural consequence of the strictness of this precept is the responsibility which weighs as a heavy burden on the shoulders of Jewish parents, and which they can shake off only when they have given their children a religious and moral education, when they have trained them "in the way they should go"* חנך לנער על פי דרכו: The same law of

* Proverbs xxii. 6.

responsibility was imposed by Lycurgus upon the Lacedemonians, when he enacted that parents should be punished for the crimes of their children who would not have abandoned the path of honesty if they had been carefully educated.

II.

The authority of a father over all his family was great and sometimes excessive among all ancient nations. But while there were peoples, like the Romans, who gave to the father the power of life and death over his children, the Hebrews, guided by the wisdom of the laws of Moses, limited paternal authority as regarded punishment, and made it absolute only when education was concerned. It was such power as could never degenerate into cruelty, it was an authority sanctified both by its cause and its effect. A father had, and has still among the Hebrews, a noble and holy mission. Other creeds declared that the priest alone is the mediator between the family and God. Judaism gave that responsible office to the father, and entrusted him with the duty of performing the most solemn acts: of carrying out the rites of the home worship, of introducing his sons into the covenant of Abraham, or of naming the man who was to act in his name, of blessing the union of his children with the partners their heart had chosen, of confirming or dissolving the vows of his wife and his children under age, of blessing God before the meals, and of thanking Him after the enjoyment of His gracious favors, of consecrating the festivals, of bestowing when on his death bed such benedictions as were considered to come from divine inspiration. And is it not natural and consistent that a father who has so many great duties to fulfil, and is in a certain manner responsible for the religious and moral obligations of his own children, should be urged to teach them such obligations, and held accountable for their education ?

And of what is this education to consist? Should it be only religious, or should it be composed of various elements? There is the Mosaic Law; consult it, and it will answer on this great point, just as it pronounces on every question concerning man's threefold duty, towards God, his neighbours, and himself. It teaches both religion and morals; it sanctions both civil and criminal ordinances, and legislates on material as well as on spiritual purity; and all these lessons on the knowledge of God and man, of heaven and earth are beautifully combined and made still more forcible by the frequent addition of narrations which are their application. Therefore, during many a century the Law was the only text-book of Jewish instruction, and never proved insufficient, for, as our sages teach, it contains all necessary knowledge. "Investigate the law in every sense, study it in all its aspects, for everything is therein; it alone can give thee understanding; spend thy life in meditating on it, never withdraw from it, for thou canst not find a better employment of thy time"* הפך בה והפך בה דכלה בה ובה תחזה וסיב ובלה בה מנה לא תזוז שאין לך מדה טובה הימנה: The union of what is earthly and what is heavenly ought therefore, to be the leading principle of Jewish education in general, but especially of that which is given at home by the tenderest teachers, the parents, who have the power, without seeming to do so, of conveying the soundest instruction. For children's curiosity is quickly excited even

* Talmud Abot, v. 25.

by indifferent things; and a broad path is thus opened before a good father who understands the sanctity of his mission; he can easily give a lesson on science, and at the same time on religion and morals.—A French nobleman, whose only means of escape from becoming the victim of the terrible and sweeping Revolution of 1789 was to retire for five years, with his wife and children, into a savage and mountainous district of eastern France, relates that his forced and long abode in that inhospitable country had its good side, for it allowed him to educate his children. And how? He had no teachers, no books, no accommodations. But he had something better—he had the great book of nature and its treasures open before him; the blue vault of the heavens and a cloudy sky, the sun and the stars, the moon and the planets, the rain and the snow, the storm and the rainbow, a firefly and a lizard, the wild plant of the forest and the stalactite of the cavern were his excellent materials and the faultless text-book which he successfully employed, and by which he made his children both well read and religious.—Even without the pressure of revolutions, the same mode of training can be efficiently adopted with children, and Moses probably thought of it when he wrote those remarkable words, whose importance we feel so deeply that we repeat them three times a day ושננתם לבניך ודברת בם בשבתך בביתך ובלכתך בדרך ובשכבך ובקומך:* "And thou shalt teach them diligently unto thy children, and thou shalt talk of them when thou sittest in thine house, and when thou walkest by the way, and when thou liest down, and when thou risest up." No circumstance, no condition in life can exempt a man from this duty. Early in the morning, this paternal mission must

* Deuteronomy vi. 7.

begin, and late in the evening it must still go on; at all times, at the occurrence of either joyous or sad events, a good father can open his children's heart to the knowledge of the Creator and give them, as it were, two lives—the bodily and material, the intellectual and spiritual. Tradition lays stress on that mission, in still stronger terms in order to secure its fulfilment. "He," say our sages, "who teaches his son the Divine law, is held to have himself obtained it from Sinai"* כל המלמד בנו תורה מעלה עליו הכתוב כאילו קיבלה מהר סיני: "A doctor," continues the Talmud, relating a simple but significant anecdote, "one morning met one of his friends, an illustrious sage, who, with his head scarcely covered, was taking his son to school in a great hurry. 'Why,' he said, 'why such haste? Why are you hardly dressed?' 'Why? Because to procure instruction for our children ought to be our first and all-absorbing care.' After that time the doctor never ate anything in the morning before having zealously taught his son." Another sage would not touch any food till he had taken his children to school : לא טעים אומצא עד דמייתי לינוקא לבית מדרשא

III.

But is the father to work alone, to be unassisted in his sacred but difficult task? Which is the divine law which teaches and upholds this principle? It may have been one of the erroneous doctrines of those nations which, when not employing woman as an instrument of pleasure or reproduction, put her contemptuously aside as though she were a useless being. But these neither were, nor are, the opinions of the Hebrews. It is a law

* Talmud Kidushin, 30.

of nature that the mother should be the first to feed her children. And it is equally a law of nature, which no legislator deemed it necessary to mention, that the mother should give her children the first ideas of knowledge. From her the child learns to lisp his first words, to utter his thoughts, the name of his father, the name of the Creator; from her he learns to join his little hands, and to whisper his first prayer to the Father of mercy; and his intellect is first prepared by her exertions for the observance of duty and the practice ot virtue. This is the law of nature and reason; and our religion, which has never opposed either reason or nature, though it often appeals to the father, does not forget to remind the mother of her moral duties; but it speaks of them as of an understood and already accepted obligation. When it rigorously commands men to honor their mother, can it refer only to the fact that she brings forth the children? But has woman more merit for the reproduction of her species than the animals for the continuation of theirs? When the wise king said: "My son, forsake not the law of thy mother," * ואל תטוש תורת אמך did he not imply that a mother must teach her children? When he asserted that a foolish son is the heaviness of his mother," § did he not mean that a mother who neglects the education of her offspring, does a great harm and will have to grieve for it? When he wrote: "The words of king Lemuel, the prophecy that his mother taught him," ‖ משא אשר יסרתו אמו did he not remind us that a mother can sometimes awaken the intellect of her sons to the highest religious meditation? Tradition, in its turn, employing an expressive oriental image, said that the *butter* of the Law is made out of

* Proverbs vi. 20. § Ibid x. 1. ‖ Ibid. xxxi. 1.

the *milk* of a mother's breast; and it meant that the observance of the Law can be most efficiently taught by early education, and that the religious life of a man depends entirely on the seed that his mother sowed in his heart when he was a child. It has been said that before he is two years old, a child has acquired more knowledge about external things and himself than he can acquire during the rest of his life; and who, during that period, has any control over, or takes care of, the child, but the mother? In fact, we read that the pious Hannah, having weaned her son, took him to the house of the Lord in Shiloh: "and the child was young"* ותעלהו עמה כאשר גמלתו וכול׳ ותביאהו בית ה׳ שלו והנער נער: Can we believe that Hannah took Samuel, when still a baby, to the temple? It is not probable, since the Bible uses the words: והנער נער "*and the child was young,*" which seems to indicate a grown up boy. Our sages teach, therefore, that Samuel had already passed "from childhood to boyhood" והנער נעשה נער שנעתק מן הילדות אל הנערות: This proves that the good and happy mother gave her son moral as well as material nourishment, that she had taught him as much as his tender mind could grasp, that she had prepared him for the great work which she felt he would have to achieve among his people.— An illustrious lady, celebrated for her skill in giving, and for her writings upon, education—the governess of the unfortunate children of Louis XVI.—was asked by Napoleon I. what, according to her opinion, was necessary in order to improve the condition of education, and she answered one word only—*mothers.*—That word conveys the noblest ideas, and is in itself a whole system of education. As long as

* 1 Samuel i. 24.

this system is not followed, the best education at school will always prove inefficient; for, as the poet rightly said, "Just as the twig is bent, the tree's inclined.* The nature of children is such that they never can overcome the impressions which they have received and which, whether good or bad, are indelible. The further instruction imparted to them can seldom modify those impressions; and if, through the mother's fault, these are opposed to wisdom and honesty, who but she will have been the cause of her children's misconduct or folly, and consequently of their misery? A mother, therefore, is not only rigorously bound to contribute to the education of her children, but she is even more responsible for it than the father himself, because she is the beginner in the sacred labour.—A sad event is related of a mother, who was left alone to take care of her only son and who, unmindful of her noble duty towards him, thoroughly neglected his training. Her culpable carelessness bore its bitter fruits. Left almost to himself, the boy spent his early years in idleness, and his mother was lenient to him; he contracted vicious habits in his youth, and his mother forgave him. The limit between disorder and dishonesty, between guilt and crime was narrow, and he overstepped it. The hand of justice fell upon him with all its weight, and he was condemned to die a violent death. His mother, whose torturing remorse came too late, followed him, at his request, on his way to execution; and approached him to hear the last word which he had asked to whisper to her. Then he bit her ear till it bled, and said: "You, mother, you alone by your leniency, by your neglect, have brought me to this frightful and untimely end!"—Un-

* Pope.

fortunately, that which gave rise to this tragic occurrence happens, although it may appear strange and almost incredible, oftener than it is believed. Is a bird satisfied with feeding its young? Does it allow them to abandon their nest before they are provided with their garment of feathers? Instinct teaches that innocent animal to perform a double duty towards its offspring, and ought reason to be incapable of doing what instinct suggests? Ought a human being, with all her softness of heart, to neglect to do on behalf of her children what irrational creatures perform so well towards theirs? A mother, who thinks that she has fulfilled all her duty because she has given life to creatures formed in God's image, loves her offspring less than a tiger loves its own. She is mistaken if she believes that she has thus enjoyed all the pleasures of maternity. She willingly exerts herself, in order to clothe her children's physical form; but she ought to think that there is another nudity, against which she ought to shield them, another nudity which exposes their tender being to worse dangers than severe cold or tropical heat. The nudity of their soul is as perilous as that of their body, and their spiritual garment ought to be prepared with as much solicitude as their material clothing. The wise woman of king Solomon "rises also when it is yet night, and giveth meat to her household and a portion to her maidens"* ותקם בעוד לילה ותתן טרף לביתה וחק לנערתיה: These words probably symbolize the early education which a good mother bestows upon her children; that education which will in time fill their heart with love, respect and veneration for her, and force them to bless her as long as their hearts beat, as long

* Proverbs xxxi. 15.

as their minds think. The children, whose mother gave them the treasure of early education, will never, never have to apply to themselves the sad words of the Prophet : " Woe is me, my mother, that thou hast borne me a man of strife, and a man of contention to the whole earth, etc.; every one of them doth curse me "* אוי לי אמי כי ילדתני איש ריב ואיש מדון לכל הארץ וכולי כלה מקללני: O parents, remember that you ought to be for your children what the Lord is for the universe. He created it and preserves it with equal solicitude by laws of wisdom and love. You have given life to your children and you ought to be their preservers according to the example of God, by preventing the order and harmony of their existence from being disturbed. Nothing on the earth could give you a joy as great as that which you felt when your dear ones lisped your name for the first time. In that sweet voice, however, you ought to have recognised a blessing and a prayer. The blessing of the created being to the author of his life, a prayer by which the new spirit destined to immortality asks to be shown the path of light and of truth. Our sages teach that "if the partners of life are equal to their mission, God will dwell between them; otherwise fire will devour them "§ איש ואשה זכו שכינה ביניהם לא זכו אש אוכלתן: This is a solemn warning to fathers and mothers who will certainly delight in the visible protection of the Almighty, on the condition only that they so train their children as to make them His true worshippers, as to make them that manly race, that *seed of men*, to obtain whom Hannah prayed so fervently unto the Lord ‖ ונתת לאמתך זרע אנשים: On the other hand, the anguish of parents when they see the bitter results

* Jeremiah xv. 10.   § Talmud Sotah, 17.   ‖ 1 Samuel i. x.

of their neglect, can only be compared to a destructive fire, which nothing can extinguish.

But that education cannot be successful unless it is both tender and strong, without weakness and error. It cannot attain its noble aim unless the parents agree with each other in the system to be followed, in the means to be employed, unless they support each other's authority, second each other's advice, and show to the child that to disobey and grieve the one is to disobey and grieve both. That education cannot prosper unless the same care is taken of all the children without distinction, without partiality. Woe to those families in which the father, like Isaac, prefers one son for his physical power, and the mother, like Rebecca, loves another son for his gentler nature. Esau's implacable hatred, Jacob's eventful life, the grief of their parents should constantly be before the eyes of father and mother as a proof that favoritism is unjust and certainly disastrous. That education, thirdly, cannot be efficient unless the lessons are strengthened by example, unless the parents are the first to practise what they exhort their children to do. Their offspring will be sober, honest, charitable, religious, if they exhibit the example of sobriety, honesty, charity and religion. Parents cannot, in spite of their recommendations, hope to see their children become fond of concord and peace, of decency and reserve, if they make their homes the theatre of scandalous quarrels, if they indulge in scurrilous conversation and impure habits. "Just as the sheep follows the sheep," say our sages, "so the actions of the daughter are like the mother's actions" רחילא בתר רחילא אזלא כעובדי אמה כך עובדי ברתא:* "The prattle of children in the streets

* Talmud Ketubot, 63.

EDUCATION.

is the repetition of what either their father or their mother has said."* שותא דינוקא בשוקא או דאבא או דאימיה:

My brethren, by the careful education of your children, you will powerfully contribute to the progress of society, and at the same time preserve the traditions of our race; you will prevent the words of God from departing "out of their mouth, out of the mouth of their seed, or out of the mouth of their seed's seed." You will do good to man and serve God. Your children, whose guardian angels you will have thus been and in whose hearts you will have engraven the principles of what is good and true, will be blessed and fruitful plants; they will be "like a tree planted by the rivers of water, that bringeth forth his fruit in his season; his leaf also shall not wither, and whatsoever he doeth shall prosper."§ Evil advice will not mislead them, nor will evil example corrupt them; the sneer of the scoffer will not echo in their heart. Their happiness will be the immediate consequence of the sacred knowledge with which you will have enriched their minds: וכל בניך למודי ה' ורב שלום בניך "And all thy children shall be taught of the Lord, and great shall be the peace of thy children."‖ You will bless the Lord for the children whom He has given you, for you will have made them worthy of their heavenly Father. You will be proud of your work, and happy in its result, or, as the Talmud teaches, "you will enjoy in this world the interest of a great capital which you will inherit in a future life." In the overwhelming delight of your heart, while looking at your virtuous and

---

* Talmud Succah, 56. § Psalm i. 3.

‖ Isaiah liv. 13.

prosperous children, you will say with the prophet, "This is the branch of my planting, the work of my hand that I may be glorified"* נצר מטעי מעשה ידי להתפאר:

* Isaiah lx. 21.

AMEN.

ISRAEL'S CHARACTERISTICS.*

ואתן צאני צאן מרעיתי אדם אתם אני אלהיכם נאם ה׳ אלהים :

"And ye, my flock, the flock of my pasture, are men, and I am your God, saith the Lord God." EZEKIEL xxxiv. 31.

מה הצאן מחפררת והרועה מכנסה כך ישראל במדבר היו בוכים ומתרעמים בכל שעה ואע״פכ לא נסתלקה מהם שכינה אלא ניהגם כצאן :

"Just as the sheep go easily astray, and the shepherd gathereth them, so Israel often revolted against the Lord; yet He never withdrew His presence from them, and was at all times their affectionate guide." YALKUT ON THE PROPHETS, ccclxxiii.

MY DEAR BRETHREN,—The imagination of oriental poets is inexhaustibly rich. It is as exuberant as the flora of Palestine and as the forests of India. Their expressions are, like oriental garments, adorned, as it were, with brilliant colours. But it is the privilege of the language of the Bible, more than any other Semitic language, to penetrate deeply into the human heart; for it borrows its power from sentiment more than from fiction, and seeks its parables, not in unmeasured flights of the fancy, but in the simple charms of nature. The hardi-

* This sermon was delivered by the Author, by special invitation, in the Bayswater Synagogue, which is not under his religious care. He willingly complies with numerous requests, and inserts it in the present series, as a token of grateful remembrance of the cordial reception which was offered him on that occasion.

hood of its pictures is great, yet it never wounds the purest and most delicate taste. Among its most beautiful images are those which represent Israel. As a nation, Israel is compared sometimes with the lily among thorns, or with the fruitful apple-tree among the unproductive plants of the wood, and sometimes with the sweet date, or with the ever green olive which does not exhibit all its worth until it has been hardly pressed. He is at times likened to a happy bride, or to a divorced wife, or to a distressed widow. But the image which is most used and best adapted of all, is that in which Israel is compared with a timid lamb, or with a numerous flock whose shepherd is above all shepherds, and never fails in His mission of kindness and tender care. On this day thirty-two centuries ago, the Hebrews, about to be delivered, prepared for ·their first sacrifice and set aside the Paschal lamb. The Egyptians were mad with rage at the sight of what they called sacrilege, for their god was thus destined to be slaughtered; but agitated by a mysterious terror, they dared not to utter one hostile word. That is the reason why this is called the *great Sabbath,* שבת הגדול. On this significant day I ought, as is customary among the preachers of our nation, to speak of that memorable sacrifice, and to explain by it how we can worthily celebrate our Passover. Yet if I do not make the lamb the subject of my brief discourse, I shall nevertheless incidentally dwell upon it, for it is my intention to describe the three characteristics of Israel, which are clearly pointed out to us by the three distinctive traits of the lamb, to which Israel has justly been likened. Though concisely treated, such a subject will be replete with numerous and most timely lessons.—Yet before I commence, I

ISRAEL'S CHARACTERISTICS.

cannot help expressing the hesitation I feel in speaking for the first time before this congregation. I am told that you listen every Sabbath to eloquent language, and I fear lest I may fall into idiomatic incorrectness or into defective pronunciation, for I cannot forget that I am a foreigner. But I know that in the Law often expounded to you, is written, "Love ye therefore the stranger, for ye were strangers in the land of Egypt"[*] ואהבתם את הגר כי גרים הייתם בארץ מצרים: As a stranger I am entitled to entreat you to bestow your love upon me, in the shape of kind indulgence.

I.

The lamb has been at all times accepted as the symbol of meekness, timidity, innocence and weakness. This is the first characteristic which the lamb has derived from its own nature. But can its meekness be the means of its preservation? Look up. See how many beautiful birds fly about and charm inanimate nature with their song. They are timid, weak, harmless. But that does not protect them. See the falcon and the royal eagle which as rapidly as lightning, descend from the highest regions of the air, and make a frightful havoc among the innocent songsters. So the lamb is not protected by its weakness; it is, on the contrary, the more easily made the object of the attacks of wild beasts.—And is not Israel, in that respect, like the lamb? Is there a nation which has been more than, or as much as, Israel the victim of implacable hatred and unceasing war? None has lived so long, none has suffered so much as Israel. In the bitterness of his grief, Job described his sufferings with very impressive

[*] Deut. x. 19.

words. He said:* "I was not in safety, neither had I rest, neither was I quiet; yet trouble came" לא שלותי ולא שקטתי ולא נחתי ויבא רגז: And these four expressions of complaint correspond, according to the Talmud, to the four periods of Israel's oppression and martyrdom § לא שלותי בבבל ולא שקטתי במדי ולא נחתי ביון ויבא רגז באדום: *I was not in safety*—this means what the Hebrews had to undergo in Babylon, when after having seen the destruction of their last bulwark and the slaughter of thousands of their brethren, they were led to the land of exile, forced to bow before idols of stone or metal, exposed to the cruel caprices of proud and frantic monarchs, and asked with irony and scorn to sing unto their enemies the songs of the Lord, the hymns of Zion. *Neither had I rest*—this signifies their repeated persecutions under the Persian rule, when the hatred of a minister, and the child-like credulity of a monarch placed them on the verge of destruction, as the people "to suffer whom was not for the king's profit" ǁ ולמלך אין שוה להניחם: *Neither was I quiet*—these words refer to the horrible tortures, to which the successors of Alexander, the Seleucides, and especially Antiochus Epiphanes subjected them without regard to sex or age, slaughtering together brother and sister, burning the mother with her children. And the fourth expression, *Yet trouble came*—relates to the indescribable torments inflicted on our ancestors by the Romans, who, enraged by the heroic resistance of the defenders of Jerusalem and Bithar, indulged in such cruelties as are repugnant to human nature, and as were only rivalled by the tiger of the circus against its unarmed victim.

But why was Israel to be thus exposed like a defence-

* iii. 26.   § Shemot Rabbah, xxvi.   ǁ Esther iii. 8.

less lamb to the fury of his enemies, and to the attacks of all nations, always at war with each other, but united when they were to conspire against his safety? A touching legend, handed down to us by tradition, can convey a satisfactory answer. After the wondrous scene of Revelation, the Hebrews, timid and terrified, said unto Moses: "Thou hast commanded us to live a virtuous life, to practise justice and charity, to love peace and to hate war. We will perform towards all men those duties which the Lord has ordained; but how are we to act towards those who will not do the same to us? If we preserve peace in spite of their attacks, they will call us cowards, our meekness will be termed pusillanimity, they will hold us as despicable because we shall have allowed ourselves to be despised. What arms, then, can we employ? How are we to fight?" Moses answered by this parable: "The timid lamb, soon after its creation, appeared before God and said, 'O Lord, why hast Thou made me so weak? How can I live in the midst of ferocious animals? Some have trunks, others horns, these have claws, and those have formidable teeth; am I to remain quite defenceless, and to labor under unceasing anxiety?' The Lord said: 'Wishest thou for horns? Thou wilt thus be able to wound thine enemies.' 'No,' said the lamb, 'for I wish to wound no one.' 'Wishest thou for a large mouth armed with sharp teeth? Thou wilt be able to devour thy neighbours.' 'No, O Lord, for I wish to remain in peace with my neighbours.' 'Wishest thou for claws or for trunks? Thou wilt surely be able to fight, and to avert all danger.' 'No, O Lord, because it is my desire to have no enemies.' 'Then, what dost thou ask for?' 'I ask for defence against those who would hurt me.' 'I understand,' said the Lord;

'I will give thee mildness as a shield and patience as a sword.' Children of Israel, said Moses, you have been selected to be the depositaries of the Law of God, and you complain of being unarmed among the nations which may oppress you. 'Will you be as cruel as they are?' 'No, we will not be cruel.' 'Will you be as unjust, jealous, vindictive, bloodthirsty?' 'No, no.' 'What will you have, then?' 'Arms like the lamb's.' 'Your wish must be satisfied,' said the Lord. 'Against those who hurt you, be armed with mildness, and let your virtue be your defence against your oppressors.'" Israel was, in fact, exposed, like the lamb, to the effects of brutal force. When Israel was still a nation and dwelt in his fatherland, he had armies and every means of self-defence; no fault could be found with the nations which, either more fortunate or more powerful, could vanquish him; it was fair fighting. But when he was scattered all over the surface of the earth and deprived of all material power, power of number, of arms and of authority, he ought to have inspired his conquerors with pity; his meekness ought to have softened the dislike of the races in the midst of which he lived; his feebleness ought to have preserved him from attacks which could only be called cowardly, just as cowardly would be the attack of a king on a forlorn pilgrim passing through his dominion. But it was not so; his woeful condition made his enemies bolder and bolder, and his imploring attitude served only to increase their ferocity. All nations were cruel to him, for among all nations intolerance assumed the garb of religious zeal, and extermination was preached in the name of a God of love. Oh, if the walls of prisons could speak, if Toledo and Seville could relate past events how painful, how sorrowful would be their tales!

ISRAEL'S CHARACTERISTICS.

They would say that the words of Isaiah were sadly true, and that Israel "was oppressed and afflicted, yet he opened not his mouth: he is brought as a lamb to the slaughter, and as a sheep before her shearers is dumb, so he openeth not his mouth."* כשה לטבח יובל ובְרחל לפני גוזזיה נאלמה ולא יפתח פיו: Even in the midst of the most piercing tortures, on the stake, even when labouring in the throes of death, Israel never uttered a word of reproach against his executioners, he never cursed his iniquitous and fanatic judges; he died pronouncing the prayer of resignation, and repeating the profession of faith which he had learnt in his childhood.

II.

What is the second characteristic of the lamb? Alas! It is not much to its credit! The lamb is too easily misled. It goes needlessly astray from its fold, stops too near a ravine, or wanders too far into a forest; so that it endangers its life, either by falling or approaching the lion's den.—And this is also the characteristic of Israel. The true cause of his misfortunes is to be found in the facility with which he abandoned the path pointed out to him by religious and moral duty. We have only to open the Book of books, the Bible, and in every page we can see a proof of the obduracy with which Israel broke through the providential laws that might have secured his prosperity and undisturbed peace. "Then I said unto them, Cast ye away every man the abominations of his eyes, and defile not yourselves with the idols of Egypt; I am the Lord your God. But they rebelled against me, and would not hearken unto me" § ואמר אליהם איש שקוצי עיניו השליכו ובגלולי מצרים

* Isaiah liii 7.   § Ezekiel xx. 7, 8.

אל תטמאו אני ה׳ אלהיכם : וימרו בי ולא אבו לשמוע אלי :

Are not the destruction of man's health and premature old age, the natural consequences of vice and profligacy? So it is equally natural that the immorality and corruption of our ancestors should have condemned them to the severest trials. It is really the story repeated over and over again, of the lamb which carelessly loses sight of the shepherd and meets the wolf. But now that experience has taught Israel such hard lessons, has he divested himself of this second characteristic so condemnable and so fatal? Does he now faithfully follow his guide? "Israel," said Jeremiah, almost speaking for the present time, "is a sheep scared away"* שה פזורה ישראל: And as he was, so he is still "the wild ass used to the wilderness, that snuffeth up the wind at her pleasure, in her occasion who can turn her away?"§ The Jew has been truly called a citizen of the world. He adapts himself with marvellous facility to the peculiarities of all climates and countries, like a plant that grows on every soil. But unfortunately he is too much influenced by the opinions that prevail around him. He allows himself too often to be guided by the society which he is eager to enter, he makes his own the prejudices and the failings of the people in whose midst he dwells. So, although there is many an honourable exception, yet, generally speaking, Israel is almost a materialist in the midst of materialists. He is an unbeliever if he lives among rationalists. He is a fanatic in the land of intolerance. He is indifferent where religion is little cared for. He is only superficially religious where bigotry is the predominant sentiment. He is ignorant where civilisation has not yet penetrated.

* Jeremiah l. 17. § Jeremiah ii. 24.

Jeremiah complained that his contemporaries believed in the prophets, who "had seen vain and foolish things for them" * נביאיך חזו לך שוא ותפל: And we see, in the present time, literary men who, in their pride, call themselves prophets, as if they were the bearers of new truths. But in reality they only bring confusion into the minds of men. Their doctrine is destructive and not constructive. It consists in denying the divinity of a precept, or the authenticity of a sacred document; and impugns a long accepted and venerated belief with doubt and suspicion. Yet they have followers. Isaiah rebuked the Hebrews because they bowed to idols of silver and gold. No temple is now openly erected for such a worship. The public adoration of Plutus is now-a-days out of fashion. But our conduct is still worse; for it is in our heart that we build an altar, and that we offer daily supplications to him. We make his gifts the object of our secret aspirations. Thus Israel has allowed himself to be infected by the most contagious disease of the age. Amos preached against those who "sold the righteous for silver, and the poor for a pair of shoes."* על מכרם בכסף צדיק ואביון בעבור נעלים: And dishonest actions are every day done for the sake of gain. The basest callings are exercised by some, the sacred rules of justice are trodden under foot by others, merely for the acquisition of that which seems to endow its possessor with as much, or perhaps more, reputation than real merit can bestow. We see but too frequently in our time those who "sell the righteous for silver, and the poor for a pair of shoes." Our sages repeatedly recommended that we should be responsible for each other, that the ties of brotherhood should bind us

---

* Lamentations ii. 14.   § Amos ii. 6.

together, that mutual friendship should gather, as it were, our scattered families into one fold. But this, a precept of vital importance, is only partially complied with. Our benevolence for each other is, indeed, unbounded; but the absolute equality which existed among the Hebrews assembled at the foot of Sinai has almost disappeared. We are divided into different classes, alas! separated from one another by an impassable barrier, the barrier of pride. Our long history offers the spectacle of the torments which were brought upon our race, not only through its weakness but also through its inconstancy and levity. But are we sure, if we follow the same line of conduct, that we shall not have our own trials? Are we sure that the present delightful breeze will not turn into a fiery and destructive blast? O Israelites of modern times, reflect that it is but recently we have been made free, that a few years ago we were still kept within an iron circle of exceptional and degrading laws, and that many of our brethren are even now, in some countries, denied the rights of man. We ought not already to forget the hand which has rescued us, and raised us to an unhoped for height of prosperity and power.

III.

Happily, however, Israel is also endowed with the third characteristic of the lamb, which is in him a really redeeming feature. Look in that field. The shepherd is alone. His flock is scattered on the plain, and many sheep are even out of sight. Yet the shepherd is not uneasy, for he will sustain no loss. Hear, the wonted bell rings, the well known whistle echoes in the forest and on the hill, and the wanderers hasten back and assemble behind their leader. Happily, I repeat, Israel is in this also like the lamb. He comes back at the solemn call of his guide; and this is the secret of his wonderful preservation through so many centuries. Israel may have fallen low; but he has never fallen so low as not to be able to rise again. Yielding to the suggestions of intemperance, he may, so to say, have exhibited the miserable spectacle of intoxication; then he was called, and did not answer; he was shaken, and did not awake. But at last the Lord's voice roused him from his slumber. Then he rose and looked around surprised, ashamed of his long excesses. But when the last effects of inebriety were shaken off, he was again Israel, the Israel of old, the people devoted to God, faithful to the sublime principles of monotheism, the teacher of mankind. "It is true, I am black," says the daughter of Zion to the other nations, in the words of the Song of songs, "I am black, but I am comely" * שחורה אני ונאוה Look at me, my sisters, I am black, I have lost the brilliancy of my complexion under the influence of a burning sun, yet I have not lost all my charms, I am still comely. I have stained myself by my wild conduct and I bear the mark of reprobation. But the intemperance of my youth has not destroyed the seed of virtue which I had received within my heart. I am as black as you through my actions, for I have, like you, exalted immorality and materialised religion. Yet I am comely, because the knowledge of God, the fear and love of Him have never abandoned me thoroughly, and from them I shall derive my complete restoration to my former nobility and imprescriptible rights שחורה אני ונאוה

* Solomon's Song, i. 5.

בנות ירושלים: See the extraordinary effect of our Penitential festivals. The mystical trumpet, the Shofar, resounds, and all Israel, even those who live far away from the house of God, even those whose religion is only in their Jewish name, answer the sacred appeal. They remember their infancy and the first lesson of their mother; they remember the dying words of their father and the earnest promise of their own hearts. And when religion says unto them through the prophet, "Return, ye backsliding children, and I will heal your backslidings;" they unconsciously answer: "Behold, we come unto thee, for thou art the Lord our God"*
שובו בנים שובבים ארפא משובתיכם הננו אתנו לך כי אתה ה' אלהינו: They are truly the wandering sheep which return again to the protecting but neglected fold. Some are thoroughly regenerated by changing their heart from enmity to the love of God; some actually enter the path of sincere repentance; and others sow such seed of reparation as will in time produce fruit of consolation and unmistakable blessing.

These are our three characteristics, the first of which is, if we may say so, our destiny; the second, our fault; the third, our merit. Let us not deplore our weakness, although it has been the cause of many of our miseries. Let us not renounce our meekness, although it may expose us to the violence of the mighty. Let it always be our glory to set before our enemies the example of mild and generous feelings. It is against the second characteristic that we ought to guard ourselves. We ought not to go astray from our fold. We ought to be steady in our religious principles. Our true greatness is proportionate to our fidelity to the noble Mosaic

* Jeremiah iii. 22.

creed. If we disregard it, or if we neglect its practical laws, then, however high our social position may be, we forfeit the respect to which we are entitled as the children of the chosen people and as the members of the most ancient race. But if unable to control our propensities, we follow the example of the lamb, and turn our back to our good shepherd; then, oh then, let us fully exercise our third characteristic which is our treasure and the most precious jewel of our crown. Let us promptly answer the Lord's appeal and return as soon as we are called. Then we shall be unto the Lord not only His flock, but the flock of His predilection. Then both trunks and horns, both claws and teeth will be impotent against us, and the day will dawn when the lion will not be able to devour the meek and timid lamb. For these are the words of the Lord: "I will feed them in a good pasture, and upon the high mountains of Israel shall their fold be: there shall they lie in a good fold, and in a fat pasture shall they feed upon the mountains of Israel. I will feed my flock, and I will cause them to lie down, saith the Lord God"*

אני ארעה צאני ואני ארביצם נאם ה' אלהים :

PRAYER.

Almighty God! Thine is the greatness, and the power, and the glory, and the victory, and the majesty: for all that is in the heaven and in the earth is Thine; Thine is the kingdom, O Lord, and Thou art exalted as Head above all. Unto Thee who disposest of good and evil, of life and death, I earnestly raise my supplication in behalf of this holy community; and I entreat Thee

* Ezekiel xxxiv. 14-15.

to keep it in Thy mercy and under Thy safeguard, to shield it from misfortune and to grace it with prosperity. O bless its ministers and inspire them with conscientious zeal; warm their heart with well-understood ardor, give them the power of persuading and convincing, and may the words of their lips be always words of truth and conciliation, words of science and morality, words of praise to Thy holy Name and Thy eternal law. Bless the wardens and the directors of this congregation. Fill them with that religious energy which secures success, so that they may prosperously carry out their communal undertakings. Inspire them with true disinterestedness, so that no party spirit may ever exercise any influence over them, and their aim may be sincerely pious לשם שמים: Bless, O Lord, the schools and charities connected with this congregation, and let them be successful, so that the two kinds of poverty which most oppress mankind, the poverty of the body and the poverty of the mind may be removed by efficient remedies: benevolence and instruction. Bless, O Lord, the faithful who meet in this sacred place and show by their constant attendance their attachment to Divine worship, their fidelity to Judaism. Preserve in them these excellent qualities, but above all, never let concord be banished from among them, for there cannot be real prosperity and joy, where the hideous presence of disunion and conflict is known. Bless them all, men and women, old and young; bless the growing generation, this promising branch of a healthy tree, this hope of Judaism. Bless finally this sacred temple, and let it be the place in which all hearts are united in love and all lips are joined in prayer. For if Israel preserves the virtues which distinguished him in the past, if he obeys his religion, if he does honour to his name before the other nations by exemplary deeds, then, as we have read this morning in Malachi, "shall the offering of Judah and Jerusalem be pleasant unto the Lord, as in the days of old, as in former years" * וערבה לה׳ מנחת יהודה וירושלים כימי עולם וכשנים קדמניות :

AMEN.

* Malachi iii. 4.

THE ILLNESS OF
THE PRINCE OF WALES.

כי לא שאול תודך מות יהללך לא ישברו יורדי בור אל אמתך : חי
חי הוא יודך כמני היום אב לבנים יודיע אל אמתך :

"For the grave cannot praise Thee, death cannot celebrate Thee; they that go down into the pit cannot hope for Thy truth. The living, the living he shall praise Thee, as I do this day: the father to the children shall make known Thy truth."

ISAIAH xxxviii. 18, 19.

ן בעי רחמי עלייהו ואיתסי :

"He raised prayers unto God for them, and they recovered."

TALMUD HAGIGAH, 3.

IN one of the graceful and touching prayers that the inspired genius of David raised to the Almighty, these significant words are prominent: "For we are strangers before Thee, and sojourners as were all our fathers; our days on the earth are as a shadow, and there is none abiding."* כי גרים אנחנו לפניך ותושבים ככל אבותינו כצל ימינו על הארץ ואין מקוה : These words of the royal poet convey to us a true, although somewhat gloomy, idea of our condition on the earth. We are not inhabitants upon the earth, we are simply sojourners; that is, temporary residents. We are travellers, and halt here for awhile on our journey. Our earthly days are like a shadow, and there is none abiding. We ought to form no hope on what remains for so brief a space in our

* 1 Chronicles xxix. 15.

power, and passes so rapidly away from us. Here we have nothing but a constant alternation of prosperity and misfortunes, of pleasures and sorrows; nothing but an interminable struggle between truth and error, vice and virtue; we are always tormented by doubt and fear, seldom gladdened by a gleam of hope, and when we see at a distance some coming prosperity, when we think that we have reached the peaceful state towards which we had eagerly aspired, then illness, preceded by its painful forerunners, and accompanied by its hard struggles, its mournful retinue, throws itself upon us as a wild beast upon its prey. Then we feel our nothingness, however great our social station may be; then we become dependent; and yet just then a voice echoes in our heart and tells us: "Pray, pray, the Lord is nigh unto those who suffer." "This poor man cried, and the Lord heard him, and saved him out of all his troubles."*

זה עני קרא וה' שמע ומכל צרותיו הושיעו :

Prayer is the act by which we feel and admit our impotence, while at the same time we acknowledge a Supreme Being to whom unlimited power belongs. By prayer we confess the bitterness of our sufferings, the difficulty of finding relief, and the unwillingness or incapacity of our fellow-creatures to succour us; but we confess, at the same time, that all hope is not gone, for we have a friend above who, if it is consistent with His will and our deserts, can help us and break to pieces the fetters of our misfortunes. Prayer is unto man both a remedy and a consolation; it achieves wonders; it lessens all sorrows and heals all wounds; it gives courage to the timid, strength to the weak, light to the blind; it supports those that are vacillating, and raises those that have fallen; it is the heavenly bread which feeds and

* Psalm xxxiv. 6.

delights our soul; it places man in direct intercourse with his Creator, and purifies him by causing him to breathe the atmosphere of spiritual regions. And prayer works wonders when it is listened to; it recalls to life those who are placed in the greatest danger; it restores to existence those for whom all human powers had declared themselves impotent. So we see Hezekiah, stricken by a fatal disease, in the midst of health, prosperity and glory, and solemnly warned by the prophet to set his house in order, for he was to die"* צו לביתך כי מת אתה: Then he turned his face towards the wall and prayed; his supplication was listened to, God saw his tears, healed him, and added fifteen years unto his days. We see the terrified Jonah, who had been swallowed up in that dreadful cavern—the bowels of a monstrous whale, on the mouth of which surely was written "Abandon all hope, ye who enter." No possible safety could there have been for him, but he prayed fervently, and his wonderful rescue became a fact; he was ejected safe and unhurt, far from the voracious animal and the voracious sea. Who could have been in more fearful danger than the three noble companions of exile and misfortune—Hananiah, Mishael and Azariah, when they were cast into the burning fiery furnace? Or than Daniel, when he was thrown into the den of lions? When did the flames ever abandon their victims? When did the hungry beasts spare the man fallen under their claws? When? When the ardent prayer of the sufferers went up to the throne of the Lord, and whenever merciful Providence pronounced the consoling words, I pardon, I will rescue: כי אתך אני נאם ה׳ להצילך "For I am with thee, says the Lord, to rescue thee."

* Isaiah xxxviii. 1. § Jeremiah i. 19.

ILLNESS OF THE PRINCE OF WALES.

But, my brethren, is it necessary to go so far back in history, in order to see the terrible ravages to which illness subjects mortal creatures, the deplorable state into which it throws them? Need we consult the events of past generations, in order to see the noble effects of fervent prayer, the wonderful results of Divine mercy? Only a few days ago, the hearts of millions of human beings in this noble country were labouring under alarm, dismay and unconquerable anxiety. A great gloom hung over cities and villages, over palaces and huts, over the houses of prayer and the dwellings of pleasure, when the sad rumour reached us that a noble life was in danger, that the beloved first-born son of our sovereign was in a perilous condition, and that "there was but a step between *him* and death."* כי כפשע ביני ובין המות:

Oh! nothing is more sorrowful than to see a flower beaten down by the storm before it has run its short career, or a promising tree struck by the lightning before its full development, before it could delight by its shade, or nourish by its fruit! And how could a loyal nation have refrained from grief at seeing its future ruler assailed by a pitiless disease? So young, he was reduced to the impotency of a decaying old man; formerly strong, he became so weak that he could scarcely raise his hand to greet his august mother. Formerly handsome, his face was covered with deadly pallor, his features were distorted; formerly vigorous, he fell into extreme prostration. He might have applied to himself the prophet's words: כי כלו בעשן ימי ועצמותי כמוקד נחרו: לבי סחרחר עזבני כחי ואור עיני גם הם אין אתי: "For my days are consumed like smoke, and

---

* 1 Samuel xx. 3.

my bones are burning as an hearth."* " My heart panteth, my strength faileth me ; as for the light of mine eyes, it also is gone from me." § And paroxysm succeeded paroxysm ; paroxysms of suffocation that threatened to cut the small thread which still kept the soul united to the body; and sleepless nights followed sleepless days, so that all hope seemed entirely gone ; and the members of the Royal Family were summoned around the Prince, his august mother who would surely have offered her crown for the life of her child, and the Princess, so noble in her devotion, in her indefatigable watch, and who anxiously looked from the face of the struggling patient to the face of the ministers of science, silently imploring from them an answer which she dreaded to hear. Oh ! it was heart-rending, heart-rending to those who know what it is to see a beloved relation, a wife, a parent, a child, a brother struggle with death, and sink, and sink, while in spite of their love they can do nothing for their dearest and nearest.

In that supreme moment all hearts were open to fervour, all lips to prayer; and in the synagogue, the church, the temple, the mosque, the pagoda, by those who, while praying, keep the quiet, composed attitude of devotion, by those who kneel, by those who beat their breast, and by those who stretch themselves on the ground, one word was pronounced, one wish was formed, one supplication was raised to heaven, and was set forth before God as incense. The Lord listened to that sincere prayer, equivalent to the richest sacrifices; and surely through the heavens must have sounded the words of consolation that we read in Isaiah : שלום שלום לרחוק ולקרוב אמר ה' ורפאתיו : " Peace, peace to him that

---

* Psalm cii. 4.   § Psalm xxxviii. 11.

ILLNESS OF THE PRINCE OF WALES.

is far off and to him that is near, saith the Lord, and I will heal him."* Peace to him that was born *far* from the religion of the chosen people; but who, opposed to idolatry, follows conscientiously his own creed, and faithfully performs the noblest precepts of justice and charity. Peace to him that is *near*, who unconquerably abides by the Law of Sinai revealed to his forefathers. Peace, peace and recovery to all the sick among the virtuous men of the earth.

The dreaded bulletins have been succeeded by pleasant announcements of improvement, of slow but sure recovery; and the anxiety of a loyal nation has been turned into joy, their prayer into thanksgivings.

And which of all these prayers was efficient before the Almighty? Was it not perhaps that which arose from amidst the remnants of the holy temple of Jerusalem? From that city which, according to the prophet, is the house of God that shall one day be called the house of prayer of all nations? We dare not to answer in the affirmative; for we bear in mind that, as David taught us, the Lord is equally a father to all human creatures, that only one prayer is agreeable unto Him—that which comes from a guileless heart. "The Lord is nigh unto all that call upon Him, to all that call upon Him in truth."§ קרוב ה' לכל קראיו לכל אשר יקראהו באמת :

But at any rate Israel is proud of his loyalty; he is proud to see that his acts of fidelity to his rightful sovereign are widely known and appreciated; and you, worthy minister of the Church of England, ah, you have been right in saying that "the wonderful Israel of old has shown a loyalty and feeling second to none."|| The

* Isaiah lvii. 19. § Psalm cxlv. 18.
|| The Rev. W. L. Onslow, Chaplain to H.R.H. the Prince of Wales, spoke thus in one of his sermons at Sandringham.

Israelites have always considered it a sacred duty, wherever they resided, to be loyal towards their king. Jeremiah first recommended them to love the land of their exile, to be faithful to their new rulers, and this advice was confirmed by tradition.* : דינא דמלכותא דינא "The law of the state must be held sacred and be obeyed."§ הוי מתפלל בשלומה של מלכות שאלמלא מוראה איש את רעהו חיים בלעו: "Always pray for the prosperity of your rulers, for were it not for their authority, men would destroy each other." In spite of the oppression of which they were the victims, in spite of the tortures which they were made to suffer, they never lowered themselves to an act of infidelity, of rebellion; our nation has never bred traitors. The Jews of England have not forgotten the persecutions to which their ancestors were here subjected: they remember that King Canute banished them all from this country in 1020, depriving them of all they possessed: they remember the terrible slaughter of their fathers in 1189 at the coronation of Richard I., in London, and Stamford, and Lincoln, and York: they remember the massacre of the seven hundred Jews in London by the Barons in 1262, and their synagogue in Old Jewry reduced to ashes; they remember how many times they were plundered and banished, how many among them in various epochs, were tortured and executed on the stupid accusation that they had killed a Christian child, in order to use his blood for their Passover celebrations: they remember that until 1858 they had always been denied those sacred civil and political rights that belong to all citizens. Oh yes, they remember all this, and yet they were, and they are, peaceable citizens, faithful, devoted subjects,

---

* Talmud B. Kamah, 112.   § Talmud Abot, III.

ILLNESS OF THE PRINCE OF WALES. 229

ready to give their property and even their life for the country of their birth, for the security and glory of its monarchs.

But the Prince, to whom the Lord has been so signally merciful, the Prince, to whom the subjects of his august mother have shown so loyal and affectionate a devotion, ought never to forget the hard trial through which he has passed; he ought, on the contrary, to derive from it appropriate warnings and useful lessons, both as a man and as a prince. And first as a man. He has suffered all that it is given to man to suffer. He went down as deep as the gates of death; and yet he has been recalled to existence. He will therefore doubly appreciate the value of life. He will feel from experience how weak mortal creatures are, how easily their apparent power, and their vital energy can be impaired and destroyed. The more he will know the smallness of man, the more he will be convinced of the greatness of the Creator. Few men have come back after having advanced so far on the way of the grave. He ought to consider his severe illness as a purification. Gold is purified by fire, and man by pain and sorrow. He ought to feel, so to say, regenerated by his sufferings; and his heart ought henceforward thoroughly to appreciate the real mission of man, which consists in loving the Lord, in doing good to his fellow-creatures, in perfecting himself. The pleasures that earthly existence allows us to enjoy, and which are so liberally bestowed upon the powerful, ought not to be the object of our life; we ought to consider them as the flowers which a traveller finds on his way; he may stop a moment to gather some, and to enjoy their perfume; but should he endanger the aim of his journey for such transitory satisfactions? The words of my text ought to be our motto, and the noble Prince ought to act in accordance with their signification. The dead are mute, but "the living, the living shall praise Thee, as I do this day; the father to the children shall make known Thy truth" * חי חי הוא יודך כמני היום אב לבנים יודיע אל אמתך:

As a Prince, I am sure he will not, and he should not, forget the terrible illness that exhausted and prostrated him, since it gave rise to such warm and hearty demonstrations of affection, as not only an heir-apparent to the Crown, but not even a monarch that has long been on the throne generally receives from the nation which he has ruled with wisdom. How sweetly will his heart be moved when he hears the whole extent of the anxiety felt for him by millions of human beings; when he hears that for him the great stream of business was almost arrested and the course of amusement suspended; that crowds assembled from morning till evening to enquire after him, smiling with hope if the news were good, struck with grief if his condition were pronounced worse; that all mothers prayed for him with his own mother, all wives with his own wife, all children with his own children! But an equally strong bond of gratitude ought to unite his heart to this nation. Oh, he will surely feel his obligation to love a people so loyal and affectionate; he will constantly think of what will contribute to their happiness and glory. To increase the nation's wealth, to widen the field of its liberties, to cover all classes of citizens with the same wing of protection will, doubtlessly, be his aspiration whenever the day comes on which he shall sit on the throne so worthily occupied by the present Sovereign.

* Isaiah xxxviii. 19.

But the Israelites ask for nothing! They are perfectly satisfied under a Government that lets them enjoy all their rights, that has destroyed the barrier which separated them from their countrymen, opening to them the gates of public offices and public honours; and to those who ask us, "Can the Crown increase your welfare?" we would answer as that woman of Shunem answered the prophet Elisha when he sought to reward her for the generous hospitality granted to him in her house בתוך עמי אנכי ישבת * "I dwell in the midst of my own people;" that is, we live peacefully with our neighbours, we reap freely what our industry has freely sown, we ask for nothing. Yes, we are satisfied with our position in this great country; and whether we are called upon to teach in the seats of learning, or to defend the rights of the innocent in the temple of the law, whether we are to occupy a place in the sanctuary of justice or to be representatives in the house of legislation, whether we are to be soldiers or sailors, merchants or artisans, we will always love this land and work for its prosperity; we will always obey the laws, while we will firmly remain Jews, and do everything in our power in order to defeat the schemes of those whose aim is to convert our brethren to a religion which is not ours; who, unable to employ violent means—for they would not be left unpunished, have adopted the system of allurements in order to detach the sons of Israel from their faith, in order to attract the poor to whom indigence is a bad adviser, or the young who, through inexperience, do not see the snare. The Conversionists' Society is one which ought not to exist in a time of progress, civilisation and brotherhood; it ought not to exist where a just and

* 2 Kings iv. 13.

wise Government rules. The Inquisition was a disgrace to the Middle Ages; but the object of this society is not less condemnable at the present time, for it constitutes the profanation of the sanctuary of the human conscience. As good Englishmen, therefore, but as equally good Jews, this is our double declaration, our unchangeable profession of faith—unshaken patriotism, and unconquerable attachment to our religion.

Let us hope, in conclusion, that the beloved Prince whose return to life has filled us with joy, may be restored to his former health, to the affection of the people, that he may in time ascend the glorious throne of this powerful nation; and animated by noble inspirations, by the love of real glory, the love of peace, he may be a king according to the wish of the Lord; a king who will be a father to all his subjects; who will keep firmly in his hand the infallible balance of justice; who, opposed to partiality, "shall not respect the person of the poor, nor honour the person of the mighty," as Isaiah said: "And righteousness shall be the girdle of his loins, and faithfulness the girdle of his reins."*

And now, my brethren, arise and recite with me our usual prayer for the Royal Family, whom may the Lord cover with His eternal protection. We shall conclude with the prayer for H. R. H. the Prince of Wales, which I wrote in the moment of our anxiety, and which has formed many a time part of our daily service in this house of worship.

* xi. 5.

PRAYER FOR HER MAJESTY THE QUEEN AND THE ROYAL FAMILY.

הנותן תשועה למלכים וכול׳

"May He who dispenseth salvation unto kings and dominion unto princes; whose kingdom is an everlasting kingdom, who delivered his servant David from the destructive sword, who maketh a way in the sea and a path through the mighty waters; may He bless, preserve, guard, assist, exalt and elevate our Most Gracious Sovereign, Queen Victoria; Albert, Prince of Wales; the Princess of Wales, and all the Royal Family. May the supreme King of Kings, through His infinite mercy, preserve them, grant them life and deliver them from all manner of trouble and danger. May the supreme King of Kings heighten their power and glory, and bestow upon them a long and prosperous reign. May the supreme King of Kings, through His infinite mercy, incline their hearts and the hearts of their counsellors and nobles, to act with benevolence towards us and all Israel. In their days and in ours may Judah be saved, Israel dwell in safety, and may the Redeemer come unto Zion. O that this may be His gracious will! and let us say:

AMEN."

PRAYER FOR THE PRINCE OF WALES.

O Lord! who sittest on the throne of mercy, who openest Thy ears unto the groaning of the prisoner and unto the prayer of the destitute, and who holdest in Thine hands the thread of the life of all creatures—from the princes shining with the splendour of royalty, down to the poor, condemned to exhausting labour—oh! look on the sufferings of the first-born son of our gracious Sovereign Queen Victoria! He lies on the bed of languishing, and all rest is vanished from him. His noble faculties are impaired, and his physical strength is departed. Suddenly has this dreadful illness come upon him, and now he has almost reached the gate of death. O Lord! good and merciful, have pity on the Prince of Wales! Preserve him from death, while still so young. Cut not the tree before it has yielded fruit. Destroy not the flower, when yet in full bloom. Listen unto the prayers that all human beings in England and her colonies raise unto Thee on behalf of the sick Prince, that Thou mayest save him from the impending danger; in behalf of the afflicted Queen, that Thou mayest not wrest from her the child of her love; in behalf of the desolate Princess, that Thou mayest not force upon her the mournful garment of widowhood; and in behalf of the young Princes, that Thou mayest not cut off their support, their father. O Lord! Thou canst recall the dead to life, and art a powerful Deliverer. Oh restore the Prince of Wales to health; give him new strength, a new existence; let him live to enjoy the love of the people that repose under his august mother's rule. Bestow upon him a full recovery—a recovery of blessing and consolation. Renew his youth like the eagle's. Grant him a long life, so that he may sit on the throne of his inheritance, and reign with justice and charity. Amen!

תפלה

המלך היושב על כסא רחמים אשר אזניך פתוחות לשמוע אנקת אסיר ולא תבזה את תפלת הערער: אשר בידך נפש כל חי ורוח כל בשר איש מן הרוזנים היושבים על כס הדר עד עניי ארץ העמלים אחר הרחיים · ראה בעני בן בכור המלכה גבירתנו השוכב על ערש דוי כל משכבו הפכת בחליו פתאום אחזתו מחלה וכאב אנוש ועתה הגיע עד שערי מות:

אנא ה' אל רחום וחנון חמול נא על **אלבירט אידוארד** ואל תמיתהו בחצי ימיו אמר למות שב ·ואל תתן אל המשחית לננוף · אל תכרות העץ טרם יתן פריו למה תשדוף רוח הקדים השבלים כאשר עודן צמחות העלה מן שאול נפשו חייהו מירדו בור · היה עם פיפיות בני בריטאניא ועם פיפיות רבבות עם מזורח שמש עד מבואו העומדים לבקש רחמים מלפניך על הנשיא החולה למען תחלימהו ומצרה ונזק תצילהו · על המלכה הנאנחה למען לא תשכלה · על השרה האומללה למען לא תלבישה בגדי אלמנות · ועל ילדיהם למען בשם יתומים לא יקראו:

אנא ה' מחיה מתים אתה רב להושיע · שלח נא ידך והגן **באלבירט אידוארד** · אל נא רפא נא לו ולא תרד נפשו שאולה · החזיקהו החליפהו למען יחיה ברצון כל העמים החוסים תחת כנפי המלכה אמו ותחת כנפיו ותשלח לו רפואה שלמה רפואת הנפש ורפואת הגוף · מרפא ארוכה · מרפא ברכה · מרפא תרופה ותעלה · מרפא חנינה וחמלה · תחדש כנשר נעוריו למען יראה עוד זרע ויאריך ימים וישב על כסא נחלתו ועשה משפט וצדקה בארץ · כן יהי רצון · אמן:

MANNA.

תערך לפני שלחן נגד צררי דשנת בשמן ראשי כוסי רויה :

"Thou preparest a table before me in the presence of mine enemies; Thou anointest my head with oil; my cup runneth over."

PSALM xxiii. 5.

אימתי אמרו ישראל דבר זה כשיצאו ממצרים והיו האומות אומרים עתידין אלו למות במדבר מה עשה הק״בה הסיבן תחת עננו כבודו והאבילם מן :

"When did the Israelites repeat the above verse? When they came out of Egypt, and the neighbouring nations said with scorn that they would die in the desert of hunger. Then the Lord surrounded His people with the clouds of His honour and gave them manna."

MEDRASH SHEMOT RABBAH, xxv.

My DEAR BRETHREN,—Nothing is more frequent among men than to hear them complain of their destiny, of the part allotted to them on the earth. Whatever their condition may be, they always find cause for discontent. They cannot bear the idea of the inequality which exists in the distribution of good and evil, nor can they be reconciled to those deceptions and failures which are often unavoidable. Some, in their bitterness, do not shrink from uttering blasphemy. "There is no God," they say * אמר נבל בלבו אין אלהים : For they think that if He did exist, He would not leave their complaints and desires unsatisfied. Others, more moderate, but

* Psalm xiv. 1.

not less blamable, exclaim that if there is a Providence, it is assuredly partial and unjust. In the very moment in which they enjoy some of its boons, they declare that it has abandoned them. They are like Zion, that though miraculously preserved by God, yet despondently said:* "The Lord has forsaken me, and my Lord has forgotten me" ותאמר ציון עזבני ה' וה' שכחני: Why! there is then no Providence? And what is the power which created the beneficial light, separated the earth from the waters, and made them both the residence of millions of beings? What is the power which gave strength to the lion and movement to the imperceptible insect? Is it not Providence that gives balsamic perfume to the flower which I smell, weighs and directs for my benefit the air which surrounds me, commands silence to the whistling winds and to the roaring sea, and never fails to be obeyed? Does not the bountiful hand of Providence give wool to the lamb, daily food to the sparrow, and its winter-shelter to the ant? And can we think that it forgets man, the noblest of its creatures? Can we complain of it when things do not proceed as we wish, when our undertakings are denied success? David rightly said: "The eyes of all wait upon Thee, and Thou givest them their food in its season;" § and the Talmud commenting upon that verse, beautifully proclaims: "that the Lord prepares for each creature separately its timely material and spiritual food" ‖ בעתם לא נאמר אלא בעתו מלמד שלכל אחד ואחד נותן הק"בה פרנסתו:

I.

What is the subject of this morning's lesson of the Law? It is one of the most sublime acts of Providence.

* Isaiah xlix. 14.   § Psalm cxlv. 15.   ‖ Talmud Ketubot, 85.

SERMON XVI.

When the Hebrews left Egypt, they were but a multitude of ignorant and superstitious men, imbued with the erroneous ideas which they had learnt among their masters, almost corrupted by the idolatrous habits of which their masters had given them the example. They were in need of education and instruction, of sound principle concerning the Divinity and the destiny of man, of good laws on justice and purity, on public and private life. They were in need of spiritual food, food for mind and soul. And the Lord spoke to them as a teacher speaks to his pupil, he taught them and in the midst of wonders He gave them the Decalogue, those ten great principles, from which all religious and social laws have been derived, just as luxuriant and graceful branches grow out of a solid and powerful stem. But before granting them the food of the soul, He had bestowed upon them the food of the body. He had acted as a loving mother acts towards her son, when before letting him undertake a great mental work, she provides for the satisfaction of his material wants, so that, by the strength of his body he may be prepared for the exertions of his mind. So the Lord before revelation, gave unto Israel the nourishing and strengthening manna. He prepared them by healthy and material food, for the more purifying nourishment of the spirit. In past years I commented minutely upon the decalogue, and entertained you at a spiritual banquet. Let me this day dwell upon manna, upon real and palpable food, and the subject, I assure you, will not be less instructive and useful; nay, it will convey unto men those practical lessons which they really need.

The condition of the Israelites when they entered the wilderness of Sin, the most desolate tract of the peninsula of Sinai, was distressing. The store of provisions which they had brought from Egypt had been consumed in their hurried march. Herds and flocks were among them, but they belonged to the wealthy. A great many had nothing, and among these was that mixed multitude which had followed, those who are with us in our success, but who are the first and noisiest rioters when our good fortune abandons us, and privations begin to be felt. The Almighty was not displeased because they had expressed their wants (a good King and a loving Father, He would not have deprived them of the right of children and subjects), but because they had murmured, because they had no faith in Him who, for their benefit, had by means of the convulsed sea destroyed their enemies, and brought the slaves over to the land of liberty. Yet when they were thirsty He gave them water; when the waters were bitter, He showed Moses a tree that made the waters sweet, and when they were hungry, He did what man had not seen before, what he did not see again, He gave them manna, the miraculous food ; as David said,* ולחם שמים ישביעם "He satisfied them with the bread of Heaven."

But those who do not believe in miracles, and make their study of the Bible consist in trying to explain naturally all the wonders therein narrated, put their reasoning powers to task in order to prove that the manna mentioned in the Law is that manna which is one of the natural products of Arabia and other oriental countries. The manna now found in the wilderness, repeatedly crossed by the Hebrews during forty years, has none of the characteristics attributed to the manna of the Bible. It is collected, as botanists teach

* Psalm cv. 40.

us, from the tamarisk shrub in the month of June only; it drops from the thorns on the sticks and leaves with which the ground is covered, and after a prescribed preparation it can be preserved in leathern bottles for several years. But that cannot be the manna of the Hebrews, which was found only six days in the week, and only around the camp of the wanderers; which could not in any way be kept for the following day, unless it was the Sabbath, and which ceased suddenly and for ever, as soon as the Hebrews could make use of the corn of Palestine. Our manna was therefore properly called a heavenly bread, since it had all the conditions of a miracle.

Then the Lord said unto Moses:* הנני ממטיר לכם לחם מן השמים ויצא העם ולקטו דבר יום ביומו למען אנסנו הילך בתורתי אם לא: "Behold, I will rain bread from Heaven for you, and the people shall go out and gather a certain rate every day, that I may prove them whether they will walk in my law or not." A question naturally arises, and more than one among you must have addressed it to himself in reading that remarkable part of our forefathers' history—how could that daily and wonderful food constitute a proof of the Hebrews' fidelity unto the Lord? This is the answer. Providence is ever ready to supply what man's necessity demands, and to grant the object of his reasonable desires. But we must not expect it to exercise its inexhaustible mercy without imposing certain conditions. Men give so little and ask for so much as a reward; "their liberality," as we daily say, "is so limited, and the gratitude which they claim is so exorbitant," § שמתנתם מעוטה וחרפתם מרובה and Providence alone, which satisfies so bountifully all

* Exodus xvi. 4.   § Prayer after Meals.

our wants, should claim nothing in return? No, that cannot be. Providence fixes its own laws, and they must be complied with. These laws are applicable to all the boons which we receive at its hand, and are obligatory whatever our personal circumstances may be. They are four in number, and all of them are clearly mentioned in the passage referring to manna, פרשת המן which many of our brethren read every day, always to be reminded of their duty. Providence demands, first of all, that man should help himself in his need; it demands, secondly, that he should carefully avoid covetousness and immoderate desires; it demands, thirdly, that he should have faith in the Almighty; and lastly, that as a token of gratitude he should rigorously comply with all the Divine precepts. Let us briefly examine these four laws as they are set forth in the 16th chapter of Exodus.

II.

Early in the morning the dew lay round about the host, and when the dew was gone, "behold upon the face of the wilderness a small round thing, as small as the hoar frost upon the ground" * ותעל שכבת הטל והנה על פני המדבר דק מחספס דק ככפר על הארץ: Thus, the manna came early in the morning, and the people were to "go out and gather" § ויצא העם ולקטו: But why were the people themselves to go out? Why were not officers appointed, who might gather for all and thus prevent confusion? No; according to the Law, each of the Hebrews was to go out and gather for himself; if he waited till the sun was hot, he found nothing; the manna was melted. What a lesson! The great law of

* Exodus xvi. 14.   § Exodus xvi. 4.

labour was thus proclaimed and taught to all future generations. Providence will not allow those whom it protects to be idle. It assists men, but provided they assist themselves; it will give them bread, but on condition that they work for it. Everyone in the Hebrew camp, and even the child who had strength enough, was to gather manna for himself. We are thus taught that as soon as childhood is over, young people must depend not on their parents but upon themselves, upon their own exertions; like the birds which leave their parents' nest, the very moment they are clad in feathers and have the power to fly. Wise people never remain idle; they fill their life with useful tasks, with virtuous actions; they consider labour as the friend of man, as the first of his duties, as his consoler when gloomy thoughts haunt his mind. The ancients believed that labour only could save youths from vice; and the Athenian Draco made a law which condemned to death any one who was convicted of living an idle life. But remember, my brethren, that manna was to be found only early in the morning, that we must set to work when the day begins, for, as our sages taught שינה של שחרית מוציא את האדם מן העולם: "The morning's sleep is unto man a cause of death."* If we let the favourable hours elapse, if we miss the good opportunity, if we arrive too late, we shall see that the blessings which the Almighty had placed before us have disappeared. "The sun is hot, and the manna is melted," it is no more וחם השמש ונמס: § So labour is Providence's first Law.

Moses said afterwards unto the Hebrews: לקטו ממנו איש לפי אכלו עמר לגלגלת: "This is the thing which the

---

* Talmud Abot, iii. § Exodus xvi. 16.

Lord hath commanded, Gather of it every man according to his eating, an *omer* for every man."* Providence bestows its boons liberally upon man, but it demands that man should avail himself of them according to his eating, according to his wants, with moderation. Man ought not to ask for more than is necessary unto him, for he ought to eat in order to live, and not to live in order to eat. איזהו עשיר השמח בחלקו "He alone," said our sages, "is rich, who is satisfied with his lot, however modest and small it may be."§ But what did happen in the wilderness? Charmed by the palatable taste of the manna, many Hebrews gathered a great quantity; they would in their greediness empty the cup of pleasure; they would have secured, if possible, all the manna instead of one omer; twenty omers they gathered, and went home delighting in the thought of their abundant food. But they were disappointed, as all are disappointed who yield to the suggestions of intemperance וימדו בעמר ולא העדיף המרבה והממעיט לא החסיר וכול׳ "He that had been moderate and sober did not lack the necessary food; he that gathered much had nothing over, he gained nothing."‖ Oh! how many of like people do we not see in the midst of society! How many are there not who would have everything for themselves; all gain, all property, all honours, all distinctions. They do not reflect that if they have so much, their neighbours will consequently be deprived of what is necessary. They are unable to master their wishes, to control their desires; their cupidity has no limits; their avariciousness prompts them to unjust and uncharitable acts. They exhibit either complete ignorance, or disregard of the noble saying of our sages: "Oh, man, that which

* Exod. xvi. 16. § Talmud Abot, iv. 1. ‖ Exodus xvi. 18.

belongs to thee is not thine, for God can deprive thee of it in a moment, and that which does not belong to thee, why shouldst thou usurp it?"* Hath not the Lord said, "Woe unto him who increases that which is not his"§ את שלך אינו שלך ואת שאינו שלך למה הוא לך והיה שלך וכול׳ שנאמר הוי המרבה לא לו: Moderation is therefore the second condition which Providence imposes.

The Hebrews were to consume every day that which they had gathered, but they were expressly ordered not "to leave of it till the morning"‖ איש אל יותר ממנו עד בקר: What was the object of this command? Was the manna so corruptible a substance as so soon to become dangerous food? The Talmud asks another question, and one answer will be sufficient for both inquiries. Why did not the Lord give manna unto the Hebrews all at once, as He gives corn for all the year round? The reason is clear, answered a sage. Suppose a king who makes unto his son a yearly allowance for his food, but to whom the ungrateful son pays only once a year a tribute of devotion and respect. What will the king do in order to force his son to a daily act of submission? Will he not appoint his portion from day to day, so that he may at any moment withdraw it? Thus did the Lord unto the Hebrews, to whom the manna was to be given every morning, and who, uncertain whether bread could be found another day for them and their children, were obliged to raise every evening their earnest supplications to their Heavenly Father¶ כך ישראל היה דואג ואומר שמא למחר אין המן יורד וכול׳ ונמצאו כל ישראל מכונים את לבם לאביהם שבשמים: The Hebrews were not to leave of the manna till the morning, for, just as we expect

---

* Talmud, Derech Erez Zuta, 11. § Habak. ii. 6.
‖ Exodus xvi. 19. ¶ Talmud Yoma, 76.

that those whom we have benefited should trust us, that they should not suspect the hand which has given them relief; so the Hebrews were not to attribute the gift of manna to hazard, nor to keep it one day for the other, as if they doubted its coming. They were to have faith in Him who had the power of feeding them by supernatural means. But the Hebrews mistrusted Him; some of them left of the manna till the morning, and "it bred worms and stank" * וירם תולעים ויבאש : The Lord had declared that the manna would be granted them till they could enter the promised land; but they doubted His word; they feared lest they should be left without food.—The Talmud teaches that "Jerusalem was destroyed because men of faith were no longer to be found in her"§ חרבה ירושלים על שפסקו ממנה אנשי אמנה : That was the great fault of Israel, and the principal source of their misery. In all their trials they placed their trust in human support. They relied on the fallible wisdom of man, and rejected the advice of Him who knows future events and cannot be mistaken. Are we then to be surprised if their cup was so bitter, their sufferings so frightful? We may surely have foresight, that is both a right and a duty; but we ought not to let it go so far as to give up faith in Providence, without whose help we cannot live. והבוטח בה' חסד יסובבנו "He that trusteth the Lord, mercy shall compass him about." ‖

Labour, moderation and faith are surely indispensable, but they are not all. Providence claims one thing more: a token of gratitude, a proof that its favours are not bestowed upon a thankless heart. The Hebrews,

* Exodus xvi. 20. § Talmud Shabbat, 119.
‖ Psalm xxxii. 10.

as you may imagine, could not help feeling grateful to God for the miraculous manna; but they were to prove their thankfulness by devoting one day in the week to rest and religious meditation, for the manna was not to be found on the Sabbath. שבו איש תחתיו אל יצא איש ממקומו ביום השבעי "Abide ye every man in his place," said Moses, "let no man go out of his place on the seventh day." * But some of the Hebrews, who so fully deserved the name of עם קשה ערף "A stiff-necked people," § would go out on the seventh day to gather. Alas! even now, many Israelites who can gather plenty of manna during the week, whose labour and speculations are so fruitful, are not satisfied and will *go out* on the Sabbath to gather; they deny Providence that small token of gratitude; they set a bad example to their brethren, and call upon themselves the contempt of other nations by their scandalous disobedience to the law of Sinai. But as the Hebrews of the wilderness could find no manna on the Sabbath, so we cannot derive a real blessing from the transactions even successfully carried out on the day of rest; the gold which we gain in improper time will, sooner or later, burn our hands, it will in the end result in a decided loss. Just as our soul and our body are joined together by an indissoluble link, so our cares for what is material ought to be blended with our cares for what is spiritual. Our earthly nature prevents us from devoting ourselves entirely to the exigencies of the soul; but if we fall into the same extreme with regard to the body, then we renounce our nobility as men, we repudiate our divine origin, we descend to the level of the brute. This, Providence taught us by supplying the material wants of

* Exodus xvi. 29.   § Exodus xxxii. 9.

MANNA. 247

Israel with the manna, and by making them afterwards, by revelation, a kingdom of priests and a holy nation. After the granting of bread, the decalogue; after material work, religious contemplation, after the weekly labour, the rest of the Sabbath; the former is necessary to our body, the latter to our soul; but both are indispensable to the welfare of our being, that is, the association of body and soul.

And now that we know the various conditions by which we may secure the blessings of Providence, can there be any doubt of the conclusion at which we are to arrive? We ought to consider ourselves as the guests of Providence upon the earth, and to accept its hospitality with warm gratefulness. We ought constantly to repeat the beautiful words which the Talmud puts into the mouth of the grateful guest אורח טוב מהו אומר כמה טרחות טרח בעל הבית בשבילי כמה בשר הביא לפני כמה יין הביא לפני וכולי וכל מה שטרח לא טרח אלא בשבילי "How much has my host exerted himself for me! how much good has he brought before me! how much excellent wine has he handed to me! how many delightful things has he prepared for my benefit! All this he has done for me alone!"* The way which Providence has traced before us is the securest; the guide which it has placed within ourselves, conscience, is our best guide. Sometimes, it is true, we unavoidably meet with bitter waters, and that is one of the features of earthly existence. But let us not forget that as it occurred in the wilderness, Providence points out unto us the tree which can make them sweet; and that by the side of the evil is always placed its remedy. To find it out is, at times,

* Talm. Berachot, 57.

our very difficult task. Guided by faith in Providence, we cannot miss our way; during the night we shall see before us the pillar of fire, during the day the pillar of cloud; the Lord will be our leader. The Talmud, speaking of the manna, says that it was adapted to the various ages of man, and tasted differently according to the nature of those who ate it, that "it tasted like bread to the young, like honey to the old, and like oil to the children,"*
בחורים היו טועמין טעם לחם זקנים טעם דבש תינוקות טעם שמן :
And our own bread, if honourably earned, will taste delightfully; it will keep up the vigour of manhood, it will strengthen childhood, and restore vigour to old age. If we comply with the four conditions imposed by Providence, labour, moderation, faith, and gratitude, our bread will be the bread of the Lord, the bread which He invites us to eat at His eternal table; as it is written in the book of Proverbs § לכו לחמו בלחמי ושתו ביין מסכתי "Come eat of my bread and drink of the wine which I have mingled."

PRAYER.

Almighty God, who art merciful towards those who suffer, who art a guide to those who wander, and a shield to all those who trust in Thee, we cannot meditate upon the distress experienced by our ancestors, and upon the wonders which Thou didst achieve for their relief, without remembering our own wants and the wants of our fellow creatures. We look around us and on the one hand observe old age, infirmity and helpless poverty, and on the other, the hardest struggles in order to earn bread in an honourable manner; we see before us honest working men who, with all their labor, cannot earn

* Medrash Shemot Rabbah, xxv. § ix. 5.

food enough for their numerous children; as our sages, unconsciously describing the present state of things, said: היוקר הוה והשכר אבד ובני אדם רצין אחר פרנסתם ואין מגיעין "Everything is so dear, and no salary is given; poor men in vain look for their living, but they find it not."* And when we think of ourselves, we see how hard it is to depend upon others, to work for ungrateful masters, for people who either do not understand or do not appreciate our work. How often we find that our bread tastes truly bitterly! that it is ineffably painful to "ascend and descend other people's staircases."§ We earnestly pray therefore unto Thee, O Lord, forget us not in our wants. We do not ask for miracles, we do not ask for luxuries, we address unto Thee Jacob's supplication : ונתן לי לחם לאכל ובגד ללבש Oh give us "bread to eat and raiment to put on," provided only they are accompanied by tranquillity and peace. "Thou nourishest all living creatures יושב הק'בה וזן מקרני ראמים עד ביצי כינים from the huge rhinoceros down to the minutest insect " ‖ and unto Thee imploringly turn our eyes. May Thy blessing descend upon us, may the work of our hands prosper, may we get our daily bread, the bread of the body, and the bread of the soul! Oh, let our undertakings be successful; let the sweat of our face be the means by which we may provide for the maintenance of our family; let us be victorious in our battles against necessity, give us the power of shaking off the gloom with which poverty or dejection envelops us, the power to hope and have faith in Thee. Shield us from the two extremes, immense wealth and overpowering indigence; as King Solomon said: "Two things have I required of Thee: deny me them

* Talmud Shabat, 32.   § Dante.   ‖ Talmud Shabat, 107.

not before I die: remove from me vanity and lies; give me neither riches nor poverty, feed me with food convenient to me."* שנים שאלתי מאתך אל תמנע ממני בטרם אמות: שוא ודבר כזב הרחק ממני ראש ועשר אל תתן לי הטריפני לחם חקי:

Amen.

* Proverbs xxx. 7, 8.

THE HOME SANCTUARY.

ועשו לי מקדש ושכנתי בתוכם :

"And let them make me a sanctuary, that I may dwell among them."
EXODUS xxv. 8.

אמר הק״בה לישראל אתן צאני ואני רועה אתן אדם ואני רועה עשו
דיר לרועה שיבא וירעה אתכם :

"The Lord said unto Israel: Ye are my flock, and I am your shepherd; ye are men, and I am men's ruler; erect therefore unto me a dwelling, that I may come and feed you."
MEDRASH SHEMOT RABBAH, xxxiv.

MY DEAR BRETHREN,—Nothing could have been more soul-stirring and delightful than the enthusiasm exhibited by all the Hebrews when they witnessed the magnificent scene of revelation and heard the voice of Moses, supported by the voice of God, proclaim the Decalogue. That enthusiasm was beautifully expressed by their unanimous promise of unconditional obedience. But the multitude is like the wind which suddenly and rapidly changes direction; its enthusiasm fades away and disappears if it is not promptly utilised. Therefore the Lord immediately after revelation gave the Hebrews those important laws of justice and charity, which are the real basis of human society. As no creed can exist if moral precepts are not strengthened by religious obligations, the Lord directed that a sanctuary should be built unto Him. "Let them make me a sanctuary, that I may dwell among them."* And the sanctuary was erected which, if we make allowance for the peculiar condition of the Hebrews in the wilderness, was splendid in its simplicity. It was the place wherein the rescued slaves were to adore the God of liberty, wherein the children were to worship their merciful Father. The outlay for such a place was not to be a tax levied upon the Hebrews. It was to be the result of gratitude and pious liberality.§ מֵאֵת כָּל אִישׁ אֲשֶׁר יִדְּבֶנּוּ לִבּוֹ תִּקְחוּ אֶת תְּרוּמָתִי: "Of every man that gives it willingly, with his heart, ye shall take my offering." And in fact, as soon as Moses made that appeal in the name of God, men and women, the old and the young brought in everything precious and beautiful that was in their possession. Their ardour and emulation in offering their property to God has seldom, if ever, been exhibited by others since that period. Not only did the rich give with profusion, but the poor, whose heart is always equally, and sometimes more, generous, deprived themselves of their modest ornaments for the house of God. The whole of the offerings was so large, that Moses was at last obliged to say with joy and pride that nothing further was needed, that the wealth gathered was beyond the want. That tabernacle, grown into a majestic temple under King Solomon, was the object of the admiration of all neighbouring nations. Destroyed by the Chaldean monarch, it revived by the pious exertions of the recalled exiles, and shone with even greater splendour under the rule of the Asmonæans and their successors, until it was reduced to ashes by the Romans;

* Exodus xxv. 8. § Exodus xxv. 2.

THE HOME SANCTUARY.

and Jerusalem fell with it, the garden of the world thus becoming the dwelling of desolation.

Here, my brethren, I see your lips move; I feel that you are about to utter a question. Stay, stay, I know what you wish to ask, and I can answer it. God, you naturally say, commanded us to make Him a sanctuary in order that He might dwell among us. By the transgressions of our forefathers the temple unfortunately fell, and even its ruins have disappeared: we cannot offer our dutiful sacrifices any longer unto God. Deprived of a central, national place of gathering, we no longer enjoy the visible signs of the Divine presence among us, such as oracles and prophetic visions. But are we really to believe that the children are punished for the sins of the fathers? Are we to adopt the despondent idea that God has really withdrawn from us, because we have no temple wherein He may reside? Will He keep far from us until the sanctuary of old may arise from its ruins?—My brethren, I think I can dispel your painful doubts. God who "keeps mercy for thousands," Himself reduced to nothing the theory that the innocent should suffer for the guilty, when He said, "The fathers shall not be put to death for the children, neither the children be put to death for the fathers; every man shall be put to death for his own sin"* לא יומתו אבות על בנים ובנים לא יומתו על אבות איש בחטאו יומתו: But if He keeps away from us, how can He accomplish His consoling promises: § ונתתי משכני בתוככם ולא תגעל נפשי אתכם: "And I will set my tabernacle among you, and my soul shall not abhor you?" We may say in some sense that His presence does not depend upon the existence of a national temple. He, in fact, has lived

* Deuteronomy xxiv. 16.   § Leviticus xxvi. 11.

in the midst of Israel these two thousand years, from the day of our great misfortunes; and the proof of His presence is to be found in our miraculous safety and preservation, in the assistance which every day He bestows upon us. Remark, besides, that God did not say: "Let them make me a sanctuary, that I may dwell *in it* בתוכו ;" but He said בתוכם "*Among them.*" This seems to mean that He will dwell with any of us who can make Him a sanctuary; and according to the Medrash, "Any one among the children of Israel can erect it." "I am your father," says God, as we read further on, "and ye are my children; it is an honor unto the children that the father should dwell among them, make then a house unto the father that he may reside among his children." Thus the difficulty is explained, and we may hope that the presence of God may be preserved in our midst, even without a national temple. What, then, is this sanctuary that every one of us can erect? How is it to be understood? It can be understood in one way only. Our home is to constitute that sanctuary.

Yes, my brethren, we ought to be able to make our houses so many sanctuaries, or rather symbols of the sanctuary of which God Himself fixed the proportions, when He said unto Moses: "According to all that I show thee, after the pattern of the tabernacle, and the pattern of all the instruments thereof, even so shall ye make it" * ככל אשר אני מראה אותך את תבנית המשכן ואת תבנית כל כליו וכן תעשו: And this is not so difficult as it may appear to be; the luxuriant furniture will not be required with which our modern dwellings, by the inexorable law of fashion, must necessarily be adorned: no

* Exodus xxv 9.

statues, no paintings, no costly trifles, no senseless show of wealth. The fitting up, if we may call it so, of the sanctuary, that is, of the department which all the priests entered in order to perform the daily ceremonies, consisted of three things only, eminently useful and bearing a noble signification : the gold candlestick, the table with the shew-bread and the altar. One object was contained in the most Holy of Holies, the ark. If in our houses we make use of this sacred furniture, or if in our houses we study and fulfil the injunction of these four sacred symbols, we shall assuredly make our dwellings worthy of the presence of the Lord, worthy of the name of sanctuary. This is my firm belief, but in order to fathom it, I must briefly explain these four emblems.

I.

The first object which would have struck our eyes on entering the Tabernacle, was the golden candlestick. It was placed on the south side of the first apartment, dressed every morning, lighted every evening, and it shed joyous and brilliant light from its seven beautifully-worked branches. Light ! And can there be in our house a more cheerful ornament, a more necessary decoration than light ? What is our dwelling without it ? Light is the bearer of joy ; and when in the morning the golden rays of the sun penetrate into our house and awaken it again to active life, we open our eyes with delight, and our heart unconsciously glad, is full of courage and hope. But when we are surprised by night, and we are lonely, then we are overcome by gloom, often by fear, and sometimes by terror, especially when our conscience is not pure and reproachless. When the Bible relates the rescue of the Hebrews from Haman and their triumph over all conspirators, it finds no better expression than this: ליהודים היתה אורה׃ "The Jews had light"* and Jeremiah considered darkness alone to be a true symbol of his overwhelming misery. "He hath set me in dark places, as they that be dead of old" § במחשכים הושיבני כמתי עולם׃ Light is life, obscurity is death.

The light which ought to shine in our homes, is not that which either the mist of autumn, or the fog of winter, or the clouds of spring can cover with a thick impenetrable veil, because it is not the effect of a material cause, it is not derived from a human source. It is the light of the soul, not that of the body; the light which illuminates the earth, but which comes from heaven. King Solomon gave the proper definition of it when he said: "For the commandment is a lamp, and the Law is light" ‖ כי נר מצוה ותורה אור ודרך חיים תוכחות מוסר׃ And he thus clearly referred to religion which has the same beneficial effect for morally erring men that a beacon has for navigators without compass, and unable through the darkness of the horizon to discover the polar star. The Jewish religion, among all the creeds of the earth, is the religion of light, the religion which placed before men such simple truths as can be grasped and analyzed by any intellect, such doctrines as can be accepted by human reason after it has subjected them to the strictest criticism. In explaining the essence of God, it did not raise those metaphysical problems which will always remain a mystery, while they will always confound the strongest mind; but it revealed those of His attributes which are comprehensible and convincing, while they place before

---

* Esther viii. 16.   § Lamentations iii. 6.   ‖ Proverbs vi. 23.

us a magnificent picture of His majesty. That is light, but it is not all. Light is the means by which many of the rites of Judaism should be performed. The day of rest comes, that seventh day which God Himself sanctified by closing the great work of creation, and the sweet angel of the domestic hearth, woman, lights the traditional lamp; the assembled family pray together, and sing with pleasing unison the hymns of the Lord; those seven lights which seem a reflection of heavenly splendour, give a most cheerful aspect to the poorest house, and infuse hope into dejected hearts. The Sabbath lamp, more than any earthly pleasure, can create the purest joy, the delight which religion has sanctioned. In the midst of brilliant illumination we welcome our great national and religious festivals, and the joyous lights of Hanucha are the symbolical commemoration of the patriotism of the Maccabees, of the favours of Providence, of the deliverance of Palestine, of the crushing defeat of Antiochus. Even in the days of our mourning, light is among us the sign of tender and noble feelings. That solitary lamp which burns for seven days in the room abandoned for ever by one of our parents is the symbol of the soul of the departed. The wise king called " the spirit of man the candle of the Lord," * : נר ה' נשמת אדם and we show by that lamp that our gratitude, veneration and love to our parents have not been removed by death, that the departed being will live among us, in our heart, in our undying remembrance.

Therefore, when I entreat you to make the golden candlestick a part of your household furniture, and when I add that this candlestick will have, as in days of

* Proverbs xx. 27.

old, its seven lights and seventy ornaments, knops, lilies, pomegranates and bowls, I mean that you should accept as your guide, during your mortal career, the noble principles of Judaism, which are as clear and brilliant as the light of the sun, and that you should make your house the abode of what is becoming, of pure habits, of holy ceremonies, so that your family may never fear to be exposed to light, never be ashamed of their public or private conduct. Your reward will be sure to come, for, in accordance with our sages, God said to Israel: "Make such a candlestick unto me, and I will bestow upon you a sevenfold spiritual light." * עשיתם לפני מנורה אני מאיר לכם שבעתים :

II.

The second object in the sanctuary which fixed the attention of the visitor, was the table with the shew-bread, השלחן ולחם הפנים standing opposite to the golden candlestick. What simplicity in the worship established by Moses! All the sanctuaries of the heathens were the theatres of the scandalous intemperance of the priests; and it was a duty for the idolaters to bring to their gods abundance of choice viands, which served only to give rise to the disgusting excesses of the ministers of the temples, so that the word *orgy*, which anciently meant a sacrifice celebrated with certain ceremonies, has become the synonym of wild and frantic revelry and licentiousness. There was the table in the sanctuary of the God of Israel, and nothing but bread upon it: twelve unleavened loaves of bread, six upon each heap, one above the other. It was a lesson to the Jewish

* Medrash Shemot Rabbah, l.

priests; it is a lesson to us who ought to adorn our dwellings with a similar table and similar bread, or rather to practise the moral principles concealed under this emblem.

We cannot help remarking that this emblem itself offers a striking contrast. Why a table delicately carved and overlaid with gold, bearing two piles of bread? Why the association of two such opposite ideas as that of wealth and that of the simplest food? In the course of the year we meet with two equally striking contrasts while we perform our domestic worship. The first is in Passover, when in the midst of rejoicing, while we celebrate by songs and banquets the deliverance of our ancestors, we eat the *bread of poverty*. The second occurs in the Feast of Tabernacles, the most cheerful of our festivals, which we celebrate "after we have gathered in our corn and our wine," * when, although we are commanded to enjoy ourselves, we must dwell during seven days in booths, that is, in frail wooden huts, the image of rural simplicity and scanty means. The Passover bread, the humble tent and the golden table with the shew-bread bear a common explanation. All three represent the contrasts so constantly observed in human life, the opposition of varied conditions appearing more impressively divergent when they are placed in juxtaposition: the darkness of night, following closely upon the brilliancy of sunset, wealth at the side of poverty, happiness at the side of grief, peace at the side of war, health and vigor at the side of weakness and infirmity. All three teach us that these contrasts are unavoidable, that men live by them just as the universe exists by the apparent opposition of its numerous

* Deuteronomy xvi. 13.

elements; and that we may attain a relative happiness, if instead of pretending that such contrasts should not exist, we prepare ourselves for them, so that we may be adapted, not only to the condition allotted to us, but also to the changes that it may undergo. They teach us that the cup of pure honey is not reserved for mortal beings.

Let the golden table with the shew-bread be exhibited in the mansions of the wealthy, as they were exhibited in the sanctuary, and the so-called fortunate of the earth will learn the lesson of frugality. They will learn that wealth is a source of pleasure and health and can be the object of the praise of man, only when it is coupled with sobriety and temperance, with that moderation which shows that they have not been inebriated by the favors of fortune, that affluence has not blinded their eyes, nor made their hearts proud. The sight of that bread will remind them of the sentence which was pronounced by God upon all the descendants of Adam, that "in the sweat of their brow they should eat bread," and from which no man is exempt. And they will not only learn to be humble and unpretending, not only will they be convinced that earthly possessions cannot place them above their fellows, or give them a nobler nature than their neighbours, but they will feel the duty of *working*—of working to earn a moral bread, their individual perfection, when their possessions exempt them from laboring for their daily food; of working for the benefit of society to which they belong, and of which all their wealth does not give them the right of being useless members. Even when we are not rich, even then, that shew-bread will remind us that there are millions of human beings who are forced to painful labor for their

living, and that charity has always been among us a household virtue; it will make our heart more and more inclined to feel pity for those who are tried by privations, whose house is the dwelling of want and hunger. If the simple sight of the table and the shew-bread can inspire us with such noble ideas and generous feelings, are we then to be surprised by the words of our sages, that "when the temple existed, sacrifices could make atonement for us; now the *table* is our advocate before God;"* and ought we not to provide for our house an ornament so likely to produce our moral improvement, and to render applicable to us the words which, according to the Talmud, the Lord said to the Hebrews, as soon as they had placed the table and the shew-bread in the Tabernacle? "As you have erected a table like this, I will save you from indigence, and place before you a table in the future"§ עשיתם שלחן
אני מציל אתכם מן הערוכה ואערוך לפניכם שלחן לעתיד לבא:

III.

Between the candlestick and the table was the altar of incense, מזבח קטרת also made of incorruptible shittim wood, and crusted over with a golden plate. We cannot hope ever to see the altar of incense adorn our dwellings; and yet I again recommend you to erect it wherever you reside; I mean that you should let the beautiful ideas with which it is associated be the principle according to which our homes are conducted. Aaron burnt incense upon the altar early every morning, and the perfume remained in the sanctuary the whole day. Thus each of us must be ready to offer incense

* Yalkut Shemot, 369. § Shemot Rabbah, l.

upon the altar in the tabernacle of our family; each of us ought to be prepared to make a sacrifice often, every day, early in the morning; each of us ought to be prepared for the duty of self-denial and abnegation. For this object we erect the altar of incense in our houses. And who is not called upon to perform this duty? By the very fact that we are men we cannot escape it. The rigorous command imposed upon Abraham to sacrifice "his son, his only son, Isaac, whom he loved" is a typical fact, it is a symbol of that which, though in a different form, is imposed upon us all. No, we are not always asked to sacrifice our children, but how many times are we not asked to sacrifice, to renounce that which is dear unto us, and which we love as much as the children of our blood? How often are we not required to abandon the possession of that object upon which all our hopes, all our happiness depends? Our heart rebels against the voice that commands the sacrifice, we shrink from the painful obedience, but we must yield, for it is the voice of duty that has spoken. Sometimes less important things are at stake; we are asked to part only with that which would be advantageous to us and raise our position; yet the sacrifice is hard, and with equally great reluctance we obey when we are called upon to give up things of even smaller import, like our habits, our opinions, or the ideas which we cherish. But these sacrifices are necessary. Our aspirations are sometimes opposed to our obligations towards our parents, or to our duties towards our offspring; and should we be unwilling to abandon that which may hurt or grieve the persons to whom we gave life, or those from whom we have received it? Our dreams of happiness could be verified only at the expense of peace and concord, of the comfort and welfare of our neighbours; and should we not renounce such advantages or pleasures as would be followed by the tears or the curses of those whom we have injured? This should be our rule. Whenever to comply with our self love, with our interests or our affections, is inconsistent with the peace of our family, with the just claims of our fellow-creatures, with the exigencies of society, with the dictates of prudence, with the rights of brotherhood, we ought to be ready to practise self-denial, to exhibit that silent and passive obedience for which the Patriarch is justly glorified among men. The voice of duty is the voice of God, and we must obey it; that is the condition upon which depend the satisfaction of our wants and the gratification of our prayers. "Renounce thy own will," say our sages, "for the sake of His will, and He will annul the will of others for the sake of thine." He will blunt all the arrows aimed at thy life * בטל רצונך מפני רצונו כדי שיבטל רצון אחרים מפני רצונך:

Let us, like the high priest, approach every morning the altar of incense, and thus show our readiness to undergo any sacrifice, however painful, which during the day morality and virtue may impose upon us; and the delightful perfume will not abandon our dwelling— the consciousness of our attachment to our duty will fill our heart with greater joy than the acquisition of riches. But there are sacrifices which we ought not to grudge. I mean those which are imposed upon us by God. When it is a question of defending our national name from calumnies, and Israel from his detractors; when it is a question of declining honours or distinctions, or high social position which would imply the breaking of

* Talmud Abot ii. 3.

our sacred laws, the transgression of our religious obligations, the contempt of our traditional customs, then we should undergo that sacrifice not only willingly, but with joy, with pride; and the greater our loss, the greater our merit. We shall have followed, though at a great distance, the example of the Patriarch, as well as that of our ancestors of Spain, Germany, and England, who paid with their life for their fidelity to God, and made themselves real burnt offerings, the flames of which reddened the earth and the heavens with glorious light. But remember the words of the Law: לא תעלו עליו קטרת זרה "Ye shall offer no strange incense thereon," that is, no sacrifice that has not a noble aim, no sacrifice of our principles to please the rich, no sacrifice of our dignity to obtain a smile from the great, no sacrifice of our honor to reach a higher step on the ladder of society. Then our incense will be agreeable to God, and our house will be embalmed with heavenly perfume, it will be the house of the Lord's glory; for the Lord will say : "They will come up with acceptance on my altar, and I will glorify the house of my glory" *
יעלו על רצון מזבחי ובית תפארתי אפאר :

IV.

These are the three things which adorned the sanctuary. The only object placed in the Most Holy, was the ark of the testimony : ארון העדות If we fit our houses with the three described symbols, we shall surely endear them unto the Lord; yet they cannot be called a tabernacle, unless we provide for them, morally speaking, the ark of the testimony, the most sacred thing which Israel

* Isaiah lx. 7.

possessed, and which contained the two greatest tokens of the Lord's omnipotence and wisdom : a pot of manna, and the tables of the covenant. The ark, together with its precious treasure, was the clear testimony of the intercourse of God with His own people; it was the document of the compact between the Creator and His creature. We have the glory of having been chosen as the depositaries of that document, and we must carry it with us whithersoever we go, and keep it with us with jealous care, wherever we dwell, for we testify by our existence that His power is unlimited, that His word is infallible, that His mercy is infinite. But what is the use of wearing a crown, if we wield no royal power? What is the use of handling a sword, if we have no courage to fight. What is the use of being the depositaries of the Decalogue, if we do not show by facts that it is ours? Only by carrying it out strictly and rigorously, we can show ourselves the true witnesses of the Eternal. The Lord said unto Moses: "And there I will meet thee, and I will commune with thee"* ונועדתי לך שם ודברתי אתך: So we ought to let God speak to us from the ark of testimony. If we do anything unworthy of the name of Jew, anything that savours of idolatry, or falsehood, anything that hurts our neighbour in his life, in his honor, or in his property, we are sure that an internal voice will bitterly reproach us with our fault. Let us listen to that voice, it is the Lord that speaks to us and communes with us from the ark. The Holy of Holies had no light, and needed none. The Decalogue was its immortal light. So let the Decalogue be the everlasting light of our houses, and they will never be plunged into darkness, nor be pervaded by gloom.

* Exodus xxv. 22.

Every heart in them will be filled with joy, every eye will be enlightened. And the stranger who enters them will immediately recognise them, by such characteristics, as Jewish houses, as the dwellings of the race which the Lord has blessed. And, according to our sages, the Lord will say unto us :* עשיתם לפני ארון שהתורה ניתנת בתוכו אתן לכם שכר טוב שאין בו הפסק: "As ye have made me the ark which contains the Law, so I will give you such reward as shall have no end."

This, my brethren, is the house that we are to build, this the sanctuary that we are to erect. From the brief description that I have given, from the moral proportions which I have pointed out to you, it can be clearly seen that it is no difficult task, that we can accomplish it, if we work with earnestness, if it forms the ardent aspiration of our heart. I repeat it, any Israelite can achieve the sacred undertaking. "When Moses," says the Medrash, "had heard from the mouth of God, all the details concerning the construction of the Tabernacle, he doubted the skill of his brethren, and timidly said : ' But will Israel be able to do such work ?' Not only all of them, by their united efforts, but every one among them." § בשעה שאמר הק"בה למשה על עסקי המשכן אמר לפניו רב"שע יכולין ישראל לעשותו א"ל הק"בה אפילו אחד מישראל: Let us therefore set to work. Let us furnish our houses according to the dictates of the Law, first with the burning candlestick, the light of religion which has the power of chasing from our minds the clouds of doubt, and from our heart the mist of error : a light which never sets. Secondly, with the table and the shew-bread, that is humility in the midst of greatness,

---

* Medrash Shemot Rabbah, 1.   § Shemot Rabbah xxxiii.

THE HOME SANCTUARY. 267

frugality in the midst of abundance, charity and mercy towards the needy, moderation and contentment. Thirdly, with the altar of incense, that is readiness to sacrifice our own inclinations and interests to a sense of duty, to the demands of religion. And finally, let us furnish our houses with the hallowed ark of testimony, that is, unbroken faith in our covenant, unconditional obedience to the Law, and absolute repudiation of all that is base and immoral. But the women of Israel must not forget that a great part of this religious task lies in their hands, and they, conscious of their responsibility, ought to make it a pride to follow the example of their mothers of the wilderness who worked with enthusiasm in order to beautify the tabernacle. Then upon the modern women of Israel also this great praise will be bestowed : * : וכל הנשים אשר נשא לבן אתנה בחכמה טוו "And all the women whose heart stirred them up in wisdom spun." What have they spun ? What thread have they twined? The strong thread of the morality and happiness of their families. And when we see that we have been able to turn our house into a sanctuary, then we shall almost think that we are on the verdant hill of Zion, on the summit of Mount Moriah, we shall almost fancy that we are in Jerusalem ; Jerusalem the beautiful and Divine city that "is compact together, whither the tribes go up, the tribes of the Lord, unto the testimony of Israel, to give thanks unto the name of the Lord " § עמדות היו רגלינו בשעריך ירושלים : ירושלים הבנויה כעיר שחברה לה יחדו : ששם עלו שבטים שבטי יה עדות לישראל להורות לשם ה׳ :

AMEN.

* Exodus xxxv. 26. § Psalm cxxii. 2, 3, 4.

THE HEIFER AND THE CALF.

ואיש אשר יטמא ולא יתחטא ונכרתה הנפש ההיא מתוך הקהל כי
את מקדש ה׳ טמא מי נדה לא זרק עליו טמא הוא :

"The man that shall be unclean and shall not purify himself, that soul shall be cut off from among the congregation, because he has defiled the sanctuary of the Lord : the water of separation has not been sprinkled upon him ; he is unclean."   NUM. xix. 20.

תבא פרה ותכפר על מעשה העגל :

"Let the red heifer come and make atonement for the sin of the golden calf."   MEDRASH, BAMIDBAR RABBAH, xix.

MY DEAR BRETHREN,—How, says the Talmud, how can a man show that he is really wise? By admitting that his knowledge is limited, and by being ready to receive instruction * : איזהו חכם הלומד מכל אדם   But no man was so wise as King Solomon who astounded the world by his sagacity and the soundness of his judgments, who enlightened men by his famous Proverbs, and to whom kings and queens came personally to pay a tribute of admiration. Yet he acknowledged his ignorance concerning the meaning of one of the precepts of the Law. "I have investigated," he said, "the most difficult cases and understood them, but in spite of all study, I have not been able to penetrate the signification

* Talmud Abot, iv.

of the Red Heifer; I said I will be wise, but it was far from me." * אמר שלמה על כל אלה עמדתי ופשפשתי ופרשה של פרה אדומה, חקרתי כיון שהייתי דורש וחוקר אמרתי אחכמה והיא רחוקה ממני: Nothing, in fact, appears more strange than the ceremony, by which the priest slew a red heifer and sprinkled of her blood before the tabernacle and the congregation seven times. The heifer was burnt; then the priest took cedar wood, hyssop and scarlet, and cast it into the midst of her ashes. They were preserved and mixed with water which thus became the water of separation. Anyone among the Hebrews who touched a human bone, or one slain, or one dead, or a grave, was to be unclean seven days. He was sprinkled with the water of separation on the third day, and on the seventh day he was declared clean again. Why the red heifer? Why so many different elements in the composition of that water? And, above all, why was the water to have the power of removing uncleanness? The answer is not easy. But in this, as in the most arduous occurrences, we find a reasonable solution in the Talmud, this wonderful store of practical lessons. It relates that "a heathen called upon Rabbi Jochanan ben Zaccai, the learned compiler of the Jerusalem Talmud, and questioned him in the presence of his numerous pupils, as to the signification of the ceremony of the red heifer. 'Are these not,' he said, 'arts of magic, sorcery and witchcraft? If you are unclean, can a few drops of water mixed with ashes reinstate you in your cleanliness?' 'Have you never seen,' answered the Rabbi, 'the practice with which they restore to health a man pervaded by an evil spirit? Uncleanness is a kind of evil spirit, and we banish it by the means of the ceremony of the

* Medrash Koelet, 96.

red heifer, which may be inexplicable, but is truly efficient.' 'Thou mayest " push such a man with a bit of straw,"' said the disciples to the Rabbi, when the heathen had withdrawn; 'so insignificant an answer may do for a vulgar mind, but unto us what satisfactory explanation wilt thou convey?' 'By your life,' said Rabbi Jochanan, ' neither a dead man can make unclean, nor can the water of separation purify; but it is one of the laws of the Almighty, and no one has a right to transgress it." * חייכם לא המת מטמא ולא מי נדה מטהרין אלא אמר הק״בה חקה חקקתי גזירה גזרתי ואי אתה רשאי לעבור על גזירתי: The learning of that sage, the liberality of his views, his spirit of tolerance make the importance of his answer greater and greater. It is a warning unto us really indispensable in this age of unbounded self-reliance, when every one discusses everything, and the less a philosophical or religious subject is understood, the readier people are to put forth arguments and to pronounce judgment; in this age of conceited men, of intolerant theologians, and of philosophers who miss their way in the labyrinth of their daring researches. It is a warning to us not to raise our mind to what is superhuman, and far above the reach of our intellectual faculties. We may be proud, as Israelites, that no mystery darkens our dogmas, the leading principles of religion. But if there are ceremonies, the meaning of which we do not comprehend, we must neither condemn them as foolish, nor consider ourselves exempt from their observance. The infinite wisdom which cannot err, has prescribed them to us merely to test our obedience. Shall we be unequal to the trial? If the reasons why the Lord choose that kind of sacrifice, and its

* Bamidbar Rabbah, xix.

THE HEIFER AND THE CALF.

various elements are concealed from us, at least we know that it had a moral bearing, and we can without difficulty establish its true object. It was to cleanse those who had fallen into the mire of impurity, and stained themselves by the contact of loathsome and revolting things. To the purport of His law more than to the law itself we must direct our attention, now especially that we have no longer the opportunity of carrying out its mystic rites.

The Pentateuch sums up this peculiar injunction with the same impressive words which it applies to the cardinal laws of the Mosaic legislation; it says, "And it shall be a perpetual statute unto them"* והיתה להם לחקת עולם: Should we then think that so solemn a declaration was used about the uncleanliness of the body, and that the Almighty showed so much solicitude only relating to the corporal impurity of man, which fresh and pure water easily washes away? To hold that opinion would be grossly to misjudge the wisest of all legislations. The intent of the Mosaic code, as clearly impressed in every line and every word, is to foster man's sanctification and resemblance with the divine image. It urges him to resist the allurements of passion, as well as the false splendour of life, and to master his senses which, left without control, would make him akin to the brutes, useless to himself, a burden to his neighbours, a nuisance to society. It fills up every moment in our existence with religious acts, sacred symbols, prayers and meditations, so that no time may remain for us to to yield to intemperance, to stain our lips and to profane our hearts. We must therefore conclude that the intention of the Lord was to warn us

* Numbers xix. 21.

especially against the uncleanness of the soul, against moral impurity, which is real impurity, which once deeply rooted is ineradicable, and which was so forcibly defined by Jeremiah, when he said,* "for though thou wash thee with nitre and take much soap, yet thine iniquity is marked before me, saith the Lord God" כי אם תכבסי בנתר ותרבי לך ברית נכתם עונך לפני נאם ה' אלהים: Few religious legislators have recommended the personal sanctification of man more persistently than Moses; few preachers have waged a more violent war against moral pollution than our prophets. And why? It is because Israel has no political task. His mission is entirely moral. He may be called, so to say, the *ideal-people*, the people that must always offer the spectacle of morality and virtue. Israel cannot be a holy nation if he is not the purest among nations; that is, if his children do not scrupulously abstain from dishonest professions and base vocations, which constitute an unceasing conspiracy against the honest part of society. What is judged as frivolous by other nations must be considered as sinful by Israel. That which is conventionally called laxity to be tolerated by the law, ought to be held by Israel as profanation and absolute impurity.

Israel unfortunately often forgot that his position imposed upon him the highest obligations, and that great rights cannot be claimed without the acceptance of great duties. He repeatedly overlooked his noble mission of virtue. And if you have attentively read this morning's lesson of the Law, you must have seen that our forefathers impressed upon their name such stain as never was and never will be entirely effaced. Three months had scarcely passed since God had miraculously delivered

* ii. 22.

THE HEIFER AND THE CALF.

them from the tyranny of Pharaoh. The Egyptian widows and orphans were still weeping for the loss of their husbands and fathers buried in the unexplored bottom of the Red Sea, and gratitude ought still to have ruled in the heart of the Hebrews. Only forty days had elapsed since the wondrous event of revelation, and Moses, concealed under the cloud which surrounded the mountain, was still writing under the dictation of the Lord, the Law, the תורה so justly termed "light of intellect and bread of soul." And yet the Hebrews, in a fit of impatience and madness, remembered nothing, neither deliverance nor revelation. They forgot that the Lord had no material form and would be represented by none. They would have, like all idolatrous nations, a god of metal, a golden calf, the image of Api, the Egyptian divinity. They prostituted both their body and their spirit by worshipping the inanimate work of man, by exclaiming,* : אלה אלהיך ישראל אשר העלוך מארץ מצרים "These be thy Gods, O Israel, which brought thee up out of the land of Egypt." That was surely an act of heinous ingratitude, of revolting impurity. In His just indignation the Lord said unto Moses:§ "Now therefore let me alone that my wrath may wax hot against them and that I may consume them." : ועתה הניחה לי ויחר אפי בהם ואכלם Softened, however, by the prayer of the Prophet, He pardoned; but the Hebrews had by their conduct stripped themselves of their spiritual ornaments, of that splendid crown which they had received on Mount Horeb‖ ויתנצלו בני ישראל את עדים מהר חורב: and a mark of infamy, of indestructible impurity remained from that day on the name of the Hebrews, and made them an object of scorn and contempt unto their enemies : ¶לשמצה בקמיהם

* Ex. xxxii. 4.   § Ex. xxxii. 10.   ‖ Ex. xxxiii. 6.   ¶ Ex. xxxii. 25.

SERMON XVIII.

A calf was worshipped in Egypt as well as among many other nations in their primitive state, yet the notion of the Golden Calf was identified with the Jewish name, and it was said that wherever the Golden Calf was worshipped, the Jew was to be found. That was the accusation of mankind against our race, and you understand that by Golden Calf they meant unconquerable covetousness, unrestrained cupidity, and readiness to employ any means for its gratification. From the moment when we were scattered on the surface of the earth, we were treated as the pariahs of society, the target of its abhorrence. The position of our ancestors became every day gloomier and gloomier. Unremittingly molested and harassed, plundered and banished by the very states which had eagerly summoned them, condemned to live in the most unhealthy quarters of the towns, excluded from all honourable professions, they were obliged to pay for the very air which they breathed. And what was the pretext for this cruel persecution? What was the argument advanced by intolerance and fanaticism? Always the same: the Golden Calf. They have obtained their wealth by usury, said the populace; they are sucking the blood of the people, said the demagogues who instigated the rabble; they acquire too much influence by becoming the creditors of princes and nobles, said the priests, whose intent was to increase the public hatred against the proscribed race. But our ancestors had no other resource than to exercise commerce and to lend money. They needed money in order to redeem their lives and to satisfy the rapacity of their implacable enemies; just as to stay the fury of wild beast, we throw to it from time time a piece of flesh. "We are forced to impose exorbitant interest," said Manasseh Ben Israel to Cromwell, "for our oppressors levy so many taxes upon us all at once, that after many years only can we breathe and feel some relief." * So the sin of our forefathers, the Golden Calf cost us dearly, even after many centuries, even when circumstances beyond our control should have been our defence.

But are we free from that impurity now that entire liberty has been restored to us? Are our mental faculties less devoted to the deification of what is perishable, the gathering of material possessions? Alas! I see now-a-days a great emulation among the generality of men. Very seldom emulation for religion, seldom for learning, or for virtue, but always emulation for the attainment of wealth. Every one wishes to be richer than his neighbour, to exhibit more splendid palaces, more precious jewels, and greater heaps of gold. Isaiah seems to have spoken of the present time, when he said §
"Their land is also full of silver and gold, neither is there any end to their treasures; their land is also full of horses, neither is there any end to their chariots.

---

* When the learned Manasheh Ben Israel applied personally to Oliver Cromwell for the re-admission of the Jews into England, the Protector reminded him of the three accusations that were constantly directed against the Jews. 1st. That they employed the blood of a Christian child in the performance of their Passover ceremonies. 2nd. That they impoverished by their usury the country in which they lived. 3rd. Their unremitting efforts to convert their countrymen to Judaism.—The eloquent Rabbi easily proved the injustice and futility of the first accusation. He showed that the second grievance might be averted if all trades were freely opened to the Jews. He denied the third charge which is contrary to the views of our religion. But he promised that such things should never occur in England. The Jews were re-admitted by Act of Parliament on December 14, 1655, and from that time no Christian has been converted to Judaism in this country. That was, and is still the rule of the Chief Rabbis of England.

§ ii. 7, 8, 9.

Their land is also full of idols: they worship the work of their hand, that which their own fingers have made. So the mean man is debased, the great man lowers himself; therefore forgive them not" וישח אדם וישפל איש ואל תשא להם:

But it is impossible, however, to become rich all at once, especially when capital is limited. The great competition allows honest and wise commerce to have only small profits, and progressive success. Therefore the most hazardous speculations, the most adventurous undertakings are set on foot; therefore immoral contrivances are resorted to, such as gambling and betting, which make man despicable, and which, especially in the middle classes, are so often the cause of troubles, quarrels and misery; therefore men often stake on one bold chance all that they possess; the property of their wives, the bread of their children. More than that, they stake their name and their honour. If they succeed, all is well, they are at the top of the social ladder; they are rich, and all smiles are directed to them; everyone bows to them; praises, flatteries, distinctions, all fall to their share. If they fail, then . . . . then . . . . oh, I cannot say, it is too horrible. Am I to remind you of the downfalls that occur every day, and of the failure of the greatest establishments? Numerous families are suddenly plunged into misery. The houses which, last night, were the scene of luxuriant and princely entertainments, are to-day visited by officers of justice. Shame and dishonour surround names, previously highly respected. One merchant fails and involves many houses in his ruin. Another absconds and wilfully reduces many honest traders to poverty. Oh, the Golden Calf, the Golden Calf! how numerous are its votaries and its victims! This

THE HEIFER AND THE CALF.

is a glorious age for Israel; he has a place in the most honourable assemblies, he is represented in the House of Parliament, among the ministers of justice, among the eloquent defenders of the people's rights; but unhappily, he is represented also among daring speculators, among unscrupulous money lenders, among hard-hearted usurers, among those who do not respect their engagements towards their creditors; and this ought not to be. Our brethren ought carefully to avoid the profession of money-lending, because it offers such temptations of large and rapid gain as man can seldom resist, and because, in consequence of the enormities of moneylenders, many still hate and despise the Jewish race. There are numerous money-lenders among our countrymen of other creeds, yet the hateful name is attached to us, and one Jewish money-lender is enough to disgrace the whole community. No, it ought not to be; for it is written in the Law, that the children of Israel ought always to transact business in a fair and conscientious manner: "And if thou sell aught unto thy neighbour, or buyest aught of thy neighbour, ye shall not cheat one another"* וכי תמכרו ממכר לעמיתך או קנה מיד עמיתך אל תונו איש את אחיו: "Usurers may be compared to those who shed blood"§ הוקשו לוקחי ברבית לשופכי דמים: It is true that such things are practised by the nations in the midst of which we exist, but that is no justification. We must be more rigorously honest than others. We cannot preserve the glorious name of the chosen people, unless we make our first privilege consist in the practice of virtue. If Israel is really to be the firstborn son of the Lord, we must act towards all other nations as a

---

* Leviticus xxv. 14. § Talmud, B. Meziha, 61.

firstborn son should act towards his younger brothers, that is, he should set before them the example of purity of life, of the strictest probity and of the rigid exercise of the precept "Thou shalt love thy neighbour as thyself"* ואהבת לרעך כמוך: You see, therefore, that the uncleanness to which the Golden Calf gave rise, in whatever form our forefathers may have worshipped it, was of a moral description: it was not only a proof of thanklessness towards the Lord, but also a degradation of the dignity of man. So the ceremony of the Red Heifer was a symbol of the purification of the soul, and in that sense it constituted an atonement for the sin of the Golden Calf. Of it our sages give a beautiful and striking explanation. In all sacrifices, they say, only male animals are offered up; by this law of purification, a female, a heifer was chosen. Why, in this case a different rule? A mother, they reply, is the best safeguard of her child. She knows in what he is likely to fail, and she devotes herself to his rehabilitation: so, merely as an emblem, "let a heifer, the mother come and make atonement for her child, the calf" * תבא פרה ותכפר על מעשה העגל: Let water, the symbol of purity, hyssop, the symbol of humility, and ashes, the truest symbol of the end of man, be employed in order to restore us to our former cleanness, to our former innocence, to that unspotted state in which, according to our doctrines, we *have been created* and in which we ought to remain. But these views were not held by our sages only. Ezekiel had, long before them, expressed similar ideas: Ezekiel, the Prophet who always uttered frank, though bitter truths, who is a model of the Lord's preacher, because he never flattered his audience, never let the impure actions of his contemporaries pass

* Leviticus xix. 18. § Bamidbar Rabbah, xix.

THE HEIFER AND THE CALF.

unobserved, never was afraid to call upon them the wrath of heaven. Have you reflected upon his words which we have read this morning? Was not your heart moved by the energy of his expressions, the nobleness of his images, the justice of his resentment? That chapter may be called the real explanation of this day's lesson of the Law, of the sin of the Golden Calf. "Son of man," said the Lord unto Ezekiel, "when the house of Israel dwelt in their own land, they defiled it by their way and by their doings, etc. And when they entered unto the heathens, whither they went, they profaned my holy name"* בן אדם ישראל יושבים על אדמתם ויטמאו אותה בדרכם ובעלילותם וכול׳ ויבאו אל הגויים אשר באו שם ויטמאו את שם קדשי: So, even Ezekiel proclaims, like the sages, that "a dead body cannot defile, neither can the water of separation restore cleanness"; לא המת מטמא ולא מי נדה מטהרין that it is not by touching a corpse that a man can become unclean, but by indulging in sinful actions. The Israelites profaned their land but only by their unprincipled conduct, by corrupting their bodies, by lowering their immortal spirit, by contracting vicious habits, by yielding to covetousness which refuses to know the limits of what is mine and what is thine, and the sacred boundaries of justice. And when the Hebrews were scattered among the nations, they again defiled themselves; not by coming in contact with a human bone or with a grave, but by profaning the name of the Eternal in the presence of the other races, by eluding the laws of that religion which enjoins justice towards men of all creeds and all countries, proscribes hatred and revenge, and has created the best institutions of universal charity. Then the pollution of the name of

* Ezekiel xxxvi. 17.

the Lord became even greater, because the Hebrews forced their countrymen to exclaim with surprise: "Oh, can those who act so deceitfully be the people of God"* באמר להם עם ה׳ אלה the people to whose charge God himself entrusted the Decalogue, to whom He said: "Ye shall be holy, for I the Lord your God am holy?"§ קדושים תהיו כי קדוש אני ה׳ אלהיכם: Now we understand why He visited them with such severe punishment, why He deprived them of His great inheritance, why He banished them from His land": ומארצו יצאו God could not let this profanation remain unpunished. "Wherefore, he said, I poured my fury upon them, and they were dispersed through the countries. According to their way, and according to their doings I judged them"‖ כדרכם וכעלילותם שפטתים: So our uncleanness was of immoral nature, and moral must be our purification. But the merciful God Himself, said Ezekiel, will assist us in our great work of reconstruction and regeneration. "Then will I sprinkle clean water upon you, and ye shall be clean; from all your filthiness and all your idols will I cleanse you; a new heart also will I give you, and a new spirit will I put within you; and I will take away the stony heart out of your flesh, and I will give you a heart of flesh"¶ והסרתי את לב האבן מקרבכם ונתתי לכם לב בשר: This, my brethren, ought to be our great task, to prepare ourselves for this noble change. Let us get rid of a heart of stone, which has no feeling, no sensitiveness, and cannot appreciate the beauty of our religion, the charm of a virtuous life. Let there be in its place a heart of flesh, a soft merciful heart, which shrinks from evil inspirations, feels gener-

---

* Ezekiel xxxvi. 20.   § Leviticus, xix. 2.
‖ Ezekiel xxxvi. 19.   ¶ Ezekiel ib.

ously, and can love. As soon as we have freed ourselves from our impurity, the water of the red heifer will no longer be required. The utterances of our lips replace now the sacrifices of old; and humility, faith, repentance can constitute the true elements of the waters of separation that will in future efface all our iniquity. The result of such purification, says Ezekiel, will be beautiful. Then ruin and desolation shall vanish for ever. The land that was laid waste shall become like the garden of Eden, and cities that were in ashes shall arise again and be inhabited. "Then the heathen that are left round about you shall know that I, the Lord, will build the ruined places, and plant that that was desolate: I, the Lord have spoken and will do it" * וידעו הגויים אשר ישארו סביבותיכם כי אני ה׳ בניתי הנהרסות נטעתי הנשמה אני ה׳ דברתי ועשיתי:

PRAYER.

Almighty God, in making a comparison between the past and the present, between our ancestors and ourselves, we are obliged to bow our face with shame, and whisper in confusion כי לא טוב אנכי מאבתי "I am not better than my fathers." § We have the same failings, the same shortcomings, the same defects as they had. We are ruled by the same inclinations, tempted by the same allurements, and led to the same transgressions, to the same idolatry. We forget that we bear the flag of purity and we defile ourselves; we forget that we are the depositaries of the Law of sanctification; and by indulging in the most lowering of earthly enjoyments, we profane both our spirit and the name of Israel. But our condition is worse than that of our ancestors, for we are no

---

* Ezekiel xxxvi. 36.   § 1 Kings xix. 4.

longer shielded by the holiness of the prophets. Not one will arise among us and say unto the Lord, "Yet now, if Thou wilt, forgive their sin; and if not, blot me, I pray Thee, out of the book which Thou hast written" *
ועתה אם תשא חטאתם ואם אין מחני נא מספרך אשר כתבת :
For who can wield the power of a Moses? But we all, we Thine assembled children, ardently implore Thee to exercise on our behalf Thy great attribute of clemency, to remember that we are but flesh, and above all not to try us by temptation, for our moral strength is but frail and limited. Grant, O grant this prayer, which we raise unto Thee every morning, when Thou awakenest us to labor and activity. "May it be Thy will, O Lord our God! and God of our fathers, to accustom us to Thy Law, and to attach us to Thy precepts: O suffer us not to be led into the power of sin, transgression, temptation, or contempt, remove us from evil imagination, and grant unto us this day and every day, grace, favour and mercy in Thy sight, and in the sight of all who behold us, and bestow gracious favours upon us. Blessed art Thou, O Lord, who bestowest gracious favours upon Thy people Israel" § ברוך הגומל חסדים טובים לעמו ישראל :

AMEN.

* Exodus xxxii. 32.   § Morning Prayers.

THE OMER.

וּכְפַרְתֶּם לָכֶם מִמׇּחֳרַת הַשַּׁבָּת כִּיּוֹם הֲבִיאֲכֶם אֶת עֹמֶר הַתְּנוּפָה שֶׁבַע שַׁבָּתוֹת תְּמִימֹת תִּהְיֶינָה:

"And ye shall count unto you from the morrow after the day of rest, from the day that ye brought the wave of the wheat offering; seven Sabbaths shall ye complete."
LEVITICUS xxiii. 15.

אֵימָתַי הֵן תְּמִימוֹת כָּל זְמַן שֶׁיִּשְׂרָאֵל עוֹשִׂין רְצוֹנוֹ שֶׁל מָקוֹם:

"When will these seven weeks be really complete? When Israel shall carry out the will of the Almighty."
VAIKRA RABBAH, xxviii.

MY DEAR BRETHREN,—A recommendation is frequently repeated in the Talmud, a saying which was constantly on the lips of the great author of the Mishna, and it is a warning which no good Jew should ever forget: "Be as careful in performing a light precept as you are careful in performing an important one, for it is difficult to penetrate the real import of religious precepts, it is impossible to know the recompense given for them either in this life or in the next"* הֱוֵי זָהִיר בְּמִצְוָה קַלָּה כְּבַחֲמוּרָה: The dogmas which in other religions are often mysterious and inexplicable, are extremely clear in ours; they are the light which chases from the mind the mist of doubt; instead of a perishable body and of

* Talmud Abot, ii. 1.

a limited existence, they concern that spirit which is immortal, like its Creator, and that spiritual life which has no end. But in the midst of the six hundred and thirteen precepts of which the Law consists, there are some religious acts, some simple ceremonies for which the Law apparently gives no reason, but which are equally binding upon us while it is left to our mental power to find their real meaning. But the ignorant, under the pretext that those pious acts are incomprehensible, consider them as unimportant, and devoid of authority. In the apparent senselessness of such precepts a new arm is afforded unto those who wage war against all forms, and who make use of this new argument in order to find objects for their destroying zeal. That is the reason why many beautiful and poetical ceremonies have fallen into neglect and disuse in numerous Jewish families. Our sages were right, therefore, in denouncing ignorance as a fatal poison; they were right in recommending us not to neglect the precepts which are apparently unimportant.

I apply this principle, to-day, to the *Omer*—the Omer, a precept which in this seemingly enlightened age, I have seen more than one of our brethren mention with a smile, as if to say, " Who will now count the Omer, a meaningless practice?" " Let that be performed by those who seem unable to appreciate the achievements of modern progress." Yet, if some of those who think so are here to-day, they will be astonished to hear the explanation of that precept, to hear its great meaning, to hear me call it, in consequence of its profound signification, almost as important as one of the Ten Commandments.

THE OMER.

I.

It is thus written in chap. xxiii. of Leviticus, "And ye shall count unto you from the morrow after the day of rest, from the day that ye brought the wheat of the wave offering; seven Sabbaths shall be complete: even unto the morrow after the seventh Sabbath shall ye number fifty days, and ye shall offer a new offering unto the Lord." What was the object of these rites? Why a first offering of the fruit of the earth on the second day of Passover, and a second offering of the same nature in the festival of Shebuoth? Why were the intervening days between Passover and Pentecost to be rigorously counted one after the other? Palestine is not one of those northern countries that suffer from the implacable harshness of their climate. The climate of Palestine is beautiful; it is blessed with the constant smile of heaven upon the earth, and of the earth up to heaven; the serenity of its sky is unparalleled; unparalleled the luxuriant vegetation of its plains and hills; unparalleled the grandeur of its mountains, with their gigantic cedars; and the manner in which Moses spoke of the Holy Land well explains the enthusiasm which at all times the Jews have evinced for that country of predilection. "The land whither you go to possess it is a land of hills and valleys, and drinketh water of the rain of heaven, a land which the Lord thy God cares for; the eyes of the Lord thy God are always upon it, from the beginning of the year even to the end of the year."* Palestine, as David said, is the perfection of beauty, which reflects the splendour of the Almighty§ : מציון מכלל יפי אלהים הופיע The spring is in Tebet, when we are shivering from cold; the begin-

---

* Deut. xi. 11, 12.   § Psalm l. 2.

ning of the harvest is in Nisan, when incessant rains sadden our days. In Nisan they began to reap the barley; and in the times of old, as it is related in the Mishna,* the delegates of the Sanhedrim cut in a field, in the neighbourhood of Jerusalem, the tops of ripe barley ears. The grains were beaten out, roasted in a perforated vessel and ground in a coarse mill: a tenth of an ephah of the flour was taken and sifted through thirteen sieves, oil and incense were added to it, thus it was waved : והניף את העמר A handful was burnt on the altar as a memorial, and the rest was eaten by the priests. No cakes made with the barley were to be eaten before that offering and waving before the Lord. That was only the beginning of the harvest. That sweet labour which was accompanied by joy as the sowing had been accompanied by tears, was continued; after the barley the wheat was reaped; but no bread was to be made with the new wheat until two leavened wheaten loaves had been offered to the Lord on the first day of Pentecost. The interval between the barley and the wheat offerings consisted of seven weeks, and the Hebrews were commanded to number the days of those seven weeks which were thus to be made complete.

What could that regular counting mean but gratitude to Providence? that is, to the supreme wisdom which fathomed the world and directs everything towards its end by means of laws, dictated alike by mercy and by justice. To count all those days was to count the blessings with which the Lord had assisted them in their agricultural works, in their commercial undertakings. When they counted the first day they

* Menachod x. 19.

remembered the wearisome labours of agriculture, they
remembered their oppressive fatigue when they prepared
the soil, when they planted the seeds, when they reared,
fed and managed their live stock; they remembered the
sweat of their brow when they carried on tillage, hus-
bandry and farming; and they burst forth into a cry of
praise to the Almighty. In counting the second day,
they reflected that all the labours of agriculture could not
have any good result without the assistance of God;
they thought of the aridity of many countries, of the
burning sands of Arabia, of those skies that never give
rain, of those fields that never yield produce, and they
blessed the Almighty who, according to His promise,
had given the rain of their land "in due season, the
first rain, and the latter rain " * ונתתי מטר ארצכם בעתו
יורה ומלקוש: In counting the third day, they reflected
upon the numerous obstacles that often prevent the
success of all industrious works, the invasion of an
enemy, internal dissensions, the attacks of wild beasts,
the visits of locusts, and they thanked the Almighty
who had saved their land from such plagues, from such
disasters; and they went on counting till they reached
the forty-ninth day, which was immediately followed by
a brilliant festival.—Yes, the Omer means gratitude to
Him who is the source of all blessings, and Moses
wisely instituted it because he well knew the nature of
man, who forgets too easily the good which he has
enjoyed, as well as the hand which has ministered
unto him. In vain he said: § ואכלת ושבעת וברכת את
ה' אלהיך "When thou hast eaten and art full, then thou
shalt bless the Lord thy God." For there are a great
many who consider the products of the earth, not as

* Deut. xi. 14.   § Deut. viii. 10.

the effect of the goodness of a Supreme Being, but as the result of the immutable laws imposed upon nature at the moment of creation. There are many who in the beautiful system and harmony of the universe see the work of hazard only. And this is a prudent device in order to shake off the burden of gratitude which weighs upon them. In vain have our sages insisted upon this sacred duty when they said * אסור ליהנות מע״הז בלא ברכה "It is forbidden to enjoy anything upon the earth without pronouncing the name of the Lord with a blessing." For how many remember to thank God after their meals, after having satisfied their hunger not only by bread, but also by all those luxuries which the Lord grants to them every day, every hour? Why when a three hours' dinner is deemed insufficient, a five minutes' grace should be considered to be too much! They forget, unfortunately, that by their words of thanksgiving they would cause God to sit at their table, to bless their bread, to give a perfume of sanctity to their household. We have no longer the sanctuary whereto we might bring our barley at Passover, or our new loaves at Pentecost, but if we count the forty-nine days in the interval, we shall have the same merit, because we shall have reached the object of that precept, which is to root in our heart what constitutes our tie with the Lord—gratitude and love; the gratitude of the relieved to the generous reliever, the love of children towards the father, of the subjects towards their king.

The Talmud says: § אל תהי מצות העומר קלה בעיניך שע״י מצות העומר זכה אברהם לירש את הארץ: "Defile not the precept of the Omer, for by performing it Abraham deserved to inherit the land." And what can

* Talmud Berachot, 35. § Vaikra Rabbah, 28.

the meaning of our sages be but this, that our thankfulness to Providence will secure unto us its everlasting favor, the possession of the land, that is, the satisfaction of all our wants, a life free from the cares of poverty and from suffering? It is related in the book of Judges that when Gideon at the head of only three hundred brave Hebrews, but strengthened by the protection of God, would attack the army of Midian more than a hundred thousand men strong, he penetrated during the night with his servant Phurah into the camp of the enemies to know their order and disposition; there he heard a soldier who was telling his dream to his fellow, a dream in which he had seen a cake of barley bread which "tumbled into the host of Midian, and came unto a tent, and smote it that it fell, and overturned it, that the tent lay along" * ויכהו ויפל ויהפכהו למעלה ונפל האהל : The fellow answered, that the cake was the sword of Gideon who would surely defeat Midian, as in truth it came to pass. But the Talmud says that the *barley cake*, the צליל שעורים represented the offering of the Omer as the symbol of the gratitude of Israel towards God, the best arm by which he always could resist his most powerful adversaries. "This simple precept of the Omer," says the Zoar, "powerfully contributes to harmony and peace between man and wife" § עומר דא מקרבין ישראל וכולי ודא אתקריב למיעל רחימו בין איתתא לבעלה : And is not that natural? If in a family, thankfulness towards God is felt and practised, can there be discord? Will not the two partners of life practise the same virtue towards each other? Will they not be thankful for the help which they lend unto each other in bearing the burden of existence? Will they not feel doubly happy in their mutual assistance?

* Judges vii. 13.   § Comment. on Leviticus.

"See," say our sages, employing a simple and practical example, see what labour men must undergo before they can avail themselves of the products of the earth, before they can make them eatable. See our manifold operations before we can adapt the materials of nature to our wants, and make bread out of the corn, garments out of the sheep's wool, houses with lime and stones. Yet we have merely to modify their form, we are not called upon to achieve the more difficult (if possible) work of bringing them into existence. But for the myriads of living creatures that have neither the thought nor the power of working, God provides abundant food. "Thou givest them, they gather; Thou openest Thy hand, they are filled with good"* תתן להם ילקטון תפתח ידך ישבעון טוב : And while men quietly enjoy their nightly rest, the Lord causes the wind to blow, the clouds to gather above the earth, the plants to grow, and the fruit to become ripe. Yet we simply present Him with the modest offering of the Omer. Ought we not, then, to compensate for the insignificance and simplicity of the sacrifice with the infinite gratitude of our heart?"§ נוהג שבעולם אדם לוקח ליטרא אחת של בשר מן השוק כמה יניעות הוא יגע כמה צער הוא מצער עד שיבשלה הבריות ישנין והק"בה משיב רוחות ומעלה עננים ומגדל צמחים ומדשן את הפירות ואין נותנין לו אלא שכר העומר :

II.

The Omer thus clearly points out to us gratitude to Providence, that duty which is never sufficiently recommended. But that is not all. It can be examined under a different aspect, it can be again the source of much instruction, and bear another great signification. In establishing the various festivals which the

---

* Psalm civ. 28.   § Vaikra Rabbah, xxviii.

Hebrew nation was to celebrate, Moses generally fixed the exact time at which each festival was to take place. The 15th of Nisan is never omitted when the Law speaks of Passover; nor the first, or the tenth, of the seventh month, when the New Year, or the Day of Atonement, is mentioned. Yet when it describes the Feast of Weeks it never reminds us of its date; it never says: "Ye shall keep it on the sixth of the third month." Instead of that, it orders us to count seven weeks from the second day of Passover, and the fiftieth day must be devoted to the Lord as a day of holy convocation. Is that not strange? Whence that difference with regard to the great feast of revelation? The first idea that strikes us is this: that there is a mysterious tie between the two festivals, and that the forty-nine days are the link that keeps them closely united. And in what does this consist? First of all, we must remember that Passover was marked by the barley- and Shebuoth by the wheat-harvest. The latter festival was therefore attached to the former in respect of their common agricultural character. The farmer celebrates with joy the gathering of the hay in the spring, that is the provender of his cattle; but then he anxiously counts the days which must elapse before he can reap the wheat, his own bread and the bread of his family. This prosperity is only secured when one harvest follows the other. If, after the hay, the wheat does not come, what prospect can he have but the prospect of want and poverty, dejection, and suffering? The ancient Hebrews were essentially given to agriculture, and the abundance or the scarcity of the products of the earth was synonymous for them with wealth or indigence. By the Lord's command, therefore, they were to count the days between the two festivals, that is, between the two harvests, in order that they might keep their eyes fixed upon the Lord and not upon themselves, and rely upon a merciful Providence rather than upon their own exertions. For, as Jeremiah said: " Blessed is the man that trusteth in the Lord, and whose hope the Lord is "* ברוך הגבר אשר יבטח בה׳ / והיה ה׳ מבטחו:

What is the real object of Passover and Shebuoth under their moral aspect? Passover was instituted to commemorate the deliverance of our ancestors from Egypt; Shebuoth in its turn reminds us of the portentous event of revelation. Passover celebrates the day of material resurrection, when a whole nation was freed from most degrading slavery, which condemned men to the existence of the brute, which imposed upon them intolerable labour, and cruelly punished them for their inability to perform it. Shebuoth glorifies the epoch of moral revival, when the fetters of ignorance and superstition were broken to pieces; when truth, announced in the midst of the majestic splendour of the Lord and by the Lord Himself, came to tear off the bandage of error by which the eyes of the Hebrews had been covered in the land of the Pharaohs. Passover is therefore intimately connected with Shebuoth, since the one is the complement of the other, since the one would doubtless have been inefficient without the other. In fact, what is the use of liberty and independence to a nation if it is to remain savage, idolatrous, ignorant and immoral? Liberty would on the contrary be unto it a fatal gift, which would destroy its possessor. In the same manner the revelation of sublime truths to a people of slaves would be out of place, for they could never under-

* Jeremiah xvii. 7.

stand nor appreciate them. God did not deliver Israel from Egypt for the mere sake of freedom, and in order that he might, like all other nations, run a wild career, become the victim of his own excesses, and sink at last into dissolution and oblivion. He rescued our ancestors from Egypt for the one grand object,— to bring them on eagle's wings to the foot of Mount Sinai, to the sublimity of revelation, to make them His own chosen nation. Even before beginning the work of redemption, He declared His divine will to Moses from the burning bush וזה לך האות כי אנכי שלחתיך בהוציאך את העם ממצרים תעבדון את האלהים על ההר הזה: "And this shall be a token unto thee that I have sent thee: when thou hast brought forth the people out of Egypt, ye shall serve God upon this mountain."* The Hebrews understood and accepted that noble, responsible station, for but seven weeks after deliverance, both before and after the terrific scene of revelation, they, with one united voice, promised the most absolute obedience to the warnings that had come from Heaven, to the words which had spoken truth and wisdom. The practice of counting the Omer not only is not a childish, insignificant ceremony, but it is a most instructive symbol, which establishes a mysterious union between free-will and obedience, between the benefited and their benefactor. It tacitly points out the Law as the strongest link between man and the Creator—that Law, whose fundamental principles were proclaimed from the summit of a *mountain* and amidst FIRE, probably to show that they would for ever be as firm as a rock; that they would be as vivifying as fire to the observant, as destructive as lightning to the transgressors.

* Exodus iii. 12.

III.

The Law says : וספרתם לכם "Ye shall count unto you." Let us apply this counting of days to our own existence! Yes, let us appear before the tribunal of our conscience and count the days of our life. Let us enumerate all the good actions with which we have made them meritorious, as well as the acts of immorality by which we have disgraced them. וספרתם לכם Let us number the days of our life, and see if by advancing on the road of time, we have also advanced on the road of virtue and religion, if we have made one step further towards our moral regeneration, if we have caused the Divine hand to write on our behalf one word of merit, one mark of approbation, in the adamantine book wherein every man's actions are daily registered. We are young, and the Omer that we are to count is long still; those fifty days are years; they pass on slowly, and it seems as though they would never end. Oh let us employ well the considerable time bestowed upon us; let us make a noble use of the materials which God has thus placed in our hands—just as the seed is placed in the hands of the labourer—merely to see how we profit by them and make them fruitful. Let us employ them in the accomplishment of our double calling, as children of the selected people, and as members of the Divine assembly. We are old, and the Omer that we are to count will not consist of many weeks; our days are like hours; the nearer our life draws to its close, the shorter our days appear to be. We shall not have a long distance to traverse before we reach the point at which we are to stop. Since the space allowed us is so very limited, let us try to do good, to make reparation for the

THE OMER.

wrongs in which we have indulged, and by which we have either hurt the feelings, or damaged the interests, of our fellow-men. The sun is about to set, it is late, let us purify our soul before the end of the Omer arrives and obliges us to restore our spirit to the Creator who gave it. That counting must not be carried out at intervals; it must be continuous; no earthly care ought to interfere with it, for it ought to be our all-absorbing care. The time of rest is, in that respect, like the time of labour, it must be taken into account; we ought not to forget any day, because, as it is written in the Law, "there ought to be seven weeks complete and perfect." And why, ask our sages, why that recommendation, when it has already been stated that forty-nine days were to be numbered? It signifies that all the prescribed days will really be numbered, all the seven weeks be really complete when Israel shall carry out the will of the Almighty אימתי הן תמימות כל זמן ‎*שישראל עושין רצונו של מקום: Then after the seven weeks, we shall be permitted to offer unto the Lord a *new sacrifice*—the new produce which the earth has yielded after long and conscientious labour. And will not both our body and our soul, that we shall have regenerated and rescued from the bondage of immorality, constitute a *new sacrifice*, an offering worthy to be placed on the altar of the Lord and agreeable to the pure and holy Being? The end of the Omer of our life will be a real Pentecost, the real Festival of Revelation, for a new world will be then revealed unto us, a future existence, with all its joy and its peace, with all its rewards and its everlasting enjoyments; a celestial existence § "without material food and sensual pleasures, without social inter-

* Vaikra Rabbah, xxviii.　　§ Talmud Berachot, 17.

course or degrading passions, and during which the righteous, adorned with an immortal crown, will delight in the indescribable joy of beholding the Majesty of God * העולם הבא אין בו לא אכילה ולא שתייה ולא פריה ורביה ולא משא ומתן ולא קנאה ולא שנאה ולא תחרות אלא צדיקים יושבים ועטרותיהם בראשיהם ונהנים מזיו השכינה :

PRAYER.

Almighty God! We cannot think of the eventful course of our life without feeling sad and gloomy; sometimes our undertakings are unsuccessful; sometimes our health is shattered; and when physical pain does not torment us, bitter grief is sure to come and try our patience and firmness. There are days when we must ask ourselves: Would it not be better to enjoy the passive rest of the grave, than to wander and struggle in this world of delusion? What is life but an uninterrupted series of stormy battles, of unsatisfied desires, of vain hopes and useless regrets? But then only one thing can give us some relief; only the thought of religion can heal the wounds of our heart; for we say with David,* : לולי תורתך שעשעי אז אבדתי בעניי "Were not Thy Law my real delight, I should surely have been the victim of my misery." Yes, Thy Law is our best friend, our faithful adviser, our untiring consoler, and this we declare before Thee on the eve of the Festival of Revelation, the anniversary of that day when Thou didst bestow upon us the greatest of Thy boons. Oh! keep constantly before the eye of our soul Mount Sinai with its divine flame; keep over us the immortal light of the Ten Commandments; let it be the pillar of fire that will guide us through the darkness of our sufferings; and in

* Psalm cxix. 92.

THE OMER.

spite of all obstacles we shall have no fear, in spite of all misfortunes our courage will not be shaken, our moral strength will not be impaired. Every one of us will repeat, in behalf of himself, the words of the prophet Habakkuk : " I will rejoice in the Lord, I will joy in the God of my salvation ; the Lord God is my strength, and He will make my feet like hind's feet, and He will make me walk upon my high places"* ואני בה׳ אעלוזה אגילה באלהי ישעי : אלהים אדני חילי וישם רגלי כאילות ועל במותי ידרכני למנצח בנגינותי :

AMEN.

* Habakkuk iii. 18, 19.

RELIGIOUS MAJORITY.

———◆———

והזהרתה אתהם את החקים ואת התורות והודעת להם את הדרך
ילכו בה ואת המעשה אשר יעשון:

"And thou shalt teach them ordinances and laws, and shalt shew them the way wherein they must walk, and the work that they must do."
EXODUS xviii. 20.

איזו דרך ישרה שיבור לו האדם כל שהיא תפארת לעושיה ותפארת
לו מן האדם:

"Which is the path which man should choose? It is that which honors him in his own sight, and in the sight of his fellow-creatures."
TALMUD ABOT ii. 1.

———◆———

MY YOUNG FRIENDS,—One of the prayers which we fervently address three times a day unto the Lord, and to the object of which we attach the highest importance, is that by which we ask that a sound intellect may be granted us, that we may be able to understand the works of His power, and the Laws of His wisdom. This is a proof of the constant care which our religion has at all times taken that instruction and knowledge should be spread among our nation; in fact the noble ambition of Moses was not that the Hebrews should be renowned for their power or their extensive territory, but that all other nations should call them a wise and understanding people. Judaism considers ignorance to be the lowest and most wretched state of man, for it prevents him from availing himself of the precious qualities either of his soul, or of his mind; and teaches that "those who have no knowledge cannot fear sin; nor can the ignorant be really pious" * : אין בור ירא חטא ולא ע״ה חסיד A true Israelite therefore devotes himself to study, and especially to religious study. A father exerts himself indefatigably in order that his children should learn and appreciate the simple tenets as well as the touching moral laws of Judaism, early in life, when they begin to lisp a word. And when a young Israelite has made satisfactory progress in that holy study, when by means of both instruction and practice he has rooted his religion in his heart, when he has reached the traditional age of thirteen, then he receives *his degree*, a degree which is conferred with solemn ceremonies and marks of joy, the degree of בר מצוה *son of religion*, which he ought to value as much as, or even more than, that which is conferred in universities after a successful examination.

And this, my young friends, this is the day on which that religious title has been bestowed upon you, the day to which you have so long looked forward with eagerness and anxiety, for which you have during many a month seriously prepared yourselves, and which is justly celebrated by your parents and relations as the day of a great event. You ought to feel proud of being admitted into the assembly of Israel as active members who will have their individual value, who with regard to all religious obligations are held to be *men*, admitted to all the rights of men, but also subject to all the duties of men. There is no doubt that your new position, while it becomes important in consequence of your new rights, becomes also difficult in consequence of

* Talmud Abot ii. 6.

the new efforts henceforward imposed upon you, and of the responsibility which you are now obliged to assume. But you have not been taken by surprise, your religious instruction has already made you acquainted with all these obligations; you have been told that the direction which you are to give to your journey on the earth ought to be strictly in accordance with the principles of religion, with the sound advice contained in the Law of Moses. Yet you have this morning accepted your new task, and solemnly declared in this holy place that you recognise your future duties, that you will undertake to fulfil them. You have made a promise similar to that which, as we have read this morning in the Law, the Hebrews uttered at the foot of Sinai.

Your position is indeed in many points like the position of our forefathers in that early period of their existence as a nation. When they left Egypt they were a disorganised mass of human beings. Their moral state was such as might have been expected after two hundred and ten years of lowering oppression exercised upon them by a suspicious and cruel nation, which knew that the least moral progress would have enabled them to break off their heavy yoke. During that unhappy period the Hebrews had, materially speaking, marvellously developed, and become very numerous; but they had achieved no moral advancement; they had been purposely kept in ignorance, and what they saw practised by their tyrants had not moralised or edified them. Nay, in the midst of the Egyptian idolatry, witnessing every day rites and ceremonies seldom consistent with reason, they not only acquired no knowledge of what is true, but they hardly preserved any spiritual idea of God, such as the Patriarchs had bequeathed unto them. They even learnt to worship animals, and put that wretched knowledge into practice in the wilderness, when they adored the Golden Calf, a sin which was so degrading in its essence, and so fatal in its effects. Depressed by sufferings, corrupted by bad example, although the breath of liberty animated them with new life, they did not present a pleasing spectacle to the observer, nor did they offer a fertile field to the labourer. An extraordinary event was necessary to their full revival. In some sense I may compare man's early years to the time of bondage, and say that until now you have been under a heavy yoke, the yoke of childhood, the time of insignificance and of caprice. Tenderness of age was for you what slavery was for the Hebrews. By your instability, by your inconstancy and fondness for childish amusements, you have been prevented from acquiring real knowledge and enlightenment, from appreciating the value of virtue and from making it yours. Your physical weakness stood in the way, and you did not think of a higher position, you could not strive in order to attain it. As regards religion you were not held to be accountable for your actions, to which little importance was attributed. If you conducted yourselves in a blamable manner, it was said that you could hardly distinguish between good and evil, and you were forgiven. If you acted rightly, the merit was ascribed to your instinct more than to your reflection, and you were said to deserve no reward. Your existence was considered to be useless to the community, useless to religion.

But all that has this day ceased to be, just as on one day, the sixth of Sivan, the Hebrews were at once raised to a noble condition. Revelation was the marvellous event that operated the great and blessed change. The presence of God, though under no material figure, turned an uncivilised people into "a kingdom of priests and a holy nation," : ‎* ואתם תהיו לי ממלכת כהנים וגוי קדוש The Hebrews who, fifty-one days before had been rescued from material bondage, were now all at once rescued from the moral bondage of ignorance and degradation; they could understand the most elevated principles and the wisest laws, and feeling the great honour thus bestowed upon them, unanimously exclaimed: "All that the Lord hath spoken we will do," : ‎§ כל אשר דבר ה' נעשה This day must produce the same change in you. The celebration of your religious majority must do for you what Revelation did for the Hebrews. Our religion by admitting you this day to all sacred duties, by raising you to the responsible position of men, declares that your reason has now developed itself, and is able to recognise what is good and worthy to be practised, as well as what is condemnable and must be avoided. It declares your actions to be the actions of a human being who knows what he is about, and is aware of the consequences of what he does; and it determines that you will call down upon yourselves reward if you are righteous, and punishment if you are wicked. You ought to be equal to the height of your new station; you ought to show yourselves worthy of the place that you will occupy in the midst of the family of Israel. You ought to say with all your heart, like the Hebrews in the wilderness: "All that the Lord hath spoken we will do."

The Law, whose fundamental principles God Himself proclaimed from Mount Sinai, and which He placed under the safeguard of our nation, is still in our hands,

* Exodus xix. 6. § Ib. 8.

it is still binding upon us, it ought to be our guide while we exist, and our Pharos when nothing remains to enlighten us in the ocean of life, when we are exposed to wrecks, or passing among treacherous shoals, when our eye seeks in vain to penetrate through the clouds and to find the Polar star. David surely meant that spiritual lighthouse when he said * כי אתה תאיר נרי ה' אלהי יגיה חשכי: "For thou wilt light my candle; the Lord my God will enlighten my darkness." Study the Law, my young friends, practise it, let the object of your life consist in being faithful to it, and your prosperity, your happiness will be certain, for in it you will find the wisest advice for every phase of human existence, for every condition, for every circumstance, for joy and sorrow, for greatness and humiliation, for the ebb and flow of the tide, for rise and for decay. If you are wealthy, it teaches you moderation in your enjoyments, it teaches you to make your pleasures sweeter by sharing your bread with those that are destitute. If you are poor, it teaches you not to lower your dignity by depending upon others, but to raise yourselves in your own sight and in the sight of your neighbours by patience, industry and perseverance. But whether you are rich or poor, it reminds you of the great law of labour, from which no man is exempt, and of which God Himself gave a striking example by the slow and progressive process of creation, which He could have achieved in one moment and by one word, as well as by the fact that He devoted the first six days in the week to work, and only the last to rest. It asserts that the powerful should not be proud of their possessions, or of the height of their social condition, nor should the poor be dejected and despondent when they find no

* Psalm xviii. 29.

man upon whom they can rely, for earthly treasures are not man's, but God's. He sends them to man whenever He pleases, and withdraws them from him when such is the will of His wisdom. "The Lord," said Hannah, "maketh poor and maketh rich; He bringeth low, and lifteth up" * : ה׳ מוריש ומעשיר משפיל אף מרומם And this I say on purpose, because one of you, my young friends, belongs to the wealthy, and the two others to the working classes. I wish to impress upon you that God in His infinite mercy has given to every man the instruments of wealth: strength of body and strength of mind; that by these two assistants a man can achieve wonders, he can gain material riches, and, what is better, the treasure of a good name and of celebrity. Wealthy may be called the man, even when a simple artisan, who makes a noble use of his natural gifts, who works honestly, maintains his wife and children honourably, and sets aside a small part of his earnings for the support of the helpless. But a man who, born in the midst of riches, thinks he has no duties to perform, and drags his existence in idleness, useless to himself and his neighbours, he is a poor miserable being, he deserves to be pointed out to the contempt of society. You make this day your official entrance into the community in the character of men, and your time thus becomes much more valuable than it has hitherto been; strive therefore to occupy it in a worthy manner. Our sages, who knew the terrible consequences of idleness, taught that we ought to divide our time between the study of religion and science, and the exercise of a useful art, because "the thought and work that both occupations demand, cause us to forget sin"§ : יגיעת שניהם משכחת עון

* 1 Samuel ii. 7. § Talmud Abot ii. 2.

And joining their example to their lessons, our sages who were celebrated for the depth of their knowledge, were also highly esteemed for the probity and ability with which they pursued their various professions. You must strive to be, as Moses said, "guiltless before the Lord and before Israel" : והייתם נקיים מה' ומישראל

To be guiltless before the Lord means that you ought not only to believe in the existence of a Supreme Being, invisible, eternal, omnipotent, but that you ought to act in conformity with His precepts, that you ought never to lose sight, as our sages taught, of "the eye that sees everything, of the ear that hears everything, of the book wherein everything is written"* עין רואה ואזן שומעת וכל מעשיך בספר נכתבים: A beautiful expression, by which they meant that no man can with impunity tread underfoot the laws of nature, that no Israelite can forget with impunity revelation, which distinguishes the Jews from the other nations, the chosen people from the multitude of the earth. To be guiltless before Israel means that in dealing with your neighbours you ought always to be guided by principles of the strictest honesty, to love all men and to make no distinction among them in consequence of difference of creed or nationality; just as he Lord bestows His gracious favours alike on the faithful and the idolaters, on the just and the impious. To be guiltlesss before Israel means that you should think yourselves honoured by the name of Israelites, that you should never follow the example of those misguided Jews who take the utmost care to conceal their origin, that you should act in accordance with the words of your prayer : " I will never cease to glorify the Lord's name in the face of all nations."

* Talmud Abot ii. 1.

And if my exhortation produces a deep impression upon you, if the principles which I have briefly explained, become the rule of your conduct, if you determine on this which I may call the most solemn day of your life, to practise David's words which I address to each of you * וחזקת והיית לאיש "Be thou strong therefore, and show thyself a man," then you will be able to accomplish many worthy things. You will first of all efficiently serve your religion, that Judaism, to which we owe the preservation of our race, and you will spread among men those true principles of the knowledge of God, of real benevolence and tolerance, which the majority of mankind has yet to learn. The good example you set before your neighbours will be the best way of teaching our religion. You will become useful members of the community in whose bosom you were born, you will contribute to its prosperity by the wisdom of your counsel and the kindness of your actions. You will be able to show your gratitude to those who have given you existence, who have surrounded you in your childhood with the tenderest love, who have undergone the greatest sacrifices for your education, and who are this day beaming with joy in hearing you called men. You will then perform the fifth commandment, which has just been proclaimed: for the virtues which you will possess will console them even more than riches, and compensate them for their long labour. You will finally do good to yourselves, for as my Talmudical text teaches, the right path that you will have followed will procure for you a twofold honor: that which your fellow creatures will show to you, and that which you will feel for yourselves, and which is still more precious, for it will be the result of the

---

* 1 Kings ii. 2.

satisfaction of your conscience. No feelings can be more agreeable than this, no reward can be sweeter than the right to self-esteem. Loved by men whom you will have benefited, protected by God to whom you will have offered the sacrifices which He prefers, you will feel really happy, you will bless the day of your religious majority, from which you will have derived your holy inspirations, you will say with King Solomon: "My heart rejoiced in all my labour; and this was my portion of all my labour" * כי לבי שמח מכל עמלי וזה היה חלקי מכל עמלי:

PRAYER.§

May He who blessed our forefathers, Abraham, Isaac, and Jacob, bless each of these youths, who have just reached the age of religious responsibility; may he guard and protect him from all evil and affliction, and direct him to the observance of His holy law and commandments, so that he may prosper in all his ways. May the Supreme King of kings, through His mercy, remove from him all evil temptations, incline his heart to all that is good and virtuous, and nourish in his breast the love and fear of his Creator, that he may offer an ever ready obedience to His holy will, and reap therefrom a happy harvest of peace.

May the Supreme King of kings, through His mercy, extend over him a protecting arm, and inspire him with a spirit of wisdom and understanding, fortitude, and piety, that all his actions may be entirely guided by justice and faith. May the Supreme King of kings,

---

* Ecclesiastes ii. 10.

§ This prayer, or rather blessing, which the Chief Rabbi utters while he stretches his hands over the head of the youth, is always delivered in Hebrew.

through His mercy, instil such virtue into his young heart that he may not stray and fall into the vanities of this world so alluring and enticing.

And thus, with God's gracious assistance, may each of these youths walk in the virtuous path traced by the holy law, prosper in life, enjoy happiness during all his days, witness the glories of the future Messianic redemption, and in the end deserve and obtain the eternal felicity of the future world. Amen.

Prayer which the youth, having previously undergone a religious examination, recites when called upon to read a chapter of the Law and to consecrate by that act his entrance into religious manhood: —

אלהי ואלהי אבותי·

באמת ובתמים אשא אליך את עיני ביום הגדול והקדוש הזה לאמר: הנה ילדותי חלפה הלכה לה ואנכי הייתי לאיש· עלי לשמור את בל־חקי רצונך· ועלי לענות ביום פקודתי כאשר תגמול לי כפרי מעללי: מיום הולדי בן ישראל אני· אמנם ביום הזה באתי שנית בקהל לך· ולפני כל־העמים אתפאר על שמך אשר נקרא עלינו:

ועתה אבי שבשמים שמע אל התפלה ואל התחנה הזאת· שלח עלי שפעת ברכותיך· גשם נדבות וברכות הניף עלי· למען ימי ישבעון וירויון מדשן עדניך: הורני נא דרך חקיך· הדריכני בנתיב מצותיך תן בלבי לאהבה וליראה את שמך· החזק בידי אל תרפני ולא אכשל על דרכי אשר אנכי הולך עליה היום בראשונה: הצילני מיצר הרע ותן בי כח לשמור את תורתך

הקדושה ואת פקודיך אשר יעשה אותם האדם וחי בהם : ובכל ימי אקרא בקול גדול ולא אבוש

שמע ישראל יי אלהנו יי אחד :

O MY GOD AND GOD OF MY FOREFATHERS!

On this solemn and sacred day, which marketh my passage from boyhood to manhood, I humbly venture to raise my eyes unto Thee, and to declare, with sincerity and truth, that henceforth I will observe all Thy commandments, and undertake and bear the responsibility of all my actions towards Thee. In my earliest infancy I was brought within Thy sacred covenant with Israel, and to-day I again enter, as an active responsible member, the pale of Thine elect congregation, in the midst of which I will never cease to glorify Thy holy name in the face of all nations.

Do Thou, O heavenly Father, hearken unto this my humble prayer, and vouchsafe unto me Thy gracious blessings, so that my earthly life may be sustained and made happy by Thine ineffable mercies. Teach me the way of Thy statutes, that I may obey them, and faithfully carry out Thine ordinances. Dispose my heart to love Thee and to fear Thy holy name, and grant me thy support and the strength necessary to avoid the worldly dangers which encompass the path lying before me. Save me from temptation, so that I may with fortitude observe Thy holy law, and those precepts on which human happiness and eternal life depend. Thus I will every day of my life trustfully and gladly proclaim: "Hear, O Israel, the Lord is our God, the Lord is One!"

REFLECTIONS ON THE CEREMONY OF RELIGIOUS MAJORITY AMONG THE JEWS.*

בן שלש עשרה למצות§—"At the age of thirteen a youth should assume the obligation of religious duty," asserts the Talmud, the inexhaustible source of the traditions of Israel, and by these words it merely hints at a custom which had long prevailed among the Jewish race. The laws of Moses, the eloquent appeals of the Prophets, the striking aphorisms of our sages may, through their wisdom, be called a sun that spreads a pure, equal, splendid light over mankind; but that which makes them inexpressibly beneficial, is the evidence they give of the knowledge of the human heart possessed by their authors. In the institution of religious majority for the Israelite, when still so young, may be found an instance of that invaluable knowledge.

Twofold are the objects of that ceremony which was for centuries exclusively ours, and which, if it is practised, though in another form, by other religions, is nothing but an imitation. The first is that the Israelite may be roused early in life to a sense of the dignity of man, of the value of the individual, to a sense of that responsibility which, if never lost sight of, is the best adviser, the securest guide on the path of life. Nothing is more important than to give to young people an early and clear notion of that free will which is the greatest distinction between men and the brutes, which makes them accountable for their actions before their own con-

* These "Reflections" were inserted some years ago in the pamphlet published by the Congregation, and which contained the service for the above ceremony, as established by the Author.
§ Abot v. 21.

science and the tribunal of God. And the age of thirteen is not too early to commence that self-study which is a life-long task. A boy of that age reasons more than he is credited for. He is conscious of his existence, of his own individuality. Even when his education is neglected, he feels the difference that exists between him and the animals, between him and inanimate things. He knows by intuition that the latter obey the laws of matter, and that the former act in accordance with their instinct only. He needs no teacher in order to be aware that his own will is free, and that when about to do a thing, he can do or not do it that he can achieve a good action or indulge in a bad one. The hesitation which he sometimes experiences before taking a decision shows that his will is under no control: he is the cause of his own actions. When a boy arrives at that conviction, it is not difficult to persuade him that since he is the cause of his actions, he is also responsible for them; that he must expect a reward for the good and punishment for the evil that he does; and when a boy, on the day of his religious majority, is told publicly and with the greatest solemnity the memorable words of Deuteronomy,* "See, I have set before thee this day life and good, and death and evil," ראה נתתי לפניך היום את החיים ואת הטוב ואת המות ואת הרע "thou art free to choose and thou shalt henceforward receive a retribution in accordance with thy choice"—then, unless he be of a depraved nature, his heart will be moved, agitated, and he will receive a beneficial, lasting impression; he will feel himself raised in his own eyes, in the eyes of his fellow-creatures; he will have the soul of a man in the body of a boy, and his

* xxx. 15.

aspirations will be to struggle bravely against all obstacles, to fulfil his duties as a man and an Israelite.

Education, early and sound education, and religious instruction are nowhere so frequently and energetically recommended as in the Bible and the Talmud. They are repeatedly enforced as duties to which nothing else is equivalent, from which nothing can exonerate the parents. The second object of religious majority is then to remind them of this their sacred obligation. These words "Religious Majority" ought to sound as a memento in the ears of fathers and mothers. For to prepare their children for that great day is their special mission. They give them material life, but they will have done nothing if they do not give them moral and intellectual life חנך לנער על פי דרכו "Train up the child in the way he should go,"* said King Solomon. The duty of religious instruction, says tradition,§ is imposed upon all Israelites, whether rich or poor, healthy or sick, young or old, exalted or humble. Even those who beg from door to door, even those who must work indefatigably for their numerous and needy families ought to study and teach their children religion.

Extremely impressive, as the Kolbo‖ relates, were the ceremonies formerly performed when a father took his son for the first time to school; the child was told that on that day he was compared to the Israelites at the foot of Sinai who prepared to receive the Law, and the venerable master covered him with his mantle, as if to signify that he would henceforward be put under the shadow of the Law. What has remained of these patriarchal customs so wholesome to fathers and children, so beneficial to the nation at large? The day of religious ma-

* Proverbs xxii. 6. § Yoré Deha ccxlvi. 1. ‖ Chap. lxxiv.

jority was formerly celebrated, amidst joyous festivities, by the father of the candidate; but they had a reason: That father could conscientiously say ברוך שפטרני מענשו של זה * "Blessed be the Almighty, who has given me the power of fulfilling my duty towards my son. I have prepared him morally and religiously for this day, when the burden of his responsibility falls upon his own shoulders. I shall assist him with paternal advice, but he knows that he is free, he knows how to use his free will." The festivities have been preserved, but these five words are no longer repeated. Perhaps the fathers no longer understand their meaning; it would be painful to assert that they feel they have no right to utter them.

Those parents, however, who are wise and prudent, whose eyes see far on the way of life, will consider the religious preparation of their offspring not only as the accomplishment of a duty, but as a work that will yield to themselves a harvest of blessing. Theirs will not be "love's labour lost;" as Isaiah says,§ "They shall not labour in vain, nor bring forth for trouble," לא יגעו לריק ולא ילדו לבהלה By teaching their children religion, they will ennoble their hearts, and elevate their feelings; they will give them the power of combating the difficulties of existence, of preserving hope and faith in an Omnipotent Redeemer, even when all human chances are lost; and if each of their children becomes a בר מצוה "son of religion" in the full significance of the word—if inaccessible to bad advice and to bad example, he grows an upright and honourable, a disinterested and generous man, an object of public sympathy and admiration—the parents will be the first to enjoy such happy results, to

* Orach Haym ccxxv. 2; Beresh. Rab., chap. lxiii. § lxv. 23.

delight in the consoling success of their work, their old age will be an uninterrupted series of joys, ministered to them by their grateful children, of whom Isaiah says,* "All that see them shall acknowledge them, that they are the seed which the Lord hath blessed" כל ראיהם יכירום כי הם זרע ברך ה׳:

It is often from a spark that great fires are kindled; from small but sound seed that magnificent plants grow up to adorn the earth, to delight and support man; and this simple ceremony, often considered insignificant and secondary, worthily prepared for and well performed, will create a generation of true Israelites, of those brave, indefatigable, [although peaceable champions, whom Judaism cannot spare, whom Judaism needs, if it is to accomplish its mission and verify its announced destiny,—to teach truth and preach the knowledge of God to mankind; "for from Zion shall go forth the Law, and the Word of the Lord from Jerusalem" § כי מציון תצא תורה ודבר ה׳ מירושלים:

* lxi. 9. § Isaiah ii. 3.

THE END.

www.ingramcontent.com/pod-product-compliance
Lightning Source LLC
Chambersburg PA
CBHW030748230426
43667CB00007B/891